I N V E S T I G A Ç Á O

I

IMPRENSA DA UNIVERSIDADE DE COIMBRA
COIMBRA UNIVERSITY PRESS

U

EDIÇÃO

Imprensa da Universidade de Coimbra
Email: imprensa@uc.pt
URL: http//www.uc.pt/imprensa_uc
Vendas online: http://livrariadaimprensa.uc.pt

COORDENAÇÃO EDITORIAL

Imprensa da Universidade de Coimbra

CONCEÇÃO GRÁFICA

António Barros

INFOGRAFIA DA CAPA

Carlos Costa

INFOGRAFIA

Imprensa da Universidade de Coimbra

EXECUÇÃO GRÁFICA

Simões e Linhares, Lda.

ISBN

978-989-26-1302-4

ISBN DIGITAL

978-989-26-1303-1

DOI

https://doi.org/10.14195/978-989-26-1303-1

DEPÓSITO LEGAL

425113/17

THE LISBON STOCK EXCHANGE

IN THE TWENTIETH CENTURY

MARIA EUGÉNIA MATA
JOSÉ RODRIGUES DA COSTA
DAVID JUSTINO

IMPRENSA DA
UNIVERSIDADE
DE COIMBRA
COIMBRA
UNIVERSITY
PRESS

INDEX

Chapter 1: Justifying

Chapter 2: The historical environment of the Lisbon Stock Exchange in the early twentieth century

Chapter 3: The Portuguese Share Indices

Chapter 4: Portuguese Macroeconomic Performance and the BVL Equity Index

Chapter 5: Stock Markets in Portugal. Organisational Features

Chapter 6: Globalisation of Stock Exchanges

Chapter 7: The Lisbon Exchange as an International Reference Case

Chapter 8: The Cost of Capital in Portugal

CHAPTER 1
JUSTIFYING
A HISTORY OF THE LISBON STOCK EXCHANGE IN THE TWENTIETH CENTURY

1. Why do we need a Stock Exchange?

History shows that for many types of products — food, ceramics, cheese, flowers, rice, insurance, etc. — people tend to flock to some traditional places to exchange the outputs of their own production for products they need. Concentration of buyers and sellers in one single place — often called a fair — speed and simplify the effort to find a suitable counterpart to make a transaction. Additionally, it also supplies reference prices for future transactions based either on previously agreed trades executed in the very same place or on the "tags" associated to products put up for offer. Therefore, one can say that centralised markets were created to facilitate transactions and to supply information about the prices and the quantities of the "goods" available for negotiation.

In this sense a Stock Exchange is the financial version of a common fair where people are specialised in trading financial instruments rather than in physical stuffs. This also explains the fact that many historical Exchanges started as a market for both physical commodities — agriculture products, animal food, metals, etc. — as well as for financial certificates. Specialisation in

DOI: http://dx.doi.org/10.14195/978-989-26-1033-7_1 ??????????

this type of centralised market is a rather modern characteristic of Exchanges.

Although it is common to present a Stock Exchange as a mechanism to provide tradability to financial instruments, recorded history also indicates that a number of companies and governments may have an interest in having their "papers" negotiable in such markets, even if, after admitting them to trading, they very rarely actually trade. This suggests that simple admission to a Stock Exchange may also be important for issuers for other reasons besides liquidity and easy access to information, among which visibility and credibility of listed issuer and/or issue must be included.

In fact, and in opposition to some other centralised markets (eg. fairs), Stock Exchanges tend to be rather selective in the quality of the issues that they accept in their markets. Normally, it is not enough that a government or a private corporation places an issue (debt or an equity) in the hands of the investment public to have it negotiated in a Stock Exchange. For example, small issues — and especially "bad" ones — are not usually granted permission to trade in such markets, not even occasionally.[1] All of these commercially minded centralised markets have now established a screening procedure — called a Listing process — whereby the issuer (or some relevant percentage of the investors in a particular issue) may apply to have the desired issue admitted to trading in one of its markets, meaning that, if accepted, orders can then be filled and trades executed in those markets. All Exchanges retain the prerogative to reject an initial application or to delist an issue subsequently, should it not meet a minimum set of publicly disclosed requirements of transparency, size, disclosure of information, etc.

---

[1] Whether this restriction is rational or not is not analysed in this book.

At first sight, this description of an Exchange makes it seem as a rather passive entity that exists simply to supply to the surrounding community a physical place (or mechanism) where the interested parties — the local investors — freely negotiate and execute their trades without any interference from the staff of the Exchange. But, although crucial to understanding the concept of a free market, no Stock Exchange can ever forget that it exists to satisfy certain clientele and this fact raises at least two very difficult questions debated in many countries: whose interests should such a centralised market serve, and how best to adapt that service to satisfy their special needs?

Of course, an Exchange would not be needed without issuers — private companies and governments — but it is also true that without buyers and sellers, that is, without investors, such a "fair" would be unnecessary. But other segments of "clients" cannot be neglected in the daily operation of any Exchange:

- Investors include today both retail individuals and institutional ones, ranging from the insurance industry, the banking sector, the fund management community, etc.
- Intermediaries are crucial to facilitate the relationship between investors of all types and the Exchange markets (and internal organization).

As a matter of fact, against the reality of more common fairs where customers and shop keepers negotiate directly one against another, a Stock Exchange requires the intermediation of a broker hired by the final investor for buying and another one for selling any financial product. Technicalities of the operation of these centralised markets, the sophistication of most financial products, and the advantage of providing trade guarantees recommend that the actual negotiations be conducted directly amongst brokers, one

13

representing the interests of the seller and the other the buyer's,[2] in a way rather similar to the roles played by lawyers acting on behalf of their clients in a court dispute over any subject.

As a result, an important segment of the "clientele" catered to by any Exchange is the group of financial intermediaries allowed to trade in its markets — said to be Members of that market. But here the world is now so sophisticated that it distinguishes between different types of intermediaries:

- simple Brokers: these are the ones who receive buy and sell orders from their clients, convey them to the appropriate market in the Exchange, try to execute those orders as quickly as possible and at the best price available, but none of them can guarantee the immediate execution of any order since it depends upon the existence of an appropriate counterpart in the market that matches that order; in fact, this simplest form of intermediation does not allow brokers to buy from a seller or to sell to a buyer to rapidly satisfy their clients because they are precluded from taking positions in any financial instrument; they simply broker on behalf of their clients;

- other intermediaries are allowed, in addition to the above brokerage activity, to maintain a portfolio of securities from which they can sell to a buyer, or to which some securities bought can be added, in order to speed up the execution of orders received from their clients; these are called Dealers or Broker-dealers;

---

[2] Mind that it may occur that a buyer and a different seller of the same instrument select the same intermediary to represent both sides in the market, but that broker is obliged to take both orders to the centralised market to find the best counterpart to each side. In the end both orders may close one against the other, but that solution is not selected before the whole market clears that match.

- still, within the dealers´ community, some make it public that they stand ready to buy to their portfolio some specific security from any seller — e.g. shares issued by Company X — or to sell from that same portfolio; these are called Market Makers (or Liquidity Providers) of that specific security; here, it is common that the Exchange where they inject supplementary liquidity into the market controls the time and the parameters of their supplementary offers to better respond to market needs — time of presence in the market with buy and sell orders exposed to trading, the size of those orders, and the prices indicated in them in comparison to the simultaneous level of prices in that market.

As for the segment of "clientele" made up of issuers, it is important to recognise that Governments tend to be very different from most private companies — notably because of their relative sizes, as most firms are much smaller than governments[3] — a fact that normally leads to segmentation of the whole securities market to offer listing and trading conditions more adapted to each particular case.

Additionally, Exchanges cannot mix the different roles the State plays in its market either as an issuer, or as a regulator (and supervisor) of the Exchange and even as the owner of the Exchange.[4]

---

[3] Even when States are present in the equity market via nationalised corporations.

[4] For example when an Exchange is run by a private company under joint stock form, its shares may be listed in an Exchange and this may raise problems (conflicts of interest) in case those shares are listed and traded at home.

2. Why do we need a history of a Stock Exchange?

Winston Churchill once said:

"The farther back you can look, the farther forward you are likely to see"

In financial parlance, it is common to print in legal documents a warning stating that *"past behaviour is not a guarantee of future results"*, but the fact is that, wherever humans find uncertainty about their future, they always seek guidance from the relevant historic records they can find. In fact, the world is always evolving and novelties are continuously pouring forth upon human society, that is, uncertainty is unavoidable. But there remains the constant presence of a crowd of humans that shape and influence with their characteristic behaviour the market around them.

Thus, if in a number of areas of human activity historians have been called upon to unearth the past of our societies in order to enlighten those individuals who are required to take decisions, in finance it is crucial to be able to see beyond the complexities of the present and differentiate amongst the constant innovation of products in order to better decide for the future.

Due to its role in the Discoveries initiated in the 1400s, Portugal was one of the first countries to establish a centralised market that approximated the role of modern Stock Exchanges. A survey conducted by David Justino in the beginning of the 1900s led to the publication in 1994 of the first book on the history of the Lisbon Exchange: *"A História da Bolsa de Lisboa"*.

Because this first study covers only the period until the end of the nineteenth century, and taking into account the added value of the most recent events upon the near future in Portugal — basically during the twentieth century — it was decided to complement that former book with a new one centred on the time window from 1900 on.

This book is part of a larger project that analysed the twentieth century with the help of a grant received from the Portuguese Foundation for Science and Technology (FCT). Amongst the many findings obtained from this project, reference shall be made to the construction of a time series of the values of a share index that extends backward from January 1988 until January 1900 the Lisbon Stock Exchange official index — initially called BVL-General Index, but later renamed PSI-General.[5]

This simple historic record made it possible to reach a number of conclusions that exemplify the importance of historical studies, even in such volatile areas as finance:

- as in any other equity market, the Portuguese shares have been rather volatile in the recent past, but overall that market shows a positive average trend from January 1900 to December 2013; in spite of two world wars, plus two profound changes of political regime in Portugal,[6] and the sudden decolonisation of all its overseas territories in one single year (1975), the accession to the European Communities in 1986, and the single currency in 1999, the annual average return from the Portuguese equity market was 12.7%;
- of course, there were long periods of high inflation in the country, but if subtracting from the average return the average risk-free rate[7] of 5.9% p.a., the average Equity (volatility) Risk Premium estimate is 6.8%;
- there were a number of cycles in this market expressed by long periods with a positive trend of annual returns followed

[5] PSI stands for Portuguese Stock Index.

[6] In October 1910, fall of the monarchy dating back to the twelfth century to a republican one; and in 1926, from a democratic regime to a dictatorship until 1974, when it returned to democracy.

[7] Where inflation is somehow included. Campbell et al., 2009.

by shorter periods with negative annual returns — sometimes strongly negative;

- the Lisbon Stock Market kept its doors open to trading almost always throughout that 114-year period, with the exception of two months at the beginning of WWI and during approximately three years following the April 1974 military coup.

This short list of main characteristics illustrates the importance of this type of historical survey, but it can be reinforced even further with the following external examples.

The US market is probably the most surveyed in statistical terms, but currently a number of other economies are also developing studies to cover at least the period from 1900 on.[8] Much of the credit for our current worldwide knowledge in this respect may be attributed to Ibbotson in the US and to his reference data series for the local equity market starting in 1926, but there is now a new reference book worth mentioning that was published in 2002 by Dimson, Marsh and Staunton — *"The Triumph of the Optimists: 101 Years of Global Investment Returns"*.[9] Dimson et al. put together a comparable set of time series for the evolution of share indices in 16 countries around the globe, all of them taking 31/December /1899 as their common starting date.

Spain, but not Portugal, was one of those 16 countries covered by this book and this absence raised the question as to whether investors and analysts would or would not make use of the Spanish

---

[8] The US and UK already have data for the 1800s.

[9] This book covered the period from 1900 to 2000, but since then the same authors have been able to update their statistical data base every year with their annual *"Global Investment Returns Yearbook"*, in the beginning published in conjunction by the London Business School and ABN-Amro Bank, and more recently replacing the bank with Credit Suisse.

financial statistics when looking at Portugal. In fact, this intuitive extension would contradict another result from that same book which indicates that all 16 countries had different average annual equity returns during those 101 years sampled in the book. That is, countries geographically close and culturally similar have proved to have different equity statistics. Therefore, a similar study for Portugal would make sense and this publication of ours is intended to report most of our conclusions, which we expect to help future investors and analysts.

Another important conclusion is that centralised markets do contribute to offer tradability and information to different constituencies and that they are able to guarantee those facilities even under bad "weather conditions". During the two world wars, the Lisbon Exchange was closed for only a very short time and when domestic politics led to the "suspension" of the operations in the Lisbon Stock Exchange following the coup on 25/April/1974, the local government soon realised that the liquidity provided by that centralised market was so important for placing public debt that it decided to reopen the Exchange *"only for bonds"* in January 1976,[10] although it had to postpone the authorisation for trading in shares until March 1977.[11] The importance of liquid markets and availability of the information flowing from them stands much beyond political views on economic models.

Finally, it is important to stress that, in spite of a number of catastrophic events that occurred in the period we analysed and in spite of the huge losses suffered by investors in the aftermath of some of them — for example, the 1974-75 political turmoil determined an

---

[10] First day of Bonds transaction on 12/January/1976.

[11] First day of share trading was on 4/March/1977.

average loss to investors[12] of about 80% of their wealth in shares — the fact is that investors always return in sufficient numbers to re-instate a new market after the end of such a crisis provided that certain minimum conditions are put in place.

3. Acknowledgements

Many institutions contributed to the building of the database included in this book. The researchers and students from Nova SBE (*Faculdade de Economia da Universidade Nova de Lisboa*) did the actual work, benefiting from the institutional support and excellent work conditions of the Nova scientific research centre, INOVA. The funding for scholarships, conference attendance, paper submission fees, and literature acquisition came from the Portuguese Foundation for Science and Technology (FCT). The project grant was €92,000.

Several institutions offered their archival material for the purpose of the project — especially the Lisbon Stock Exchange and the Bank of Portugal's Historical Archives — as they opened their doors to the team, and bore the respective costs, offering excellent working conditions in terms of access, staff, consultation, space, electricity, etc.

We are grateful to all the stakeholders of this book, particularly libraries and historical archives. They were all decisive partners and supporters in the undertaking:

- *Arquivo da Bolsa de Lisboa,* the main source of information were the daily bulletins kept in the archives of the Lisbon Exchange.

---

[12] Even after compensation with T-Bonds offered by the government to those investors.

- *Arquivo Histórico e Biblioteca do Banco de Portugal*
- *Biblioteca Nacional*
- *Arquivo Histórico do Ministério das Finanças*
- *Arquivo Histórico do Ministério da Economia*
- *Arquivo Histórico do Tribunal de Contas*
- *Arquivo Nacional da Torre do Tombo*
- *Arquivo Histórico Ultramarino*
- *Arquivo Histórico do Banco Nacional Ultramarino/ Caixa Geral de Depósitos*
- New York Stock Exchange Archives
- *Biblioteca da Sociedade de Geografia de Lisboa*
- *Biblioteca da Associação Comercial de Lisboa*
- *Biblioteca da FEUNL (and its historical archive)*
- *Biblioteca da Universidade Católica Portuguesa*
- *Biblioteca do ISEG*

The project funded two scholarships. We wish to stress the important work these students had in the project. These two positions were awarded to several students over thr course of seven semesters:

- Maria Belen Loor Turade
- Pedro Esperança
- Pedro Alexandre Peixoto Teixeira
- João Ricardo Pereira dos Santos
- Ana Rita Moreira Martins

who trained and performed very efficiently as assistant scholars for many tasks. All of them helped in statistical and econometric estimations for the index construction and discussion. We are thankful to them for the dedication and excellent work they developed in the study of the Lisbon Stock Exchange.

Other important contributors were Manuel Gonçalves and Pedro Silva, from Nova SBE, who helped in establishing the online database you may enjoy in this book.

The advising of Bologna Master students´ research at the Universidade Nova de Lisboa provided us good insights and global perspective:

- Ana Filipa Cruz Seabra dos Santos, *Historical Equity Risk--Premium in Portugue-se Market,* Faculdade de Economia da Universidade Nova de Lisboa, Nova SBE. (Supervised by José Rodrigues da Costa).
- Chiluva Iveth Augusto Anselmo Vilanculos, *Globalization And The Convergence Of Stock Markets,* Faculdade de Economia da Universidade Nova de Lisboa, Nova SBE. (Supervised by Maria Eugénia Mata).
- Jekaterina Bogorodova, *Vilnius Stock Market In A Global Perspective In The Last Decade,* Faculdade de Economia da Universidade Nova de Lisboa, Nova SBE. (Supervised by Maria Eugénia Mata).
- Pedro Teixeira, *The Value Of Political Connections In The Closing Years Of Authoritarian Portugal*, Faculdade de Economia da Universidade Nova de Lisboa, Nova SBE. (Supervised by José Tavares).

We are very thankful to Dr. José Luís Sapateiro, a main author of the Securities Codes of 1974 and 1991, and to Dr. Manuel Ricciardi, a former broker in the Lisbon Exchange and a long-term President of this Exchange. They both helped us to obtain a better understanding of the business environment of the Lisbon Stock Exchange, in long interviews in which they shared their extensive professional expertise in legal aspects and brokerage, respectively. Both interviews are presented in the book.

The main conclusions of this book benefited from the discussions with a large audience of Portuguese economists, in professional environments, and in the most respected Portuguese institutions, such as the CMVM[13], the *Ordem dos Economistas*, and the Bank of Portugal.

We are very indebted to Dr. Carlos Tavares, the CMVM Chairman who opened us the floor for a presentation, *The Portuguese Average Cost of Capital (1978-2008)*, at the 2010 weekly seminar, where we could meet many more Finance experts and benefit from their suggestions.

In the same way we are grateful to Dr. Rui Leão Martinho, the *Bastonário* of the *Ordem dos Economistas*, who welcomed us to a session for the discussion with dozens of economist colleagues and Finance experts.

We benefitted from the co-operation we received from Elroy Dimson, Mike Staunton, and Paul Marsh to publish the Portuguese results on the *Equity Return Premium* in a chapter of *Crédit Suisse Global Investment Returns Yearbook*. The 2014 edition included Portugal for the first time, now the 23rd country in that periodic issue, along with Australia, Austria, Belgium, Canada, China, Denmark, Finland, France, Germany, Ireland, Italy, Japan, Netherlands, New Zealand, Norway, Russia, South Africa, Spain, Sweden, Switzerland, United Kingdom, and United States of America.

As usual, the Portuguese Economic and Social History Association (APHES) also offered us a friendly environment for organizing Sections on financial markets in its annual conferences, where the provisional results of this book were presented. We are grateful to Maria Fernanda Olival and Jaime Reis, while Presidents, and

---

[13] "CMVM — *Comissão do Mercado dos Valores Mobiliários*", the Portuguese Securities and Exchange Commission.

to Cristina Moreira and Álvaro Garrido, as local organizers of the annual conferences.

We are very grateful to the members of the project Board of Advisors. Joseph Love came twice to Lisbon, and read most of our paper drafts. Elroy Dimson, Mike Staunton, and Paul Marsh were always in touch by e-mail. Elroy Dimson discussed our Section at the World Economic History Congress in Stellenbosch, South Africa; Mike Staunton discussed our paper in Antwerp, co-operated in the task of including Portugal in the 2014 issue of the Credit Suisse Global Investment Returns Sourcebook, and came to Lisbon for this purpose at the expense of the London Business School; Leslie Hannah and Larry Neal came once to Lisbon to discuss our work and (provisional, at the time) conclusions at length, and attended the pre-session of our Section at the World Economic History Congress, for Stellenbosch. Leslie Hannah also discussed our paper at the conference of Paris and our Section at South Africa. Beyond the Board, our work also benefited from Richard Sylla's appraisal and comments at Stellenbosch. His contribution went even further, at the Stern School of Management (New York University), where Maria Eugénia Mata benefited from long advising on a sabbatical leave, and participated in the Financial History weekly seminar to present on *The European Financial Thought at the early twentieth century.*

We are also very grateful to our papers discussants, referees, EURHISTOCK colleagues, and participants of Sections we organized, for all their encouragement to continue and for improving the conclusions of this book. We are very grateful to John Huffstot for correcting our English. All remaining mistakes are ours. We dedicate this book to our families. Our joy at this moment results from accomplishing an aim that we pursued for long, and the opportunity to have been in touch with parallel international research on this issue, in joining the European History of Stock Exchanges research group EURHISTOCK.

We hope that our readers will share our joy and satisfaction.

Maria Eugénia Mata,
PhD., Associate Professor, Nova SBE,
memata@novasbe.pt
http://docentes.fe.unl.pt/~memata/
Universidade Nova de Lisboa, Faculdade de Economia,
Campus de Campolide, 1099-032 Lisboa, Portugal

José Rodrigues da Costa
Former Invited Professor at Nova SBE (1989-2010);
Lisbon Stock Exchange, EURONEXT,
jcosta@euronext.com
Av. da Liberdade, 196, 1250-147, Lisbon, Portugal

David Justino,
PhD., Associate Professor
david.justino@fcsh.unl.pt
Universidade Nova de Lisboa, Faculdade de Ciências Sociais e Humanas,
Avenida de Berna, 26C, 1069-061 Lisbon, Portugal

CHAPTER 2

THE HISTORICAL ENVIRONMENT OF THE LISBON STOCK EXCHANGE IN THE EARLY TWENTIETH CENTURY

Introduction

Although the focus of this book is the twentieth century, during the second half of the previous century, and especially in the last decades, Portugal went through a succession of important events that culminated in a kind of a *"partial-default"*, which was declared in 1892 by the government in response to a series of acute difficulties in managing the stock of public debt with a very large component of external loans. The activity of the Lisbon Stock Exchange in the early twentieth century thus developed in a difficult historical background.

In particular, in October 1910, there was a violent change of the political regime from a Monarchy that had governed the country since its independence in 1143, to a Republican regime that immediately promised to implement a new political blueprint based on new citizenship values. This change of the political regime also expresses the consequences of the failure of the financial policies of the monarchy.

1. Participation of Portugal in the Gold Standard

An additional financial turmoil plagued the Portuguese economy in the last decade of the nineteenth century. The 1890s Baring crisis affected the Portuguese economy severely, and had considerable consequences for stock markets. It may be considered as a global crisis. Its negative influences on the Portuguese balance of payments came via Brazil. Slavery abolition in 1888 in this ex-Portuguese colony increased local production costs and affected Brazilian production, reducing the opportunities for Portuguese exports. Additionally, as Brazil had for long decades been the main destination of Portuguese emigrants, Brazilian local difficulties decreased the emigrants' earnings sent back home.

The heavy Portuguese dependency on public borrowing throughout the nineteenth century had led to the accumulation of a huge stock of Public Debt, the service of which also expanded the government´s annual spending, demanding ever greater financial resources that tax revenues could not cover entirely, thereby forcing the use of ever increasing short-term external loans — namely from the Baring Brothers bank — in order to be accepted by other foreign lenders (via reduction of their credit risk) and also to secure lower interest rates aimed at reducing the annual burden of debt service upon the state budget.

While Brazil provided important remittances and the debt burden was manageable, Portugal was able to maintain its participation in the gold-standard regime for some decades. In fact, Portugal had adopted the gold-standard in 1854, and maintained the convertibility of its currency, the *Real*[1], thanks to the equilibrium of the

---

[1] The monetary unit of the monarchy — the *Real* — was converted into a brand new unit — the *Escudo* — in 1911 by the republican regime implanted in 1910 in order to avoid a repeated reference to a word that in the Portuguese language is closely linked to the previous royal regime. See Decree of 22 May 1911.

Portuguese balance of payments obtained with those remittances and foreign direct investment (FDI) inflows, in spite of the large outflows produced by servicing the foreign public debt.

The Baring crisis led to the abandonment of the gold-standard in 1891, because of the inability to maintain that convertibility. The market value of the Portuguese government bonds declined after leaving the gold-standard regime and the exchange rate of the domestic currency in terms of other currencies depreciated, making it increasingly more difficult to service the externally contracted public debt.

2. The 1892 government bankruptcy

With all these difficulties, residents and non-residents weighed the outlook of the Portuguese economy and its financial conditions when taking their decisions to invest in the country either as Foreign Direct Investment or when granting loans to the government.[2]

Political developments were also unfavourable for producing positive expectations about Portugal in the foreign capital markets. The 1885 Berlin Conference had discussed Europe´s division of sub--Saharan African territories with the aim of European colonization, but Portugal could not guarantee the presence of local administrations in all the huge territories stretching from the Atlantic-Angolan coast to the Indian-Mozambican coast — the so called "*Mapa Cor--de-Rosa*".[3] In fact, this requirement followed the British interests of the time which sought to establish a British administration over all the territories extending along the central strip running from Cairo in the north to Cape Town in the south. In 1890 the UK sent

---

[2] Flandreau, 2013: 12-13.

[3] This stands for "pink-coloured map". Wheeler, Pélissier, 1971.

an *Ultimatum*, to force Portugal to abandon the hinterland part of that map and reinforced that "order" with a British Navy fleet sent to the Tagus river in Lisbon.

These political events affected the financial markets: Portuguese T-Bonds lost value due to the loss of respectability of the Portuguese government, and the Portuguese currency depreciated externally because of the declaration of its inconvertibility into gold — abandonment of the gold-standard in 1891 — both leading to higher real public-debt interest rates and increasing the difficulties in managing the external public debt.[4] Moreover, foreign short-term loans required by Portugal to honour its foreign public debt became more and more difficult to obtain in the international markets.

In the end, a package of diplomas[5] increased to 30% the income tax upon the coupons paid to domestic investors in T-Bonds, imposed a two thirds reduction in the payment of the interests to external creditors, and "offered" these last investors the option to convert their securities (external debt for the Treasury) into similar domestic bonds denominated in the Portuguese currency (and paying coupons in the same currency). This was in fact a partial bankruptcy of the national Treasury.[6]

The bankruptcy represented a violation of all financial market rules, as it means that assumed commitments were no more respected. Long negotiations with bondholders of foreign public debt were then initiated that dragged out for a decade, as conversion could be declared only in 1902.[7]

---

[4] Mata, 1987. Rambaud, 1884. Royal Commonwealth Society, 1962.

[5] Law of 23 February 1892, Decree of 13 June 1892, Law of 20 May 1893, and Law of 25 June 1898.

[6] Mata, 1993. Only 33% of the periodic interest initially contracted was actually paid out to external creditors (in foreign currency).

[7] See Law of 14 May 1902 which converted three external issues — the 3% Consol, the 4% Bond issued in 1890 and the 4.5% Bond issued in 1888 and 1889 — into a single new Bond paying 3% coupons and amortised along 198 semesters.

3. The interim period

During this period the country was not fully excluded from international Capital Markets. As a matter of fact, during the 1890s and in the subsequent decades, Henri Burnay, a Portuguese banker, was able to raise short-term loans abroad for funding the Treasury through his own *Compagnie des Tabacs Portugal,* thanks to an exceptional business network he maintained with a number of important financiers including Baring Brothers, Comptoir National d'Escompte, Banque de Paris et des Pays Bas, Neuflize et Cie., Crédit Lyonnais, Société Générale, Deutsche Bank, Bank fur Handel & Industrie, Dresdner Bank, M. Jacob H. S. Stern, and the Deutsche Effecten & Wechsel Bank from Frankfurt.[8]

4. Gold hoarding

As Portugal declared the inconvertibility of the Portuguese currency into gold following the abandonment of the gold-standard (1891), the devaluation of the Portuguese *Real* in international terms led economic agents to avoid its use as reserve currency because of its loss of international value (Figure 1 illustrates that more and more *Reis* were required for each pound). From an initial parity defined under the Gold Standard of £1 = 4500 until 1891, the *real* lost value until 1898, rebounded back and almost reached the old par value in 1906, lost value again but did not depart much from par until WWI, fell sharply during this war and mainly after 1918

---

[8] Mata, 2010. Bodenhorn, 2013.

in a heavy inflationary period, and hit its minimum in the middle of 1924.[9]

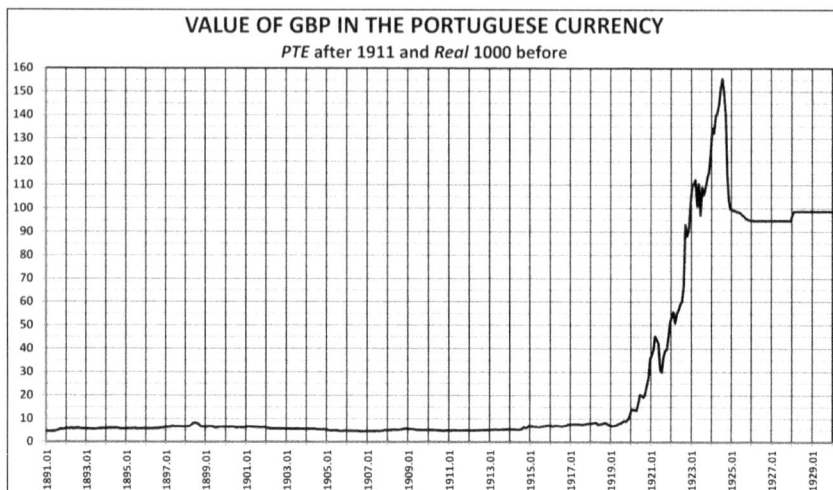

VALUE OF GBP IN THE PORTUGUESE CURRENCY
PTE after 1911 and Real 1000 before

Figure 1 — Evolution of the Portuguese currency in relation to the Great Britain Pound (GBP) from an initial par value of £1.00 = 4500 *real* and using the domestic ratio of PTE1.00 = 1000 *real* from 1911 onward. Source: Banco de Portugal internet site www.bportugal.pt.

Physical Gold and other currencies that remained in the gold-standard regime were then preferred by Portuguese investors as a reserve of value and so Portuguese bonds could no longer easily attract new investors. Gold coins (such as the British sovereign, the international currency at the time) disappeared from circulation in Portugal as they were hoarded. This meant that financial difficulties of a bankrupted Treasury coupled with political instability brought uncertainty and pessimism to both savers and investors.

---

[9] Text inserted in paragraph j) of the preamble of the Decree n.º 19869 published in the Portuguese Official Gazette (*"Diário do Governo"*) nº 133, dated from 9 June 1931.

As the Portuguese economy was also sluggish in this global crisis, hedging mechanisms for stock market investors in general were also required.

5. The necessary government budget equilibrium. The role of the Bank of Portugal to fund small Government deficits

The difficulties of the Portuguese Treasury with successive annual deficits, the abandonment of gold-standard, the declaration of bankruptcy by the government and the subsequent inability to access foreign capital markets, and the lack of domestic savings imposed the absolute need to pursue an effective budget equilibrium of public accounts. Even some funding in the domestic market to service foreign debts (interests and amortisations) required international means of payment that the country could not obtain.

Looking at the performance of public accounts after 1892 the efforts of the monarchic governments to balance the Portuguese public accounts are evident. However, some smaller annual deficits still had to be financed and these required loans from the Bank of Portugal, that is, funding by monetary creation.

The Central Bank was a traditional short-run lender to the Portuguese government, but after the 1891/92 crisis and the abandonment of gold-standard it became a significant source of funding.[10] After the Baring crisis it boosted its importance in the Portuguese banking system, and therefore, after 1892 became the anchor of the Portuguese Treasury.[11]

---

[10] As well as the state-owned bank "*Caixa Geral de Depósitos*".

[11] Reis, 1996. Besomi, 2012.

6. Regulation consequences

In the beginning of the twentieth century and as in other countries, the legal framework regulating the Portuguese Stock Exchange was the one that had been designed in the late nineteenth century, following the periods of bubbles and crises.[12] In spite of the long--rooted European experience in trade and insurance affairs (particularly in the Netherlands, Belgium, and France), most Exchanges in the world are today recognised as nineteenth-century markets (New York, London, Berlin, Milan, and Vienna).[13] Current main differences in corporate finance amongst these Exchanges may be due more to political events (such as the different kind of participation in the world wars) than to differences between the civil law and the common law systems for their legal environment in the beginning of the twentieth century.[14]

The liberal regulations offered by Portuguese governments in the early nineteenth century, such as in the Commercial Code, promoted a legal convergence toward other markets in Europe and America. But the first Portuguese Commercial Code (enacted in 1833) did not regulate any kind of transaction and/or operation in Stock Exchanges. This together with other reasons made it obsolete only 55 years after its publication.

Stock market growth and economic development demanded an appropriate legal framework around it, and it was only during the first industrialisation phase — from the 1860s to the 1890s — that the Lisbon's Exchange grew large enough to really drive legal changes. If economic growth requires liquid Stock Exchanges, a clear set of

---

[12] Philips, et al., 2013 presents a methodology and identification of asset market bubbles. Horta, 2010. Phillips, 2013. Le Bris, 2014.

[13] Ulrich, 1906: 64-69, 153-170, 414-416.

[14] Roe, 2006: 1. Frey, 2000.

rules for trading also contributes to economic growth, providing protection and confidence to investors. Rathinam and Rajá (2010) observe precisely that under weak legal systems, corporate management discretion can be used to expropriate revenue from financiers through various means such as outright expropriation, transfer pricing, or asset stripping. In particular, *"Minority shareholders do not have the resources and expertise to monitor the managers and due to rational inaction, there would be too little monitoring. The presence of agency costs and the inability to implement complete contracts give the management some discretionary power"*.[15]

Figure 2 — Francisco da Veiga Beirão (1841-1916), author of the second Commercial Code, belonged to the *Partido Reformista* that later gave origin to the *Partido Progressista*. He was a lawyer, professor, and Prime Minister of Portugal between 1909-1910.

---

[15] Rathinam and Rajá, 2010, page 307. Edersheim, 2004.

The enactment of a second Commercial Code authored by Francisco António Veiga Beirão (Figure 2) and published by the Law of 28 June 1888, to be enacted in the beginning of 1889, was an attempt to regulate and to avoid bad practices.[16] This Code did away with the freedom to create new Stock Exchanges, either official or not, by forbidding the existence of more than one such market in any one city (article 85°).[17]

Unfortunately this *"Veiga Beirão Code"* was followed by the abandonment of gold-standard in 1891 and the government bankruptcy of 1892 — both very detrimental for Stock Exchange businesses. It suffices to recall the 1882 crash in France that *"had led to 14 defaults among (...) brokers"* in the Parquet of the Paris, making *"some of their clients — mostly bankers — to lose money"*, particularly when two more brokers went bankrupt in the 1886 (Vueaflart) and 1888 (Bex) events.[18]

In Portugal this influenced the contents of the two regulating decrees of 8 October 1889 and 29 January 1891 consecrating a strict regulation for the Lisbon and Porto Stock Exchanges, respectively. In spite of giving the surveillance of both markets to the government (to the Ministry of Public Works, Commerce and Industry, in particular), the issuing of bonds did not yet require any authorisation.[19] In the aftermath of the crisis bond issues became subject to government authorization, even in banking, through the decree of 12 July 1894, which was converted into a law on 3 April 1896.

---

[16] Published at the Official Gazette *Diário do Governo* of 6 September 1888.

[17] In Spain the 1885 Commercial Code already included regulation for all Spanish Stock Exchanges, but recognised the existence of private Exchanges. Valencia, Santander, and Seville had their own markets and in 1915 a fourth one was created in Barcelona. Cagigal, 2009: 45. Carreras, 1993.

[18] Hautcoeur, 2010: 10.

[19] For a general view on the available concepts for economic life, see Duarte, 1881.

In the historical context the following 1901 Regulations offered a real first package of state rules, a real founding structure for corporate finance in Portugal.

7. The new organisational framework of the Lisbon and Porto Stock Exchanges

The Commercial Code of 1888 confirmed all the features established in the law of 22 June, 1867 that regulated joint stock companies ("*Sociedades Anónimas*") in Portugal. Decisions about listing on Exchanges remained with each Chamber of Brokers except for domestic T-Bonds, which were automatically listed.

In spite of the publication of the Stock Exchange regulations, it was still missing some regulation for the brokerage profession ("*Regimento dos Corretores*"), which was published by the decree of 10 October 1901, and would last until April 1974.

There was also a need for more flexible rules on limited liability firms to help the necessary economic recovery.[20] Following a German inspiration coming from a law of 20 April 1892 on partnership associations,[21] the Portuguese law of 11 April 1901 made any auditing requirements optional.

---

[20] A synthesis of the commercial law is available in Saldanha, 1896.

[21] A Gesetz bettrefend die Gesellschaften mit beschränkter Haftung, of 20 April 1892. Duarte, 2008: 27.

8. Failure of the Monarchy and the military coup that established the Republic

The abandonment of the gold-standard in 1891 coupled with the 1892 bankruptcy put an end to any possible survival strategy for the monarchic regime in Portugal into the twentieth century.

The Lisbon government´s submission to the British Ultimatum (1890) brought large discredit to the Portuguese monarchy which in conjunction to the fact that, in a period of general financial constraints, the royal family routinely ignored the ceiling fixed in the state budget for their annual expenditures led the Parliament to discuss this issue with negative consequences in the local public opinion. Some newspapers openly criticized the King and the Queens' poor financial management. This atmosphere isolated the royal family and the Portuguese monarchy in the small circles of the Portuguese aristocracy,[22] while urban middle classes clearly supported Republican ideals, and the Republican Party associated all the country´s financial problems with the monarchy.

On 2 February, 1908, the King Carlos I and the Crown Prince Luís were both murdered in an assault on the royal carriage by two gunmen in downtown Lisbon. Although the second Prince (Manuel) could still reign, the 10 October 1910 revolution installed a Republic in Portugal, ending the monarchy that had lasted since the independence of the country in the 12th century.

This broad political disappointment and economic and financial uncertainty were a poor backdrop for businesses, corporations, and Stock Exchanges.

---

[22] Machuqueiro, 2014.

9. The Size of the Market

The Stock Exchange market was very small in the beginning of the twentieth century for a number of different reasons:[23]

- first, corporations in Portugal tend to be small and do not tap the market directly to raise funds; for their financial needs banks are traditionally preferred by most companies, small or large;
- second, listed companies are even less numerous as transparency requirements tend to apart owners from any open markets where disclosure is demanded by fund suppliers;
- third, listed issues — equity and debt — are also small due to the prevalence of that bank funding, even for listed companies, and their small size, both features restricting liquidity and demotivating investors to take large positions;
- fourth, the number of brokers at the time (members or not of the Exchange) was also reduced — to be able to survive — and their effects constrained because they had to make their living only out of their trading commissions, as they were not allowed to act as dealers (much less as market makers).[24]

The most important corporations listed in the Exchanges were the banks, utilities, and companies having colonial businesses. Most entrepreneurs preferred to avoid the Exchange market as it required some minimum transparency, which made them more exposed to

---

[23] And still is by very similar reasons.

[24] These restrictions explain the adoption of a roll-call system for trading securities and of a reduced daily schedule for the market to work. The 3 to 5 p.m. schedule was enough for the stock-market transactions in 1901, and in 1910 was even reduced to the period from 2 to 3:30 p.m. Duffie, 2002.

political interference, as had occurred a number of times in Portuguese history.

That same long memory also advised enterprise owners to allocate the minimum amount of capital to their companies to reduce potential losses, in case of nationalisation or expropriation. This explains the frequent credits supplied by the owners of a firm to that firm even for long periods of time, but without integration of those credits in the share Capital of that company.

A daily bulletin was (and still is) published every business day with an indication of the agreed prices — legally binding prices[25] under the legislation — along with the end-of-the-day best Bid and Ask prices per asset, as indicators of the potential trend of their markets. Additionally, listed companies must periodically publish, in the most important daily newspapers and in the Official Government gazette, a minimum set of financial data.

10. The Capital Market role in financing the Corporation

The decision by a corporation to raise money to finance its activities and its investments along with the instruments it selects and their quantities is always and fully concentrated in the hands of the management of that very firm, and no Stock Exchange plays any role in that context. However, it may facilitate such decision due to the liquidity, credibility, and visibility they provide to any security that is listed in its markets.

As a matter of fact, Exchanges are not all equal and some may cater better to corporations and investors' needs than others. As Ranald Michie says,

---

[25] Binding in the sense that prices discovered through trades agreed in the Stock Exchange are legally understood as the "true" value of a security.

Although all Exchanges serve the same basic function of providing a fair and transparent market, Exchanges were neither identical nor unchanging. (...) The need to devise sophisticated rules and regulations, and adapt them to meet changing commercial and technological circumstances, constantly created differences between Exchanges; (...) Exchanges were human constructions devised to meet the needs of advanced economies. As such, they both arose from economic growth and contributed to it"[26]

According to Hannah,[27] taxes, listing fees, or any kind of legal enactment should be equated and interpreted in terms of the economies of scale and scope that may produce network externalities for efficiency with spillover effects in terms of creating massive centrifugal forces from one Stock Exchange to another, and explaining the concentration in a special financial city of much of the world's securities trade.[28] So, the secret for world hegemony should not rest only on cultural contexts and historical traditions, but consider also the quality of the securities settlement systems, and the level of taxes and listing fees.[29]

For example, the success of the American economy in the twentieth century may explain the success of most local Stock Exchanges, but that may be misleading when extrapolated to other national economies. Europe is a good case as the twentieth century was a "step-mother" due to a number of events that negatively affected its development, if not its very survival: the two world wars were real "civil" wars in Europe, and the political "engineering" of

---

[26] Ranald Michie, 2010: 14.

[27] Hannah, 2011: 2

[28] Schwert, (2002). Poitras, 2005.

[29] London, the largest nineteenth-century exchange, has long been notably hospitable to foreign listings. Preda, 2004. Reddy, 1995.

fascism and communism very much affected the development of such financial markets.

In this respect, the Portuguese case is paradigmatic on a number of grounds: the survival of the local Capital Market as mirrored in the continuous functioning of the Lisbon Exchange under the successive and "volatile" political and economic conditions the country experienced throughout the twentieth century; the importance of that market for the financing of many economic initiatives in the Portuguese African territories; the participation of that Lisbon Exchange in the unparalleled experience of the European integration.

Historians look at these aspects as illustrations of capital market performance under the institutional framework of Stock Exchanges. It is believed that their organisational adaptive efficiency has been very important for businesses and productive activity, in promoting the conditions for capital availability and entrepreneurship that historically have produced the modern economic growth of nations.[30] However, we cannot forget that *"If we fail to account for the 'losers' as well as the 'winners' in global equity markets, we are providing a biased view of history, which ignores important information about investment risk. (...) We feel it is important to learn from history"*.[31]

---

[30] Sylla, 2010. Sylla, 2014. Donaldson,1996.
[31] Jorion; Goetzman, 2000, p. 19.

CHAPTER 3
THE PORTUGUESE SHARE INDICES

1.Stock Exchanges as Important Sources of Information

It is likely that Exchanges initially resulted from the simple need to facilitate the encounter between buyers and sellers, simply by concentrating in a single known place and during some established periods of the day those individuals that have the intention to buy or to sell some securities. In that sense, an Exchange is basically a fair specialised in financial instruments. For example, the New York Stock Exchange traces back its formal beginning to 1792 as symbolised in Figure 1.

Figure 1 — Signing the Buttonwood Agreement, outside of 68 Wall Street in New York, under a tree, on May 17, 1792, by 24 brokers[1] to found the New York Stock Exchange

---

[1] This photo is an image from the Gottscho-Schleisner Collection, which was given to the Library of Congress in the early 1980s. According to the library, the

However, that geographic concentration soon turned Stock Exchanges into important sources of financial information made easily available to a multitude of interested parties:

- one type of data describes the daily trades agreed on during the intervals of negotiations: number of issues actually traded, quantity of securities traded per issue, prices agreed in those trades, and the variation of all those figures in relation to previous days, weeks, months, or years; in opposition, similar information relative to trades agreed at the counters of banks (OTC) or in the offices of lawyers or other intermediaries, is more difficult to gather due simply to their natural geographic and temporal dispersion;

- another kind of data stems from the requirements Exchanges traditionally put on listed companies when they apply for their securities to be tradable in their markets and also to remain so, such as periodic disclosure of updated accounting figures — frequently, per quarter — and any relevant information about the businesses pursued by each such firm (e.g. the appointing of a new president, the discovery of a new technology, etc.);

- a third group of information relates to the geographic origin of orders flowing to an Exchange during, for example, one year, such as the division between residents and non- -residents or the size of the accumulated in/out cash flows from/to the domestic securities listed; in a similar direction is the common requirement to disclose the list of the largest

images in this collection have been placed in the public domain by the heirs of the photographers. Museum of the City of New York, 104th St. and 5th Ave., New York City. Stock Exchange, Buttonwood diorama. Werner, 1991.

participants in the share capital or in bond issue along with their relative importance;

- and because all this information is produced and made available every day, it is not difficult to use these statistics either to measure average behaviours — like share indices — or to organise historical time series to express time trends (if any); in particular, time series from different countries and/ or Exchanges can be compared to each other in order to detect correlations amongst them, or other connections with other macroeconomic variables like GDP, foreign exchange rates, interest rates, etc.

That is, by their very nature Stock Exchanges accumulate vast amounts of economic data that are frequently relevant for issuers, investors, and governments to take their own decisions. But while Exchanges offered basically a physical room where individual brokers met and negotiated securities in oral terms, the quantity, modernity, and diversity of such information was somewhat restricted due to the labour force needed to gather and "mine" many different types of statistics. As soon as computers and telecommunications were introduced in this business, there was an explosion of data offered by Exchanges to any interested party, making this another segment of business explored by all Exchanges — information, especially real-time data, is disclosed at a price. And that availability also explains the numerous academic papers published about security markets in all countries.

The emergence of Exchanges specialised in trading Futures and Options Contracts added a new dimension to this theme of information. As derivative instruments, such contracts call for the postponed delivery of some underlying asset and that means that their current equilibrium prices depend upon the simultaneous quotations of those underlying assets. Such interconnection between those two markets creates two additional demands in terms of information flows:

- current prices of the underlying asset must be available to the parties negotiating in the corresponding derivatives; and the trades agreed in these "second order" instruments may influence that underlying "first order" market;
- measures of risk control in Derivative Exchanges demand real time flows to supervisors of a large set of data relative to derivative trades — volumes, quotations, open-interest — along with a number of other financial variables that may affect both quotations (e.g., interest rates) and that level of risk (ratio between open-interest and cash positions).

Finally, it is debatable whether Exchanges show a capacity to anticipate economic breaks separating bull years from bear ones and vice-versa. Because rational investors in securities are supposed to make their investment decisions thinking first about what might be their future market values, their current prices should incorporate a market consensus as to their time evolution from today. In that sense, Exchanges should constitute an important source of information for governments when designing their annual economic and social policies. And in the case of derivatives, because they are always promises of gains to be realised in a distant future, these particular Exchanges should be more reliable than the cash Exchanges in terms of that price anticipation.

The progressive introduction of telecommunication and cyber technologies in all Exchanges only reduced the burden necessary to collect, to memorise, process and disclose/broadcast all those financial variables that are of interest to so many parties, from intermediaries to issuers, and to investors.

The case of the Lisbon Stock Exchange is a typical example. Until the introduction of electronic trading in September 1991, all trades were conducted orally and therefore information was mainly disclosed in paper form. Only during the middle of the 1980s were timid steps taken to automate information collection and its subsequent disclosure:[2]

- an internal data base called SIIB[3] was constructed to receive and accumulate figures from the daily trading session and work them out to produce periodic statistics (per month, quarter, and year)
- an agreement was reached with Reuters to have one of their journalists present in the trading room during the session to introduce manually in their broadcasting system all the figures relative to the negotiations as they were unfolding during the session.

The big step came only after February 2002, when the Lisbon Exchange merged with the Euronext Group — Paris, Brussels, and Amsterdam — and subsequently shared common trading engine with the three partner Exchanges, naturally benefitting from common access to a large number of information disclosure networks — Reuters, Bloomberg, etc. — and also of a visibility of orders and trades in the trading rooms of the large number of non-resident financial intermediaries that subsequently became members of the Portuguese market.

---

[2] In 1901 and at a cost of 46$130 per month, telegraph facilities connected the Lisbon market to Paris, London, and Berlin, thanks to a contract established with the Havas' agency intended to allow a closer following of European markets' behaviour.

[3] **SIIB** — *Sistema Integrado de Informações de Bolsa* (= integrated system of Exchange data). Gorham and Singh, 2009.

The possibility to broadcast daily quotations to a much vaster geographical area, and therefore of adding new orders received from distant investors, had profound impacts in Lisbon:

- it brought new business to the Exchange
- it improved the quality of the trading facility (and settlement services) since more investors added new layers of liquidity that attracted additional orders
- it gave to quotations obtained a more solid economic value, as they expressed an enlarged consensus obtained from a much broader audience
- the information extracted from the orders entered into the Lisbon markets and from the trades executed became more valued and therefore searched by a much larger "audience".

2. Impact of European Integration upon Lisbon

Historical records indicate that in many countries natural economic and business evolution led to the creation of small Exchanges in a number of towns distributed geographically in each country. Their numbers may have been excessive in a number of places, but, even as recently as the end of WWI, there were still many local trading centres in some of them. For example, the UK then had 22 Exchanges; Switzerland had 7, and Brazil 14.

Although centralisation of trading in a common place brings in liquidity and cost reduction to Exchange transactions, in the beginning such local entities were so small that they could obtain large benefits if two or more of them concentrated their operations in a single Exchange. In fact, this first step did occur and was facilitated by the development of telecommunications and transportation technologies that made it physically possible and economically viable to transform a number of local markets spread over a geographic region into a single regional Exchange. This brought in relevant economies of scale to their operations along with wider visibility to each listed issue in a larger community, which added extra tradability to issues and extra capacity to raising funds.

As technology further penetrated financial markets — in particular telecommunications like telephones and telegraphs — a second step became possible and appropriate, which led to the concentration of all regional markets of a country in one single national Exchange. Other "minor" positive consequences could also be found in this second step such as cost reductions due to the replacement of man--power and paper archives, due to the calculation speed of computers and their extended electronic memories. Even new businesses could be developed as the broadcast of share indices in real time and the sale of statistical data from trades and accounting figures about listed companies.

In the UK the London Exchange amalgamated the entire spectrum of centralised regional markets, and in Switzerland, Zurich concentrated the whole Swiss market. Another important example is the French case where the initial concentration of the seven[4] regional Exchanges in the "Bourse de Paris" in 1988 was completed in 1999 with the integration of the Derivatives Exchange MATIF (*"Marché à Term International de France"*) in what was then called *"Paris Bourse SBF"*. Outside Europe, Brazil had initially 14 Exchanges, merged some of the smaller ones located in the capitals of minor states, and now has everything concentrated in the huge Exchange of São Paulo.[5]

---

[4] Paris plus regional Exchanges in Lyon, Bordeaux, Lille, Marseille, Nancy, and Nantes. Houpt, Cagigal, 2010.

[5] In Brazil some Exchanges headquartered in some minor federal states first agreed on some form of regional cooperation as were the cases of the Exchanges

The globalisation process that also accelerated after WWII — and within that global process, the unification of Europe after 1957 — raised the question of whether that consolidation at the domestic level should not go one step further and embrace all Exchanges within the European Union. In fact, in the beginning of the 1990s and within the Working Committee of the then Federation of European Stock Exchanges (FESE), discussions began amongst representatives of European countries on whether or not the concentration movement observed in most of the European landscape that led to only one Exchange per country[6] ought to proceed and lead to a single such entity for the entire European Union.

Nordic countries were pioneers in this European-wide process field in the 1990s, under the leadership of the Stockholm Exchange, which first initiated some form of agreements with the Copenhagen and the Helsinki markets — which later evolved to controlling them — and to expanding that domain into the three Baltic states of Estonia, Latvia, and Lithuania.[7]

---

headquartered in Minas Gerais (created in 1914), Espírito Santo (first two to merge — 1974), and Brasília (added to the former two in 1976) in the centre of the country; Bahia, Sergipe (the first two to merge - 1978), Alagoas, Pernambuco and Paraíba in the northeast. Besides these merged cases there were other independent cases in Rio de Janeiro (the first Exchange in the country), in the city of São Paulo, in Fortaleza (Ceará state) in the port of Santos (São Paulo state), Paraná, and Rio Grande do Sul (covering also the state of Santa Catarina). From 2000 on, all markets closed and concentrated in BOVESPA in the city of São Paulo, although some of the former regional institutions remained active as centres of local education and promotion of this market.

[6] Exceptions in Europe worth mentioning are the German case where a number of *länder* still maintain their regional Exchange, and the Spanish one where the four legal Exchanges share one single trading engine located in Madrid.

[7] OM AB (*Optionsmäklarna*) was a Futures Exchange founded by Olof Stenhammar in the 1980s to introduce trading in standardised option contracts in Sweden. OM acquired the Stockholm Stock Exchange in 1998. On 3 September 2003 the Helsinki Stock Exchange (HEX) merged with OM, and the joint company became **OM HEX**. On 31 August 2004 the brand name of the company was changed to OMX. OMX then acquired the Copenhagen Stock Exchange in January 2005. On 19 September 2006 the Iceland Stock Exchange owner announced it would be acquired by OMX and the transaction was completed by the end of the year. Between 2001 and

The big step was taken by Euronext, which announced in June 2000 the project to fully merge the three Stock Exchanges of Paris, Amsterdam, and Brussels. In September 2000 this plan was indeed implemented and a holding company — Euronext NV — was created in the Netherlands to take control of the three companies that operated the three legacy markets.

Portugal registers only two Exchanges in her history, one in Lisbon, which can be traced back until the 1400s — when it played an important role in financing and securing the endeavours of the overseas discoveries — and another one, authorised only in 1891 in the northern town of Porto, intended to "lubricate" the important wine market due to producers located around that port. The merger of these two regional markets happened only at the end of 1999 following the process of European integration. Portugal decided to join this undertaking in February 2002.[8]

3. Share Indices

Soon in history specialised newspapers began devoting attention to corporations from all continents, even in the most remote regions of the world. Capital gains and dividend pay-outs are currently announced worldwide. But to facilitate the expression of daily market evolutions they have invented an economic indicator that, although

---

2004 the group incorporated the three Baltic exchanges and respective CSDs. The company also took a 10% stake in Oslo Børs Holding ASA, the owner of the Oslo Stock Exchange, in October 2006. OMX acquired the Armenian Stock Exchange and Central Depository in November 2007.

[8] As a matter of fact, in 1994 there was an agreement signed between the members of the Lisbon and the Porto Stock Exchanges to specialise each one in a segment of the domestic market: Lisbon took the entire cash market previously divided between the two, and Porto took the derivative market to be launched in 1996 (a Derivatives Exchange). In 1999 these two entities merged into a single Exchange named Lisbon and Porto Exchange.

not restricted to them, is more frequently available from Exchanges: indices, especially for the share market.

In the United States of America, in 1882 three financial journalists, Charles H. Dow, Edward Jones, and Charles Bergstresser, joined together in a partnership in New York for developing their own financial news corporation. They began publishing an index for transportation stocks in 1884, so that a time-series comparison could be established for stock market returns in this sector. To disseminate this information they also created The Wall Street Journal (first edition was on July, 8, 1889), a specialised morning newspaper having the purpose of meeting the curiosity of the financial market clients on the evolution of financial news, but also including many other aspects that were considered to have a possible impact on economic issues in order to provide information for decisions on portfolio management.[9]

Then, in 1896, Dow and Jones inaugurated the publication of an industrial average index, the Dow-Jones Industrial Average, DJIA, which received their names and which continues until today. It is the most influential exchange index in the world.

In 1902 Clarence Barron paid $130,000 for Dow Jones & C°, when the Wall Street Journal published only 7,000 copies[10] but before the Great Depression its circulation already amounted to 50,000 (reaching 2.4 million today).

The initiative of issuing a financial newspaper in London arose in 1888. The Financial Times and the making of an index based on the capitalisation of the 500 largest corporations listed on the London Stock Exchange belonged to a financial services company, the Standard & Poors.

---

[9] Rosenberg, 1982: 15.
[10] Morris, 2014.

In continental Europe other important (and old) indices are the CAC-40 from the Paris Stock Exchange, the DAX-30 from the Frankfurt market, the IBEX-35 for the Spanish market, etc., although currently all Exchanges produce more than one equity index in an attempt to satisfy specific needs of different groups of investors. Even the bond markets today have indices of their own from a number of places.

Portugal started its first share index[11] in 1928 when the Central Bank ("Banco de Portugal") started producing a time series that went uninterrupted until April 1974, at which time the Exchange markets were suspended for around three years.[12] After 1977, when the Lisbon Exchange resumed its operations, that series was never restarted and so the Exchange decided to develop its own equity index from January 5, 1988, but now on a daily basis — the so called BVL-General Index[13] — and adopting international standards. In 1993, this index was complemented with a shorter one — the so called PSI-20 — conceived to be used as an underlying asset for derivative products (Futures and Options) to be launched in 1996.

---

[11] The Portuguese Statistics Office also launched a share index in 1938 but initially only on a quarterly basis (March, June, September, and December) but extended to a monthly basis from January 1969. In any case this series ended in April 1974.

[12] The Central Bank time series begins with only two figures per year — from 1928 to 1934 — but turns to one per month in 1935 and until April 1974.

[13] Later renamed PSI-General (Portuguese Stock Index).

4. History of Indices in Portugal

As summarised above, only very late in the twentieth century did Portugal start to compute share indices. It was only in February 1991[14] that the Lisbon Stock Exchange launched a capitalisation--weighted share index — then called the BVL-General Index — with a time series dating back to the first trading day of 1988 (January, 5). This index is still being calculated today but since October 15, 2012, it is calculated in real time throughout the trading session (Figure 2).

This initiative of the Lisbon Exchange was a response to the drawbacks arising from the two share indices that existed at the time (beginning of 1990s):

Figure 2 — The most diversified Equity Index developed and disclosed by the Lisbon Exchange

---

[14] Included in the Daily Bulletin of the Exchange, for the first time, on 25th February, 1991.

- the Totta & Açores Index was calculated and published every day by the local Totta & Açores Bank, but with a methodology for the selection of the companies to be sampled, and a set of rules for translating the corporate events in the daily index value — dividend payments, stock splits, etc. — that were never made public, thereby casting a shadow of representativeness over the values of this index;
- the Bank of Portugal index was based on all the companies listed in the main market of the Lisbon Exchange, but it weighted each share price by the corresponding traded volume (not the capitalisation), a method that overvalued those securities having more trades, not those with more capital placed in the market.

It is important to note that the reason for the Lisbon Stock Exchange to start that index time series only in 1988 is connected to the liquidity problems of many listed shares, therefore reducing the economic representativeness of those agreed prices.

The reasons that led us to emphasise the BVL-General index in our analysis were the following:

- it uses the largest and most diversified sample, as it uses all corporations with shares listed in the main market, not only the 20 most "representative" ones, as popular PSI-20 index;
- it is the longest time series available: against a base date of 5/Jan/1988 for this index, all indices by sector of activity start at the beginning of 1991, and the PSI-20 index starts on the very last day of 1992;
- it includes large and small corporations, therefore any potential size effect is diluted in the sample; [15]

---

[15] This criterion excluded all published sector indices from our choice;

- it corrects for dividend pay-outs of the sampled shares, a feature that the PSI-20 index does not include.

5. Technical Purpose of an Index

Before calculators and computers made their entrance in statistics, indices were always a demanding endeavour due to the large number of computations they required and the potential for mistakes stemming from those calculations which would always accumulate as the time series expands day by day. Therefore, some Exchanges published other indicators instead aiming at the same purpose of characterising the market evolution during each trading session.

A typical example is the publication of the number of issues that witnesses at least one transaction in the session along with the number of rises and the number of falls of quotations within the same period.

Instead of detailing the periodic evolution of each and every listed security, an index translates the average evolution of the whole market during that same time interval. That is, an index is a summary giving the central trend showed by the entire portfolio selected to be analysed.

From such historical registers an investor may judge about what he may expect to be the future expectable price evolution of that portfolio along with the uncertainty — confidence interval — around that average.

It is important to keep in mind, however, that an index should never "be used as the sole predictor of economic ups and downs, but "simply as a tool, an instrument that could be helpful in providing sound guidance to an investor's overall business and market strategy".[16]

---

[16] Rosenberg, 1982: p. 14.

A financial index is "an ingenious barometer of the relationship between stock market trends and general business activity".[17]

6. Weighted Averages

Although a share index averages a group of share prices observed at some specified moments — most commonly, at the closing of each trading session — calculation constraints led some markets to initially simply average those market prices. Weighting each of those prices with specific individual factors would require the execution of many multiplications and possibly the previous search for the weights to be used in each day. This explains why some initial indices — the most known example being the famous Dow Jones index — only summed the quotations of all the shares selected for the index and divided that sum by their number.[18]

This simplification introduced an important drawback, however: the daily percentage variation of the index depended only on the amplitude of the quotations of the shares used in the average and not on the economic size of the different companies that issued those same shares. In fact, a small company with a few large shares (large unit quotations) listed in an Exchange will have a larger influence upon the index value than a large company represented by a large number of penny stocks.

This led to a new type of indices in which each quotation is multiplied by the number of shares in circulation in order to introduce the impact of the size of the issuing company upon the final sensitivity of the index to their daily variation. And because each company selected for an index enters into the average by the

---

[17] Rosenberg, 1982: 13.

[18] Or some other fixed divisor translating corporate events.

product of price and outstanding shares — that is the capitalisation value of that particular corporation — these indices are said to be capitalisation weighted averages of observed quotations.

Using weights based on the number of shares seeks to replicate the composition of the market portfolio in order to guarantee that an investor whose investments in shares are proportional to the quantities circulating in the market can use the daily variations of that index as an indication of his own simultaneous gains and losses.[19] But this requires that, ideally, every day those weights should be adjusted according to the changes in the number of outstanding shares after taking into account the issuer buys and sells of its own treasury shares, besides any new shares issued following a capital increase. In practice those adjustments are less periodic, unless when large changes occur in their numbers.

7. Capital Gains versus Total Return Indices

Prices of shares reflect future benefits to investors but they must also adjust their value on the very day companies pay-out dividends to them because these cash-flows eliminate one of those future benefits. This means that averaging only share quotations in an index — with or without weighting them — only measures the capital gains or losses that investors collect from investing in a portfolio that is similar to the sample of corporations used by that index.

However, it is also interesting to measure the whole gains received from such portfolio, which demands the inclusion of those dividends paid-out during the interval of time the index is used to

---

[19] Other weights have also been used like the trading volume of each sampled issue — as in the case mentioned above of the former equity index used by the Portuguese Central Bank — but the trend is to use capitalisation weights and not any others.

analyse those complete gains. Therefore, there are basically two types of equity indices:

- average price indices that measure only capital gains and losses
- total return indices that include dividends in their calculations to express the whole benefits — gains and cash-flows — received by investors.

Because these dividends may be used from the perspective of the paying company — that is, before taxes applied upon those dividends — or from the perspective of the investor — after that same taxation — Total Return indices can measure either gross returns or net returns.

It is not easy to define the calculation rule of a net return index, as taxation upon dividends normally depends on the particular type and statute of the investor (e.g. resident or non-resident). This non--uniform tax rate upon dividends makes these net return indices less used because of that uncertainty.

In the Portuguese case, the BVL-General index is a gross total return index, but the PSI-20 is a capital gains index.

In this study only the General Index was used because it uses a broader sample of the Portuguese market and because it was the longest time series already available, thereby reducing the work needed to extend it backwards until the year 1900. Also the same basic rules of that official index were used to compute the new historical figures.

COMPANIES LISTED IN THE LISBON STOCK EXCHANGE

Number of Companies

- Total Number of Companies Listed
- Companies sampled for the Indices

Figure 3 — Comparison between the number of listed companies
and those used in the indices

However, for the period 1900-1987 not all share issues listed in Lisbon could be used due to liquidity constraints: some issues did not trade or show price offers (Bid and/or Ask prices) every week, which forced to exclude them from the index sample. Figure 3 compares the total number of share issues that were listed per year in the time window 1900-1974 with the number of issues used to compute the general index and the overseas index.[20]

8. Handling the Impact of Corporate Events upon the Index

Since the BVL-General Index covers all shares listed in the main market of the Lisbon Stock Exchange, the sample had to be modi-

---

[20] The Overseas Index uses a subset of the issues selected for the General Index. About the Overseas Index see point 13 of this Chapter and also Chapter 8.

fied and the index adjusted whenever a company entered the market or left it:

- for the case of a new company entering the market, the index did not consider the first day of its quotation, but added its capitalisation only on the second day of the time series:

$$I_{t+1} = I_t \cdot \frac{\sum_{1}^{n}(Capitalisation_i)_{t+1}}{\sum_{1}^{n}(Capitalisation_i)_t} \qquad \begin{cases} t = \text{first day of the new company} \\ t+1 = \text{second day of the new company} \end{cases}$$

where the denominator already includes the capitalisation of the new company on the first day of trading. Of course, calculating the index for the first day of the new company, the numerator excludes that added capitalisation in order to reduce the index variation to simple changes in the sentiment of the market.

$$I_t = I_{t-1} \cdot \frac{\sum_{1}^{n-1}(Capitalisation_i)_t}{\sum_{1}^{n-1}(Capitalisation_i)_{t-1}}$$

- when a company leaves the market for any reason, the denominator excludes that company for the computation of the index on the first day without the old company:

$$I_t = I_{t-1} \cdot \frac{\sum_{1}^{n-1}(Capitalisation_i)_t}{\sum_{1}^{n-1}(Capitalisation_i)_{t-1}} \qquad \begin{cases} t = \text{first day without the old company} \\ t-1 = \text{last day of the old company} \end{cases}$$

This index measures the total return of the market including the yield due to cash dividends paid-out by some of the companies in the sample. To include this impact of the dividend, the numerator of the formula was expanded to include the total amount of cash dividend outflow from that firm:

$$I_t = I_{t-1} \cdot \frac{\sum_{1}^{n}(Capitalisation_i)_t + N_j . D_j}{\sum_{1}^{n}(Capitalisation_i)_{t-1}} \qquad \begin{cases} t = \text{first Wednesday after dividend pay-out} \\ t-1 = \text{the previous Wednesday} \end{cases}$$

For all other days, only the sum of capitalisations without those paid dividends were used in the formula.

9. Weekly Sampling

When extending the existing time series of the BVL-General index backwards to 1900, a decision was taken to restrict the sampling to a weekly frequency in order both to reduce the number of moments to be analysed and to better cope with the traditional lack of liquidity of the domestic equity market.

The aim was to sample on every Wednesday because:

- this placed any potential weekend effects at a distance
- and allowed some room to use another day of the week in case of a no-session day or of a Wednesday without quotation; then preference was given to the adjacent Tuesday or Thursday, using Monday or Friday only as the last alternative.

Even so, there were weeks when no single trade was registered and that led us to use the Bid and Ask offers, also available in the

Daily Bulletins of the Lisbon Exchange.[21] The idea was that the simple average between those two prices gives the second-best indication as to the level of prices the market was working with during such a week. Therefore, the following methodology was adopted:

- when no trades had occurred, the average between Bid and Ask was used as a proxy for the real traded price; however, preference was given to a traded price from another day of the same week, if available
- when only the Bid or the Ask was available, that single value was used as that proxy;
- when none of the three values were present on a particular Wednesday, the value from the previous Wednesday was (repeatedly) used; however, if two or more weeks without data occurred in a row, that company was temporarily excluded from the sample according to the rules mentioned above for new entrants and for old companies leaving the market.

Measurement Errors

As mentioned above, in a significant number of days the listed shares included in the index did not trade at all. In spite of that, when no agreed price existed, the daily index was computed using the average value between the Bid and the Ask prices as a second

---

[21] Note that the Stock Exchange used the Roll Call system of trading during this period, in which each listed share was called once at a time, and a single equilibrium price was discovered after confrontation of all the orders carried by the brokers for that particular asset. The prices of those orders closest to that equilibrium, but already excluded from trading, produced the daily Bid and Ask prices.

best alternative to such an equilibrium quotation. Of course, all those approaches introduced a source of errors, because

- we knew only the range within which any equilibrium price could have been struck;
- when companies only offered either a Bid or an Ask price, that puts a limit to the range of potential equilibrium prices on one side only; it was not possible to make an estimate of an individual error for those days and for those shares for which only one side is disclosed;
- even for those shares with an equilibrium price struck for the day, very low volumes of shares actually traded raise the question of the representativeness of that quotation.

All of this suggests that the fitted straight line is estimated in the context of an input data $(\mathbf{Y}, \mathbf{X})$ with some measurement errors but only in $\mathbf{Y}$, not in $\mathbf{X}$. Since those sampling errors are not correlated with the quotations, they do not affect the value for the estimated slope β, but lead only to a confidence interval for that estimate that is larger than the real one. This specific source of error does not affect our estimate of the average annual return, and can be left for future work.

10. Estimating the Average Return

a. Historically Realised Return or a Trend Curve?

From a series of historical index values, the first impulse is to estimate the historical annual return from the arithmetic average of the **n** periodic returns observed during the entire sample

$$\overline{R}_{historic} = \frac{\sum_{1}^{n} R_i}{n}$$

However, if as usual, we use logarithmic periodic returns (see below), this average is

$$R_{realized} = \frac{Ln(S_T) - Ln(S_0)}{T - t_0},$$

and that raises an important issue: this estimate does not take into account the particular time evolution of the index between those two extreme dates. That is, it is irrelevant whether the initial S_0 and/ or the final value S_T happen to be simply a peak (or to a trough) of an otherwise euphoric (or pessimistic) period, because the final average obtained is always determined solely by those two extreme prices.

The consequence is that the estimate obtained from a short slice of history is crucially sensitive to the starting and closing dates, especially if either of those two prices is significantly deviated from the "average value" of the index.

We took the view that more than comparing two extreme quotations, it is the average annual trend of gains (or losses) that better characterises a random behaviour if there is such a growing trend beneath the visible uncertainty. In that sense, the common Black, Scholes, and Merton (BSM) model captures both simplicity and a capacity to measure annual growing trend and volatility.[22] Therefore this was the model we adopted to estimate the historical average return of the Portuguese Stock Exchange from 1900 on:

$$dS = \mu.S.dt + \sigma.\sqrt{dt}.\varepsilon_t \quad \text{where} \quad \varepsilon_t \sim N(0,1)$$

Although it is known that this stochastic model does not correctly describe the random behaviour of the share prices — at least, it is known that the random term is not Gaussian — we chose that model to justify the regression that we used to estimate the historical average return provided by the Portuguese shares during the years of our sample. That differential equation can be transformed into

$$d[Ln(S)] = \left(\mu - \frac{\sigma^2}{2}\right).dt + \sigma.\sqrt{dt}.\varepsilon_t$$

or, after integration from **t = 0** to **t = T**

$$Ln(S_T) = Ln(S_0) + \underbrace{\left(\mu - \frac{\sigma^2}{2}\right).(T - t_0)}_{deterministic\ term} + \underbrace{\sigma.\sqrt{T - t_0}.\varepsilon_t}_{random\ "noise"}$$

---

[22] Some scholars have studied other Stock Exchanges and found that for some of them a Mean Reverting model of periodic returns could well describe their stochastic behaviour. In our case and for the period after 1988, an adjusted autoregressive model AR(1) produced an R^2 of only 0.07. However, this is not a universal view, and some countries have even shown a change from such a mean reverting model to a random walk behaviour. Due to that low R^2, and because there is yet no consensus in academia about this question, and since mean reverting is against the logic of market efficiency, we adopted the B&S model.

This expression suggests that the *log* values of the share prices — or of the index — tend to follow some straight line with a slope given by $\left[\mu - \dfrac{\sigma^2}{2}\right]$.

It was this suggestion that led us to fit a straight line to the historical *log* values of the Portuguese share index recorded during the years from January 1900 to December 2013.

Mind that according to this BSM model:

- the deterministic term of the difference between the final and initial *log* prices grows linearly with the time interval between those extreme dates;
- but the disturbing random term grows only with the square root of that same time span;
- therefore, even if the slope $\left[\mu - \dfrac{\sigma^2}{2}\right]$ is small, this deterministic term will sooner or later dominate the random component, for intervals of time long enough to compensate for that reduced slope.

That is, according to the BSM stochastic model and for very long time series, most of the difference between **Ln(S$_T$)** and **Ln(S$_0$)** is due to the deterministic term — the slope of the line — because the random term affects that average only marginally.

It is this fact that justifies the use of the realized return — the actual difference between the two extreme values — for estimates of the historical cost of capital when one has more than one century of continuous time series: the series is already long.

In any case, we decided to estimate that average annual return adopting the logic of a linear curve fitting.

BVL-GENERAL INDEX

Example of Exponential Fitting. Jan 1988 to Dec 2013

$y = 2.6571e^{0.0002x}$
$R^2 = 0.6883$

Figure 4 — The pre-existing share index for the Lisbon market

b. Fitting an Exponential to the Historical Index Curve

Our decision to fit a straight line to the *log* values is also ground-ed on another reason. Since there is a consensus that shares must provide investors with a certain expected periodic return — although disturbed by a permanent "noise" — one can anticipate that all share indices will tend to evolve through an "oscillating flight" around a "middle of the road" exponential line (Figure 4 illustrates the 1988-2013 period). The degree of deviations from that ideal trend curve will depend on the level of volatility σ around that average expected periodic return.

Of course, things can be linearised by taking the logs of all index values.

c. Fitting a straight line

That same purpose of fitting a straight line to the series of *log* values of the index comes also from the idea of estimating the parameters of the BSM model using the maximum likelihood method:

$$Maximize \prod_{1}^{n} \exp\left[\frac{\left(Ln(S_i) - Ln(S_0) - \left(\mu - \sigma^2/2\right)t_i\right)^2}{\sigma_i^2}\right],$$

which leads, in essence, to the minimisation of the square distances between the measured points of the *log* index and the estimated best-fitted line.

In summary, we estimated the average historical annual return of the Lisbon Stock Exchange by fitting a straight line to the *log* values of the share index covering that entire sample, not forgetting that this time series could show strong autocorrelation and some heteroskedasticity.[23]

11. Historic Sources used

Our main source of numerical data was the collection of Daily Bulletins published by the Lisbon Stock Exchange for the period December 1899 to December 1987, available in the Documentation Centre of the Lisbon Exchange (now called Euronext Lisbon).[24]

---

[23] Heteroskedasticity does not affect the estimate of the slope through the use of the Ordinary Least Squares methodology. However it has to be replaced by a more elaborated alternative that takes into account the variability of σ and the intense autocorrelation along the time series of log prices in case of estimating confidence intervals..

[24] The collection goes uninterrupted from 1900 to current days on a daily basis except for the second semester of 1919 for which there are no Bulletins. To cover this semester, use was made of information published in the *"Jornal do Comércio e das Colónias"* available in the *"Hemeroteca de Lisboa"*.

Similar data from the Porto Stock Exchange were not used because this market remained closed until 1981 and also because, even after that date, it accounted for only a minor share of the total domestic secondary market (quotations potentially less representative due to liquidity problems).

Prices and quantities were collected once per week: first option was the Wednesday in order to minimise the potential impact of the weekend effect, if any,[25] but another day of the same week was selected in case no trade occurred on that Wednesday because traded prices were preferred in comparison to Bid and Ask offers.

For the purpose of constructing a share index, it was crucial to have information concerning all the corporate events that affected all the firms included in the index. Three main sources were used for this:

- from the Lisbon Stock Exchange Historical Archives: Daily Bulletins, Annual Reports of Activities of the Exchange when available, and some other statistical publications on listed companies;
- the Annual Reports of the selected companies, available in Banco de Portugal Historical Archives;
- other statistical news published by the Exchange on newspapers.

Based on these sources it was possible to adjust the weekly values of the index for all the corporate events that were detected for each of the firms included in the sample of the index. Note that

---

[25] Note also that until 3 May 1989 the Lisbon Exchange traded only four days a week. Reasons were mainly connected to the manual workload associated with Netting and Settlement of all past trades. Also, from the reopening in 1976 until 20 September 1978, there were only three sessions per week, on Mondays, Wednesdays, and Fridays.

this means that the reconstructed index measures the total return of the market — dividends plus capital gains/losses — not only price averages.

12. Historic Results

The oldest Portuguese share index still being calculated is the BVL/PSI-General[26], which started its daily series on 5 Jan 1988 with a defined base value of 1000 points. This index includes all shares that are listed in the Main Market of the Lisbon Stock Exchange[27] and weights each component of the sample according to the number of shares listed.

All corporate events affecting the price of any share beyond market sentiment are taken into account through proper adjustments in the formula of the index, either implemented in its numerator or its denominator.

However, for dates before January 1988, there was nothing compatible with this index since the different series known either never disclosed the methodology adopted to calculate the index, or followed solutions incompatible to the above index[28].

The new time series from 1900 replicates as closely as possible the methodology of the BVL-General index of the Lisbon Exchange for the entire century.

---

[26] It was launched as BVL-General in 1991, but was later re-baptized PSI-General, the name still in use today.

[27] Following the first version of the DMIF Directive introduced in Europe in 2004, this segment is now called a Regulated Market.

[28] See number 3 of this same chapter.

Market without Quotations

From February 1983 on[29], the Exchange market was divided into two segments:

- the so called "Official Market" — the main market — where the larger and "senior" companies could list their shares;
- and the "Market without Quotations" created to trade (but not list) some junior companies and/or the provisional certificates of shares (and bonds) issued by corporations already listed, while their final paper certificates were being printed and distributed amongst the investors.

These differences between the two segments suggested to us to use only the firms listed in the Official Market, but to take into account all the shares already issued by a listed corporation (if fully liberated) when computing the capitalisation weight of that particular component of the index.

---

[29] See Daily Bulletin for 13 January 1983.

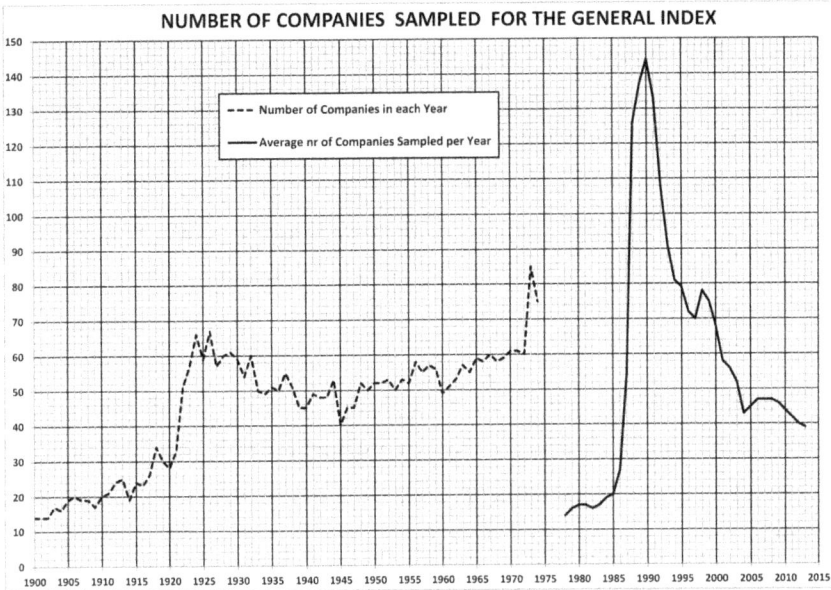

NUMBER OF COMPANIES SAMPLED FOR THE GENERAL INDEX

--- Number of Companies in each Year
—— Average nr of Companies Sampled per Year

Figure 5 — Evolution of the number of companies sampled for the Lisbon General index

Selection of Companies to compute the BVL General Index

Due to the restricted number of corporations that had their shares listed in the main market of the Lisbon Exchange, we decided to use almost all of them, with the few exceptions of those so small or so infrequently traded that their contribution to the final value of the (capitalisation weighted) index would be negligible. Figure 5 depicts the evolution of the number of companies sampled for the Lisbon General index.

The entire index estimated comprises three segments:

- from the end of December 1899 until April 24, 1974 which is brand new, as this is the first estimation, but forgets the very long closure of the market in 1974;

73

- from January 1978 until December 1987, also a new series that seems to show a desire of the market to recover from the heavy losses of the 1974-75 period;
- from January 1988 to December 2013, selecting all Wednesday values of the daily series routinely computed and disclosed by the Lisbon Exchange, already impacted by the accession of Portugal to the then European Economic Community in 1986.

Figure 6 uses three different colours to distinguish these segments. Chapter 4 discusses this evolution from a macroeconomic perspective, in considering events that occurred in Portugal and elsewhere.

It is also interesting to mention that it is now clear that the initial time series of this BVL-General index — the one that started in 1988 — suffers from two important impacts that influence significantly the average returns estimated from that series:

- the base date adopted for the BVL-General index — beginning of 1988 — is still somewhat influenced by the excessive speculation of the two previous years, which culminated in the spectacular crash of October 1987; that is, that initial index value seems to be "overvalued";

HISTORICAL EVOLUTION OF LISBON STOCK EXCHANGE GENERAL INDEX
Jan/1900 to Dec/2013. Natural Logs and Weekly Sampling (Wednesdays)

Figure 6 — BVL index from December 1899 to 31 December 2013,
based on data collected

- the Portuguese share market was in the 1980s still recovering from the "wounds" that followed the economic and social events of 1974, in particular the "suspension" of the Exchange operations for about three years;[30] Pessimism permeated the investment community, which seems to have demanded an extra average return to accept returning to the local share market.

13. The case of the Overseas Listed Companies

Evidence on the presence of joint stock companies and private capital in the Portuguese colonies abounds.[31] In one way or an-

---

[30] The Exchange closed for trading on 25/April/1974 and reopened for share trading only on 4/March/1977.

[31] The studies produced until now focus on the political (and military) aspects of the empire, and on the ethnographic descriptions of those territories. It is also

other, Portuguese economic historians are unanimous in signalling the presence of economic groups in the Portuguese motherland, although they care less about its presence in the Portuguese overseas territories.[32]

In the twentieth century the old dreams to build a rich and powerful Portuguese nation returned to the fore of political discussions and to projects of political parties. This empire was to be based on the Portuguese continental territory and on the collection of vast and rich overseas territories.

Economic development of colonial territories as a road to prosperity and economic growth became a fundamental blueprint of the Portuguese Monarchists, but the Republican Party also subscribed to this enthusiasm for the role of colonies in material progress and prosperity.[33] Later, Salazar's political regime also supported these projects of the Portuguese learned class and political parties of the day, on how to manage this fourth colonial empire. Pragmatism and a fascination with modernity were hallmarks of the epoch in Portugal, and Corporations emerged as the institutional framework to achieve business progress in Africa.[34]

The legal environment for national and foreign direct investment that prevailed in the Portuguese motherland was extended to her overseas territories, and tropical businesses began flourishing there.[35]

known that during Pombal's eighteenth-century government trade corporations were created, aiming at an increasing economic integration with Brazil. That corporate model seems to have been extrapolated to other territories of the Portuguese empire to complement the Portuguese state in the task of running large slices of the empire. (Duarte, 2000).

[32] Reis, 1993. Valentim, 1979.

[33] Laíns, 1998 (a).

[34] Lisbon Stock Exchange Historical Archive. Lisbon Overseas Historical Archive. Banco de Portugal Historical Archive. Baumol, 2006.

[35] Mata, 2007 .

There is now ample historical evidence on the Portuguese and foreign companies operating in the Portuguese offshore. Their presence comes from the pre-World War I decades when globalisation led to the capacity of investing in economic activities on other continents.[36]

As a result, overseas businesses became a new profitable sector and came into fashion very suddenly, giving place to corporations requesting to be listed in the Lisbon Stock Exchange.

Figure 7 — Provisional certificate of 25 bearer shares of "*Companhia de Moçambique*", one of the "majestatic" firms used by Portugal to develop Mozambique.

---

[36] Mata, 2007. Bordo, 2003.

Annex 1 describes the companies operating in overseas territories that were listed at the Lisbon Stock Exchange, specifying those that were used to compute the Overseas Index.

The 1885 Berlin Conference established the borders for the European overseas empires in Africa in the 1880s. It adopted the principle of effective occupation as the main rule to legitimise international claims to each territory. Historical arguments were useless as effective settlement and administration were required for this purpose.

The administrative seizure of those territories through settlement and effective occupation can explain corporations' rush to the African colonial territories.[37] Individual businesses also existed, but corporations were the most representative actors.

By giving concessions to special Portuguese joint-stock companies in Mozambique[38] — the so-called "Companhias Majestáticas" due to their extended powers in their allocated territories — in a region where a Portuguese administration did not yet exist, the government transferred the responsibility for establishing a Portuguese administration and authority in the territory to those free-standing companies during their period of the concession.[39] Figure 7 exhibits a provisional certificate of 25 bearer shares of *Companhia de Moçambique*, one of the "majestatic" firms used by Portugal to develop Mozambique.

The government also minimised public expenditure by allowing religious missions to provide education and health care to overseas populations.[40]

---

[37] Foreman-Peck, 2001 and 2001a.

[38] *Companhia de Moçambique* is a good example: Duarte, 2000.

[39] Wilkins, 1998. The extended sovereign powers transferred to these firms explain the "*majestatic*" classification of them.

[40] For the role of tribal power in Mozambique and local rebellions see Garrett, 1907: 214.

There is a widespread and spirited discussion on the character of colonial businesses. Both Marxist and Imperialistic approaches point to exploitation in colonial investment.[41] On the opposite, globalisation studies identify internationalisation of capital behind overseas investments as a consequence of the increasing integration of the world economy, thanks to the improving technology that provided better and more efficient transportation, implying proximity and decreasing information costs.[42] However, this approach considers only macro-economic perspectives.[43]

This book departs from both interpretations because those methodologies lead to misunderstanding the internal logic of private corporations, by forgetting their microeconomic views in conceiving their individual businesses. The views from strategic management suggest that entrepreneurship, international business, and investors' expectations command the flows of capital to new regions.[44]

In Portugal nobody discussed the perspective of investors in terms of the cost of the capital that was required for these firms to operate in African offshore. Our proposal is to elect investors' perspectives concerning their rewards. For this purpose all corporations operating in the Portuguese overseas territories that were listed in the Lisbon Stock Exchange were considered for the period extending from 1900 to the decolonisation that occurred in 1974-75, in the aftermath of the 25 April military revolution.

The amount of reward achieved in investing in the Portuguese offshore is the important question to be examined, because one may see this exercise as the discovery of the equity return premium that investors required to invest their capital in start-ups and other

---

[41] Lenine, 1917. Wheeler, 1971. Bastien, 2001.

[42] Foreman-Peck, J, 1995, 1999.

[43] O'Rourke, 1999.

[44] Zahra, Ireland, R. D., and Hitt, 2000, pp 925-50. Chandler, 1997, 1999.

entrepreneurial activities in those endeavours, instead of applying it in alternative less risky initiatives in known geographic regions.

Unknowns in the territories, severe tropical climate, the lack of local public utilities, the absence of local trained labour force, the need of moving European employees to head local activities, and the difficulty of controlling management decisions at a distance, were surely great problems to be equated and solved for those investments "abroad".

The greater the difficulties and risks, the higher the equity return premium required, because the comparison was done with the rewards that alternative assets could provide. For these reasons we might expect that the equity return premium for those who invested in the Portuguese offshore should be higher than the equivalent premium for identical activities developed in the more tranquil and known European territory. Of course they also benefited from the government rule over those territories, which represented a positive externality for businesses. The private incentives to invest capital depended upon the new opportunities stemming from the needs to finance local central-state expenditures, on the one hand, and the political support from the Portuguese government, on the other.

The Portuguese dominance over this empire was partially guaranteed by a number of joint-stock companies operating in the realms of agricultural plantations and livestock raising, mining, felling and carrying timber, shipping, transportation (for mail, passengers, and goods), insurance, and banking.[45] Shipping and insurance were the two sectors in which established firms decided to expand their activities to overseas geographies, as vessels were already plying coastal waters and shipping required insurance for the cargoes. Together with local crop production, these activities profited from

---

[45] On colonial banking see Nunes et al., 2011. Chandler, 1977, 1990.

the favourable geographic positioning of the African offshores on the sea routes from northern Europe to Brazil and other South American territories, and also to Asia. Commerce, ports and railway construction, telegraphs and telephones, water, gas and fuel provision, banking, and industrial activities were very active sectors of economic activity in the Portuguese empire. An example of a special role is banking,[46] and, on another front, *Diamang* was a special case in Angola (mining diamonds), after 1956.[47] Figure 8 exhibits a multilingual certificate of a five-bearer share of "*Companhia de Mossamedes*" operating in Angola.

Additionally and for other sectors of activity one can also consider that geographic expansion was due to market-seeking investment to broaden the customer bases of the established firms, as local populations had a low standard of living for demanding their products, but the rising number of Portuguese settlers and the rising standards of life throughout the century were increasing the demand for all kinds of goods and services.[48]

---

[46] The issuing bank *Banco Nacional Ultramarino* and the unique case of *Banco de Angola*, a completely private corporation, are very illustrative. Valério, et al. (2011).

[47] It was given so many powers that this company had an independent police force to fight against smuggling of diamonds, easily unearthed in the geographic areas whose concession was granted to the company.

[48] Cassis, 1997 states the same aspects, globally.

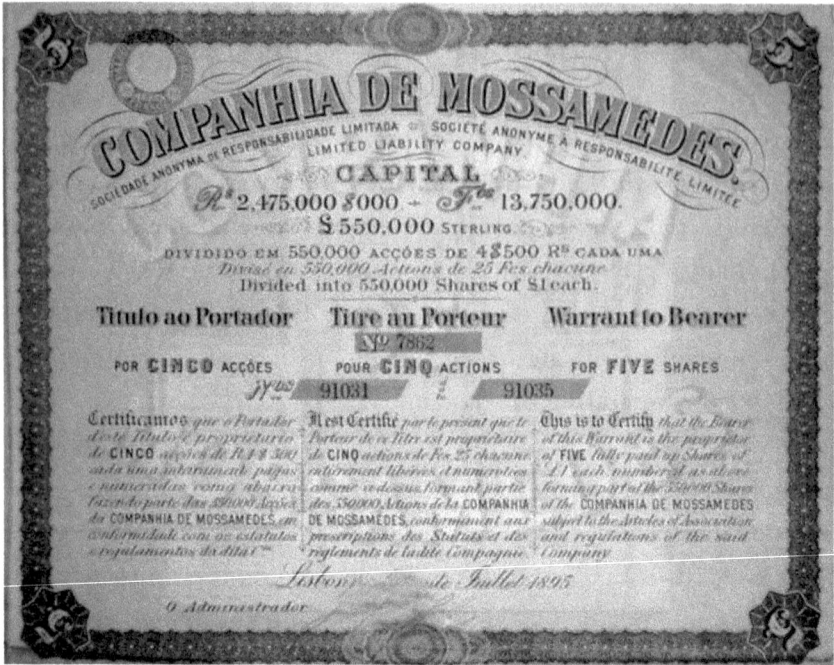

Figure 8 — Multilingual certificate of a five bearer share of "Companhia de Mossamedes" operating in Angola.

The desire for new production conditions might also have been a force driving the companies to the Portuguese territories.

Smaller territories seem to have been unattractive to private investment, and as a result, most of the private companies and corporations were concentrated in Angola and Mozambique, but farming prospered in the tiny archipelago of São Tomé e Príncipe because of cocoa and the international market for chocolate, and some of the farms were listed in the Lisbon Stock Exchange.[49]

---

[49] Although history attributes to India the underlying motivation for the extraordinary project of the Portuguese discoveries from the beginning of the 1400s — to by-pass the Italian cities that supplied Europe with spices imported from India — it was not in the Portuguese State of India that private companies played a significant auxiliary role to the state. Macau probably deserves a different and independent

In the last years of the nineteenth century, the largest territories (Guinea, Angola, and Mozambique) were carefully visited and inspected by geographers, who mapped and described them under the surveillance of the Lisbon Society of Geography,[50] thanks to scientific expeditions carefully planned for this purpose, while rebelled tribes were submitted thanks to military campaigns. Public goods received by corporations from the government include all these aspects, particularly peace, as well as a legal background definition, the existence of courts for conflicts arbitrage, and material facilities.

In the early twentieth century these facilities were scarce, because the main government aim was to fund regiments to protect the borders of southern Angola and northern Mozambique from German attacks, on the eve of and throughout WWI.[51] Only after this War was it possible to launch a programme of administration, thanks to the appointment of colonial governors — so called *"Altos Comissários"* — who were awarded with extensive functions and decision-making autonomy from the Lisbon government to begin the implementation of settlement policies in order to secure the most interior and remote zones.[52]

Urbanisation was another aim, as well as communications, schooling, and health-care provision. The 1920s, however, were disappointing times concerning the behaviour of the colonial stuffs. Because of agricultural mechanisation in the American continents, the formidable production increase for the global world supply led to risible

---

study, as it always (even today) operated as an entry and exit door for China to trade with the outside world.

[50] *Sociedade Portuguesa de Geografia.*

[51] All financial documents on these military campaigns are available at the Lisbon Overseas Historical Archive (*"Arquivo Histórico do Ultramar"*). Birmingham, 1978.

[52] The action of *Altos Comissários* such as Norton de Matos and Vicente Ferreira in Angola is frequently remembered.

prices in the context of the Great Depression market surpluses.[53] In Lisbon pricing was carefully watched thanks to the foundation of a Commodities Exchange, where glass cases exhibited samples and quotations of these commodities for the people to trade in.[54]

Normality returned in the early 1930s. Salazar's government pursued policies that always sought to preserve the Portuguese empire.[55] Not only could the overseas territories offer a "relief valve" for emigration when cyclical fluctuations afflicted the motherland's economy and other destinations were closed-door outlets, but could also be a good source of revenue for mainland traders and investors.[56] Statistical information began being published in annual yearbooks, indicating high political interest of the Portuguese government for administration management, a decisive feature of public goods provision from corporations' perspectives.[57]

The expression "colonial business" was a catch-all legal phrase that embraced more than "business". Alliances between firms point to "several benefits including the minimization of transaction costs, increased market power, shared risks and better access to key resources such as capital and information". The overseas empire had a significant impact on the motherland as it joined, on the one hand, a small European territory, and on the other hand, a collection of much larger territories geographically dispersed from the middle of the Atlantic — Azores Islands — to the Indonesian archipelago —

---

[53] "Ministério do Comércio, Indústria e Agricultura", 1933.

[54] "From the two large lateral entries for the people one can see a large floor and a frontal semi-elliptic balcony for the brokers. Back, on a stage, will be located the blackboards for writing the quotations". Associação Industrial Portuguesa, 1930, p. 64.

[55] Cardoso, 2012.

[56] Laíns, 1998.

[57] Note, however, that the first demographic censuses were organised only in 1940, and their quality for remote countryside regions is much lower than for "civilized" regions, terminology that was used in these documents. Instituto Nacional de Estatística, Lisbon.

East Timor.[58] In the twentieth century the economic growth of the motherland was accompanied by these overseas territories´ economic growth, especially after the Second World War.[59] Adding to the policies defined and implemented by the successive national governments in overseas territories, two additional types of organisations helped to mould those overseas regions to the European financial template. Religious missions always went hand in hand with the national political forces to Christianise and educate local populations.[60] However, private companies and corporations had a central role here, as well.[61] They always sought to obtain profits from all of their efforts, independently of the places where they undertook their activities. In spite of this selfish view, they brought to Africa significant improvements to consumption, standards of living, and also to the motherland in Europe.

In such a short period of time — less than half a century — there was a herculean change in infra-structures, modernisation, economic growth, and development. According to (Valério; Tjipilica, 2008), the Angolan GDP per capita index multiplied 5-fold between the immediate post-World War II period and the late 1950s, stagnated for a while in the late 1950s, and resumed its growth in the 1960s, more than doubling until decolonisation. The Mozambique U-shaped character of the GDP per capita index in the 1930s and the first half of the 1940s was a consequence of the Great Depression and WWII, respectively.

In any event, the guerrilla operations after 1961 never affected the urban centres as well as most production areas, while the necessary military spending was launching Keynesian multiplicative effects on

[58] Boxer, 1969. Bethencourt and Curto, 2007.

[59] Valério, N., Tjipilica, P., 2008. Eichengreen, 1996a, b.

[60] Asiedu, 2002: 107-19.

[61] The project cannot embrace the less measurable impacts such as education, health care, transport infrastructures in the overseas territories, etc.

each individual economy.[62] Its growth between the mid-1940s and the early 1970s was similar to the Angolan. The worst consequences of the overseas war seem to have occurred in São Tomé and Príncipe due to the specialization in a single crop — cacao — which explains the stagnation of its per capita GDP in the 1960s and early 1970s due to "the boycott on Portuguese products by countries that actively opposed the Portuguese colonial policy".[63]

Government defended the idea that Portugal was not a coloniser, but a cohesive nation made up of diversified citizens that lived in territories spreading throughout all continents of the earth, from northern mainland in Europe to East Timor in Asia, using the same language, having the same political rights, framing the Portuguese national brotherhood under the same flag. The youth coming from the overseas territories who graduated in Portuguese universities contested this official philosophy, and founded political movements advocating the independence of Guinea, Cape Verde, Angola, and Mozambique.

In the Portuguese historiography 1961 is considered as a dramatic year and a real turning point for the Portuguese economy. The peaceful environment that prevailed in the Portuguese overseas territories was dramatically interrupted by guerrilla actions in the northern provinces of Angola in March 1961 and later extended to Guinea and Mozambique. The reaction of the Portuguese government was immediate in sending large military resources to preserve the empire. The political project of the Portuguese government to assure normality in everyday life in those territories was successful, particularly in urban centres. Moreover, the public goods provision was tremendously improved thanks to the needs of building a road network in order to move troops, and install them throughout

---

[62] Laíns, 2004.

[63] Valério, N; Tjipilica, P., 2008: 1780.

the territories. The military engineering helped in many technical aspects, such as water provision and electricity production, while education (including high-schools and universities) and hospitals were spread throughout denser urban networks.

For foreign firms the existence of a colonial linkage between a territory and a European partner provided special safety in terms of available knowledge on the locally dominant political organisation, respect for established legal aspects, governmental administrative practices, and contract regimes.[64] For Portuguese firms the overseas empire also had these advantages, but it presented the same uncertainty regarding the ability to interpret the fitness of the business in global markets, the capacity to control it at a distance, or the possibility of performing in a different environment where tropical diseases were dangerous, especially malaria. The need to send confident staff, and the plan for training local employees was similarly demanding.

Two indices are estimated, one for the total number of companies listed in the Lisbon Stock Exchange, another for companies operating in the overseas territories, listed in the Lisbon Stock Exchange. Figure 9 accounts the number of companies we sampled to estimate the general and the overseas indices until 1974, using the methodology of the BVL-General index as closely as possible.

[64] Mata, 2007.

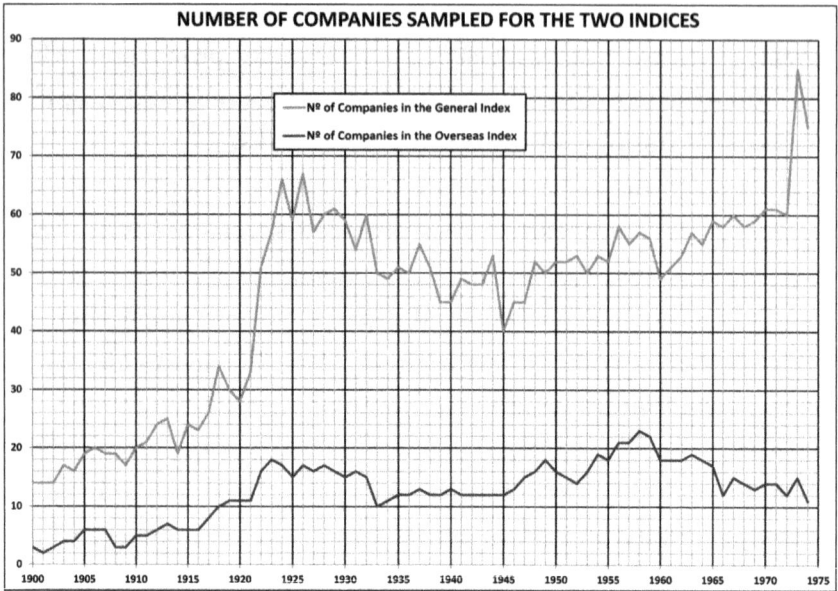

NUMBER OF COMPANIES SAMPLED FOR THE TWO INDICES

Nº of Companies in the General Index
Nº of Companies in the Overseas Index

Figure 9 — Number of companies used to compute the general and
the overseas indices until 1974

The number of corporations operating in the Portuguese offshore
listed in the Lisbon Stock Exchange varied from year to year, and
the statistical information that is recorded in the daily bulletins
shows that stock transactions were sparse. Table 1 summarises the
total number of corporations listed in the Lisbon Stock Exchange
and their distribution by sectors of activity (banking, insurance,
cotton-weaving and textiles, railways, other sectors, and overseas
businesses). Table 1 also refers the territories where the colonial
corporations sampled were at work. The sample that was selected
amongst the listed colonials includes all those that had frequent
transactions recorded in the daily bulletins.[65]

---

[65] Some of them even benefited from foreign capital investment. For global
explanations see Jones, G; Schröter, H., 1993.

Shipping companies were amongst the largest, especially the two sister corporations "Companhia Nacional de Navegação" and "Companhia Colonial de Navegação". Their existence was quite related with the existence of the empire and its geographical spread across three continents, reflecting the character of business opportunities that were involved. Other important sectors of activity were mining (including the diamonds company in Angola after 1956), farming (plantations of tropical crops and animal husbandry),[66] electricity production and distribution,[67] oil distribution,[68] and industrial activities (mainly sugar refining and alcohol production).[69]

The sample does not include the two banks listed in the Lisbon Stock Exchange, "Banco de Angola" (issuing bank for Angola) and "Banco Nacional Ultramarino" (issuing bank for all other overseas territories). This decision resulted from the huge weight they represent in the sample, commanding the evolution of the index and minimising the impact of all the others.

Most of the overseas corporations (including railway companies) were small organisations when compared with these two banks, and the aim is to discuss the equity return premium for private investment overseas, given the risk that was involved in those ventures and in those geographical endeavours.

Moreover, the inclusion of the two banks would not make sense, because both were headquartered in Lisbon, and also had an intense activity in the motherland.

---

[66] *Cotonang* was a cotton cultivation firm in Angola, using Belgium-Portuguese capital, founded in 1926. Riots and revolt against the company labour conditions in 1961 have been pointed out as the beginning of the colonial war.

[67] *Hidroeléctrica do Revué*, in Mozambique, listed since 1957.

[68] *Fina* do Lobito, in Angola, listed since 1958.

[69] *Companhia Agrícola do Cassequel*, in Angola, listed since 1937.

COMPANIES LISTED IN THE LISBON STOCK EXCHANGE

SECTOR	(Dec. 1900)		(Dec. 1905)		(Dec. 1910)		(Dec. 1915)	
	All Listed	In the Indices	All Listed	In the Indices	All Listed	In the Indices	All Listed	In the Indices
Banks (including BNU and BA)	7	5	6	5	6	5	8	7
Insurance Companies	7	0	9	1	15	1	11	4
Cotton, Weaving and Textiles	6	0	2	0	1			
Railways	1	1	4	2	3	2	3	1
Others	14	5	11	5	14	7	11	6
Total Overseas	10	3	10	6	13	5	10	6
Overseas — More than 1 Territory							1	
Guiné-Bissau								
S. Tomé e Príncipe*	4	1	3	1	4	1	3	3
Angola	1		2	1	2	1	2	
Mozambique	5	2	5	4	6	3	4	3
Timor					1			
TOTAL	45	14	42	19	52	20	43	24

SECTOR	(Dec. 1920)		(Dec. 1925)		(Dec. 1930)		(Dec. 1935)		(Dec. 1940)	
	All Listed	In the Indices	All Listed	In the Indices	All Listed	In the Indices	All Listed	In the Indices	All Listed	In the Indices
Banks (including BNU and BA)	12	7	10	11	10	10	9	8	8	7
Insurance Companies	18	5	23	10	15	8	15	10	17	5
Cotton, Weaving and Textiles	1		3	1	4		4		5	
Railways	4		4	2	4	3	4	1	4	1
Others	19	5	42	20	44	23	40	20	45	17
Total Overseas	24	11	33	15	35	15	26	12	25	13
Overseas — More than 1 Territory	1	1	2	1	2	2	2	2	2	2
Guiné-Bissau					1		1		1	
S. Tomé e Príncipe*	9	3	12	5	16	5	12	3	11	3
Angola	5	2	10	6	10	5	6	3	7	3
Mozambique	9	5	9	3	6	3	5	4	4	4
TOTAL	78	28	115	59	112	59	98	51	104	43

90

SECTOR		(Dec. 1945)		(Dec. 1950)		(Dec. 1955)		(Dec. 1960)		(Dec. 1965)	
		All Listed	In the Indices	All Listed	In the Indices	All Listed	In the Indices	All Listed	In the Indices	All Listed	In the Indices
Banks (including BNU and BA)		10	9	11	9	11	10	12	10	13	10
Insurance Companies		18	3	17	3	20	4	19	2	20	5
Cotton, Weaving and Textiles		5		5		5	1	5		5	
Railways		5	1	3	1	3	1	2			
Others		43	15	49	23	54	18	58	19	64	27
Total Overseas		23	12	25	16	30	18	36	18	35	17
Overseas	More than 1 Territory	2	2	2	2	2	2	3	3	3	3
	Guiné-Bissau	1		1		1		1		1	
	S. Tomé e Príncipe*	10	4	11	6	10	5	10	3	10	2
	Angola	6	3	6	4	8	4	11	6	10	6
	Mozambique	4	3	5	4	9	7	11	6	11	6
TOTAL		104	40	110	52	123	52	132	49	137	59

SECTOR		(Dec. 1970)		(Dec. 1973)		(Apr 1974)	
		All Listed	In the Indices	All Listed	In the Indices	All Listed	In the Indices
Banks (including BNU and BA)		12	11	17	16	17	16
Insurance Companies		24	4	25	17	25	15
Cotton, Weaving and Textiles		5	1	4	1	4	1
Railways				2		2	
Others		60	31	63	36	64	32
Total Overseas		35	14	36	15	37	11
Overseas	More than 1 Territory	3	3	3	3	3	2
	Guiné-Bissau	1	1	1	1	1	
	S. Tomé e Príncipe*	10	1	10	0	10	5
	Angola	11	6	12	7	12	
	Mozambique	10	4	10	5	11	4
TOTAL		136	61	145	85	149	75

Table 1 — Territories of operation of the overseas corporations listed in Lisbon

* The company "Agrícola de Fernando Póo", located in the spanish island of Fernando Póo was added to S Tomé e Príncipe.

The Overseas index had higher volatility. However, the general trend of the Overseas Index presents a steeper slope when compared to the General Index. It improved expected returns. The most successful firms had more expansive operations, just in the overseas territories and not in Europe. Their names evoke the region of operation or the business they addressed, and their annual reports frequently identify crossed-capital participations.

The net result of those private corporations has never been studied, and this chapter helps to investigate some of the consequences of the cost of capital in Portugal and in those overseas countries in terms of the economic value-added and diffusion of corporate culture. Long-term goals of most of the corporations operating in the empire may have ended in 1974, but the legacy of market rules to sub-Saharan territories was made available, entrepreneurship in novelty was learned, and decentralised leadership was experienced. Figure 10 presents the General and the Overseas indices of the Lisbon Stock Exchange over the twentieth century until decolonisation.

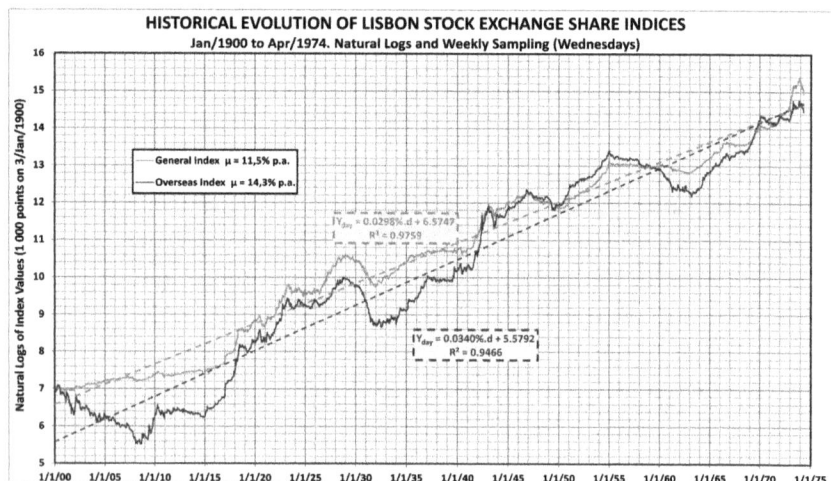

HISTORICAL EVOLUTION OF LISBON STOCK EXCHANGE SHARE INDICES
Jan/1900 to Apr/1974. Natural Logs and Weekly Sampling (Wednesdays)

General Index μ = 11,5% p.a.
Overseas Index μ = 14,3% p.a.

$lY_{day} = 0.0298\%.d + 6.5747$
$R^2 = 0.9759$

$lY_{day} = 0.0340\%.d + 5.5792$
$R^2 = 0.9466$

Figure 10 — The general trend of the Overseas Index compared to the General Index is for an extra volatility but improved expected return (steeper slope).

The capitalisation index represents the shareholders' rewards for their invested capital and risk, and those rewards contribute to the national income. Thanks to this measure for the investment success in these decades, both in the overseas empire and in Portugal as a whole, it is possible to suggest that from the end of the Great Depression to Decolonisation, there was a positive engagement in entrepreneurship initiatives, corporations' businesses, and Western management culture, while increasing levels of GDP per capita were achieved in the Portuguese overseas territories. The results are robust and particularly relevant in considering the current economic growth of these countries and the current difficulties of economic growth in Portugal. [70] The corporations performing in the overseas territories successfully provided higher returns (steeper slope of the fitted line) to their shareholders, in comparison to the whole sample of corporations listed in the Lisbon Stock Exchange. According to economics and National Accounting definitions, the national income corresponds to the total income from the remuneration of *productive factors*, including the remuneration of labour (wages) and return on capital (rents, interest and profits distributed by companies to their owners), as estimated here. There is equivalence between national income and GDP if depreciation and direct taxes are deducted from national income.[71]

The consequences of these estimates for the Portuguese historiography cannot be traced here. Out of any kind of prejudice, this chapter leaves objective information to be interpreted in the context of discussions on globalisation, risk, and colonial contributions for studying the modern economic growth.[72]

---

[70] Krugman, 2009. O'Brien, 1999. Spierdijk, 2010.

[71] Taxes levied directly on income from labour and capital.

[72] Hertner; Jones, 1986.

ANNEX 1
Companies Listed at BVL and those used to compute the Overseas Index

Dec/1900		
Name of Company	Listed at BVL	Overseas Index
Assucar de Moçambique	Moçambique	
Moçambique	Moçambique	Moçambique
Agrícola do Príncipe	São Tomé e Príncipe	
Agricultura Colonial	São Tomé e Príncipe	
Zambézia	Moçambique	Moçambique
Luabo	Moçambique	
Ilha do Príncipe	São Tomé e Príncipe	
Minas de Manica	Moçambique	
Agrícola de São Tomé	São Tomé e Príncipe	São Tomé e Príncipe
Mossamede	Angola	

Dec/1905		
Name of Company	Listed at BVL	Overseas Index
Assucar de Moçambique	Moçambique	Moçambique
Agrícola do Casengo	Angola	Angola
Moçambique	Moçambique	Moçambique
Congo Português	Angola	
Agrícola do Príncipe	São Tomé e Príncipe	
Agricultura Colonial	São Tomé e Príncipe	São Tomé e Príncipe
Zambézia	Moçambique	Moçambique
Luabo	Moçambique	Moçambique
Ilha do Príncipe	São Tomé e Príncipe	
Minas de Manica	Moçambique	

Dec/1910		
Name of Company	Listed at BVL	Overseas Index
Assucar de Moçambique	Moçambique	Moçambique
Colonial do Buzi	Moçambique	
Agrícola do Cazengo	Angola	Angola
Ilha do Príncipe	São Tomé e Príncipe	São Tomé e Príncipe
Luabo	Moçambique	
Moçambique	Moçambique	Moçambique
Agricultura Colonial	São Tomé e Príncipe	
Zambézia	Moçambique	Moçambique
Agrícola do Príncipe	São Tomé + Príncipe	
Agrícola Bela Vista	São Tomé + Príncipe	
Nyassa	Moçambique	
Timor	Timor	
Congo Português	Angola	

Dec/1915		
Name of Company	Listed at BVL	Overseas Index
Navegação (Nacional de)	Angola + Moçambique	
Assucar de Moçambique	Moçambique	Moçambique
Agrícola do Cazengo	Angola	
Ilha do Príncipe	São Tomé e Príncipe	São Tomé e Príncipe
Luabo	Moçambique	
Moçambique	Moçambique	Moçambique
Cabinda	Angola	
Agricultura Colonial	São Tomé e Príncipe	São Tomé e Príncipe
Zambézia	Moçambique	Moçambique
Agrícola do Príncipe	São Tomé e Príncipe	São Tomé e Príncipe

Dec/1920		
Name of Company	Listed at BVL	Overseas Index
Açúcar de Moçambique	Moçambique	Moçambique
Agrícola da Beira	Moçambique	
Agrícola de Bela Vista	São Tomé e Príncipe	
Agrícola do Cazengo	Angola	Angola
Agrícola do Ganda	Angola	
Agrícola das Neves	São Tomé e Príncipe	
Agrícola do Príncipe (Empreza)	São Tomé e Príncipe	São Tomé e Príncipe
Agrícola Ultramarina	São Tomé e Príncipe	
Agricultura Colonial (Sociedade)	São Tomé e Príncipe	São Tomé e Príncipe
Boror	Moçambique	Moçambique
Cabinda	Angola	Angola
Colonial do Buzi	Moçambique	Moçambique
Comércio de Moçambique	Moçambique	
Congo Português	Angola	
Ilha do Príncipe	São Tomé e Príncipe	São Tomé e Príncipe
Luabo	Moçambique	
Moçambique	Moçambique	Moçambique
Mossamedes	Angola	
Navegação (Nacional de)	Angola + Moçambique	Angola + Moçambique
Niassa	Moçambique	
Roça Aliança	São Tomé e Príncipe	
Roça Angra Toldo	São Tomé e Príncipe	
Roça Laura	São Tomé e Príncipe	
Zambézia	Moçambique	Moçambique

Dec/1925		
Name of Company	Listed at BVL	Overseas Index
Açúcar de Angola	Angola	Angola
Açúcar de Moçambique	Moçambique	
África Ocidental Portuguesa	Angola	
Agrícola de Bela Vista	São Tomé e Príncipe	
Agrícola do Cazengo	Angola	Angola
Agrícola do Ganda	Angola	Angola
Agrícola das Neves	São Tomé e Príncipe	São Tomé e Príncipe
Agrícola do Príncipe (Empreza)	São Tomé e Príncipe	São Tomé e Príncipe
Agrícola Sant'Ana	Angola	
Agrícola Ultramarina	São Tomé e Príncipe	São Tomé e Príncipe
Agricultura Colonial (Sociedade)	São Tomé e Príncipe	São Tomé e Príncipe
Amboim	Angola	Angola
Boror	Moçambique	Moçambique
Cabinda	Angola	Angola
Colonial do Buzi	Moçambique	Moçambique
Comércio de Moçambique	Moçambique	
Congo Português	Angola	
Govuro	Moçambique	
Ilha do Príncipe	São Tomé e Príncipe	São Tomé e Príncipe
Luabo	Moçambique	
Moçambique	Moçambique	
Mossamedes	Angola	
Navegação (Nacional de)	Angola + Moçambique	Angola + Moçambique
Navegação Colonial	Angola + Moçambique	
Niassa	Moçambique	
Roça Aliança	São Tomé e Príncipe	
Roça Angra Toldo	São Tomé e Príncipe	
Roça Ió Grande	São Tomé e Príncipe	
Roça Porto Alegre	São Tomé e Príncipe	
Roça Vista Alegre	São Tomé e Príncipe	
Roça Saudade	São Tomé e Príncipe	
Sul de Angola	Angola	Angola
Zambézia	Moçambique	Moçambique

Unknown or doughtful localion

96

Dec/1930		
Name of Company	Listed at BVL	Overseas Index
África Ocidental Portuguesa	Angola	
Agrícola de Angola	Angola	
Agrícola de Bela Vista	São Tomé e Príncipe	São Tomé e Príncipe
Agrícola do Cazengo	Angola	Angola
Agrícola do Ganda	Angola	Angola
Agrícola das Neves	São Tomé e Príncipe	São Tomé e Príncipe
Agrícola do Príncipe (Empreza)	São Tomé e Príncipe	São Tomé e Príncipe
Agrícola Ribeira Palma	São Tomé e Príncipe	
Agrícola Sant'Ana	Angola	
Agrícola Ultramarina	São Tomé e Príncipe	
Agricultura Colonial (Sociedade)	São Tomé e Príncipe	São Tomé e Príncipe
Amboim	Angola	Angola
Açúcar de Angola	Angola	Angola
Açúcar de Moçambique	Moçambique	
Boror	Moçambique	Moçambique
Cabinda	Angola	Angola
Colonial Agrícola	S. Tomé e Príncipe	
Colonial do Buzi	Moçambique	Moçambique
Colonial Portuguesa	S. Tomé e Príncipe	
Comercial Ultramarina (Sociedade)	Guiné	
Comércio de Moçambique	Moçambique	
Ilha do Príncipe	São Tomé e Príncipe	São Tomé e Príncipe
Mossamedes	Angola	
Navegação (Nacional de)	Angola + Moçambique	Angola + Moçambique
Navegação Colonial	Angola + Moçambique	Angola + Moçambique
Niassa	Moçambique	
Roça Aliança	São Tomé e Príncipe	
Roça Angra Toldo	São Tomé e Príncipe	
Roça Ió Grande	São Tomé e Príncipe	
Roça Plateau e Milagrosa	São Tomé e Príncipe	
Roça Porto Alegre	São Tomé e Príncipe	
Roça Vista Alegre	São Tomé e Príncipe	
Roça Saudade	São Tomé e Príncipe	
Sul de Angola	Angola	
Zambézia	Moçambique	Moçambique

Unknown or doughtful localion

97

Dec/1935		
Name of Company	Listed at BVL	Overseas Index
África Ocidental Portuguesa	Angola	
Agrícola das Neves	São Tomé e Príncipe	São Tomé e Príncipe
Agrícola Ribeira Palma	São Tomé e Príncipe	
Agrícola Sant'Ana	**Angola**	
Agrícola Ultramarina	São Tomé e Príncipe	
Agricultura Colonial (Sociedade)	São Tomé e Príncipe	São Tomé e Príncipe
Açúcar de Angola	Angola	Angola
Açúcar de Moçambique	Moçambique	Moçambique
Boror	Moçambique	Moçambique
Cabinda	Angola	Angola
Colonial Agrícola	**S. Tomé e Príncipe**	
Colonial do Buzi	Moçambique	Moçambique
Colonial Portuguesa	**S. Tomé e Príncipe**	
Comercial Ultramarina (Sociedade)	**Guiné**	
Comércio de Moçambique	Moçambique	
Ilha do Príncipe	São Tomé e Príncipe	São Tomé e Príncipe
Mossamedes	Angola	
Navegação (Nacional de)	Angola + Moçambique	Angola + Moçambique
Navegação Colonial	Angola + Moçambique	Angola + Moçambique
Roça Aliança	São Tomé e Príncipe	
Roça Ió Grande	São Tomé e Príncipe	
Roça Plateau e Milagrosa	São Tomé e Príncipe	
Roça Porto Alegre	São Tomé e Príncipe	
Roça Vista Alegre	São Tomé e Príncipe	
Sul de Angola	Angola	Angola
Zambézia	Moçambique	Moçambique

Unknown or doughtful localion

98

Dec/1940		
Name of Company	**Listed at BVL**	**Overseas Index**
África Ocidental Portuguesa	Angola	
Agrícola de Cassequel	Angola	Angola
Agrícola das Neves	São Tomé e Príncipe	São Tomé e Príncipe
Agrícola Ribeira Palma	São Tomé e Príncipe	
Agrícola Sant'Ana	**Angola**	
Agrícola Ultramarina	São Tomé e Príncipe	São Tomé e Príncipe
Agricultura Colonial (Sociedade)	São Tomé e Príncipe	São Tomé e Príncipe
Açúcar de Angola	Angola	Angola
Boror	Moçambique	Moçambique
Cabinda	Angola	Angola
Colonial Agrícola	**S. Tomé e Príncipe**	
Colonial do Buzi	Moçambique	Moçambique
Colonial Portuguesa	**S. Tomé e Príncipe**	
Comercial Ultramarina (Sociedade)	**Guiné**	
Comércio de Moçambique	Moçambique	Moçambique
Ilha do Príncipe	São Tomé e Príncipe	São Tomé e Príncipe
Navegação (Nacional de)	Angola + Moçambique	Angola + Moçambique
Navegação Colonial	Angola + Moçambique	Angola + Moçambique
Mossamedes	Angola	
Roça Aliança	São Tomé e Príncipe	
Roça Ió Grande	São Tomé e Príncipe	
Roça Plateau e Milagrosa	São Tomé e Príncipe	
Roça Vista Alegre	São Tomé e Príncipe	
Sul de Angola	Angola	
Zambézia	Moçambique	Moçambique

Unknown or doughtful localion

Dec/1945		
Name of Company	Listed at BVL	Overseas Index
África Ocidental Portuguesa	Angola	
Agrícola de Cassequel	Angola	Angola
Agrícola das Neves	São Tomé e Príncipe	São Tomé e Príncipe
Agrícola Ribeira Palma	São Tomé e Príncipe	
Agrícola Ultramarina	São Tomé e Príncipe	São Tomé e Príncipe
Agricultura Colonial (Sociedade)	São Tomé e Príncipe	São Tomé e Príncipe
Açúcar de Angola	Angola	Angola
Boror	Moçambique	Moçambique
Cabinda	Angola	Angola
Colonial Agrícola	S. Tomé e Príncipe	
Colonial do Buzi	Moçambique	Moçambique
Colonial Portuguesa	S. Tomé e Príncipe	
Comercial Ultramarina (Sociedade)	Guiné	
Comércio de Moçambique	Moçambique	
Ilha do Príncipe	São Tomé e Príncipe	São Tomé e Príncipe
Mossamedes	Angola	
Navegação (Nacional de)	Angola + Moçambique	Angola + Moçambique
Navegação Colonial	Angola + Moçambique	Angola + Moçambique
Roça Aliança	São Tomé e Príncipe	
Roça Ió Grande	São Tomé e Príncipe	
Roça Plateau e Milagrosa	São Tomé e Príncipe	
Sul de Angola	Angola	
Zambézia	Moçambique	Moçambique

Unknown or doughtful localion

Dec/1950		
Name of Company	**Listed at BVL**	**Overseas Index**
Agrícola Bela Vista	São Tomé e Príncipe	São Tomé e Príncipe
Agrícola de Cassequel	Angola	Angola
Agrícola de Fernando Poó	Ilha de Fernando Poó	Ilha de Fernando Poó
Agrícola das Neves	São Tomé e Príncipe	São Tomé e Príncipe
Agrícola Ribeira Palma	São Tomé e Príncipe	
Agrícola Ultramarina	São Tomé e Príncipe	São Tomé e Príncipe
Agricultura Colonial (Sociedade)	São Tomé e Príncipe	São Tomé e Príncipe
Açúcar de Angola	Angola	Angola
Angolana de Agricultura	Angola	Angola
Asfaltos de Angola	Angola	
Boror	Moçambique	Moçambique
Cabinda	Angola	Angola
Colonial Agrícola	**S. Tomé e Príncipe**	
Colonial do Buzi	Moçambique	Moçambique
Colonial Portuguesa	**S. Tomé e Príncipe**	
Comercial Ultramarina (Sociedade)	**Guiné**	
Comércio de Moçambique	Moçambique	
Ilha do Príncipe	São Tomé e Príncipe	São Tomé e Príncipe
Navegação (Nacional de)	Angola + Moçambique	Angola + Moçambique
Navegação Colonial	Angola + Moçambique	Angola + Moçambique
Moçambique	Moçambique	Moçambique
Roça Aliança	São Tomé e Príncipe	
Roça Plateau e Milagrosa	São Tomé e Príncipe	
Seles	Angola	
Zambézia	Moçambique	Moçambique

Unknown or doughtful localion

101

Dec/1955		
Name of Company	Listed at BVL	Overseas Index
Agrícola Bela Vista	São Tomé e Príncipe	São Tomé e Príncipe
Agrícola de Cassequel	Angola	Angola
Agrícola de Fernando Poó	Ilha de Fernando Poó	
Agrícola do Incomati	Moçambique	Moçambique
Agrícola das Neves	São Tomé e Príncipe	São Tomé e Príncipe
Agrícola Ribeira Palma	São Tomé e Príncipe	
Agrícola Ultramarina	São Tomé e Príncipe	São Tomé e Príncipe
Agricultura Colonial (Sociedade)	São Tomé e Príncipe	São Tomé e Príncipe
Açúcar de Angola	Angola	Angola
Angolana de Agricultura	Angola	Angola
Asfaltos de Angola	Angola	
Boror	Moçambique	Moçambique
Boror Comercial	Moçambique	Moçambique
Cabinda	Angola	Angola
Cabinda Comercial	Angola	
Colonial Agrícola	S. Tomé e Príncipe	
Colonial do Buzi	Moçambique	Moçambique
Comercial Ultramarina (Sociedade)	Guiné	
Comércio e Construções	Angola	
Comércio de Moçambique	Moçambique	Moçambique
Hidro Eléctrica Revué	Moçambique	
Ilha do Príncipe	São Tomé e Príncipe	São Tomé e Príncipe
Moçambique	Moçambique	Moçambique
Navegação (Nacional de)	Angola + Moçambique	Angola + Moçambique
Navegação Colonial	Angola + Moçambique	Angola + Moçambique
Roça Aliança	São Tomé e Príncipe	
Roça Plateau e Milagrosa	São Tomé e Príncipe	
Seles	Angola	
Sena Sugar	Moçambique	
Zambézia	Moçambique	Moçambique

Unknown or doughtful location

Dec/1960		
Name of Company	**Listed at BVL**	**Overseas Index**
Águas de Montemor	Moçambique	
Agrícola Bela Vista	São Tomé e Príncipe	
Agrícola de Cassequel	Angola	Angola
Agrícola do Encoge Micula	Angola	
Agrícola de Fernando Poó	Ilha de Fernando Poó	
Agrícola do Incomati	Moçambique	Moçambique
Agrícola das Neves	São Tomé e Príncipe	São Tomé e Príncipe
Agrícola Ribeira Palma	São Tomé e Príncipe	
Agrícola Ultramarina	São Tomé e Príncipe	
Agricultura Colonial (Sociedade)	São Tomé e Príncipe	São Tomé e Príncipe
Açúcar de Angola	Angola	Angola
Angolana de Agricultura	Angola	Angola
Asfaltos de Angola	Angola	
Boror	Moçambique	Moçambique
Boror Comercial	Moçambique	
Cabinda	Angola	Angola
Cabinda Comercial	Angola	
Colonial Agrícola	S. Tomé e Príncipe	
Colonial do Buzi	Moçambique	Moçambique
Combustíveis do Lobito	Angola	Angola
Comercial Ultramarina (Sociedade)	Guiné	
Comércio e Construções	Angola	
Comércio de Moçambique	Moçambique	
Diamantes de Angola	Angola	Angola
Hidro Eléctrica Revué	Moçambique	Moçambique
Ilha do Príncipe	São Tomé e Príncipe	São Tomé e Príncipe
Moçambique	Moçambique	Moçambique
Navegação (Nacional de)	Angola + Moçambique	Angola + Moçambique
Navegação Colonial	Angola + Moçambique	Angola + Moçambique
Roça Aliança	São Tomé e Príncipe	
Roça Plateau e Milagrosa	São Tomé e Príncipe	
Seles	Angola	
Sena Sugar	Moçambique	
Sonefe	Angola + Moçambique	Angola + Moçambique
Turismo de Moçambique	Moçambique	
Zambézia	Moçambique	Moçambique

Unknown or doughtful localion

Dec/1965		
Name of Company	Listed at BVL	Overseas Index
Águas de Montemor	**Moçambique**	
Agrícola Bela Vista	São Tomé e Príncipe	
Agrícola de Cassequel	Angola	Angola
Agrícola do Encoge Micula	Angola	
Agrícola de Fernando Poó	Ilha de Fernando Poó	
Agrícola do Incomati	Moçambique	Moçambique
Agrícola das Neves	São Tomé e Príncipe	
Agrícola Ribeira Palma	São Tomé e Príncipe	
Agrícola Ultramarina	São Tomé e Príncipe	
Agricultura S. Tomé e Príncipe	São Tomé e Príncipe	São Tomé e Príncipe
Açúcar de Angola	Angola	Angola
Angolana de Agricultura	Angola	Angola
Asfaltos de Angola	Angola	
Boror	Moçambique	Moçambique
Boror Comercial	Moçambique	
Colonial do Buzi	Moçambique	Moçambique
Cabinda	Angola	Angola
Colonial Agrícola	**S. Tomé e Príncipe**	
Combustíveis do Lobito (FINA)	Angola	Angola
Comercial Ultramarina (Sociedade)	**Guiné**	
Comércio e Construções	**Angola**	
Comércio de Moçambique	Moçambique	
Diamantes de Angola	Angola	Angola
Hidro Eléctrica Revué	Moçambique	Moçambique
Ilha do Príncipe	São Tomé e Príncipe	São Tomé e Príncipe
Moçambique	Moçambique	Moçambique
Navegação (Nacional de)	Angola + Moçambique	Angola + Moçambique
Navegação Colonial	Angola + Moçambique	Angola + Moçambique
Roça Aliança	São Tomé e Príncipe	
Roça Plateau e Milagrosa	São Tomé e Príncipe	
Seles	Angola	
Sena Sugar	Moçambique	
Sonefe	Angola + Moçambique	Angola + Moçambique
Turismo de Moçambique	Moçambique	
Zambézia	Moçambique	Moçambique

Unknown or doughtful localion

104

Dec/1970		
Name of Company	**Listed at BVL**	**Overseas Index**
Águas de Montemor	Moçambique	
Agrícola Bela Vista	São Tomé e Príncipe	
Agrícola de Cassequel	Angola	Angola
Agrícola do Encoge Micula	Angola	
Agrícola de Fernando Poó	Ilha de Fernando Poó	
Agrícola do Incomati	Moçambique	
Agrícola das Neves	São Tomé e Príncipe	
Agrícola Ribeira Palma	São Tomé e Príncipe	
Agrícola Ultramarina	São Tomé e Príncipe	
Agricultura S. Tomé e Príncipe	São Tomé e Príncipe	São Tomé e Príncipe
Açúcar de Angola	Angola	Angola
Algodões de Angola (Cotonang)	Angola	
Angolana de Agricultura	Angola	Angola
Asfaltos de Angola	Angola	
Boror	Moçambique	
Boror Comercial	Moçambique	
Colonial do Buzi	Moçambique	Moçambique
Cabinda	Angola	Angola
Colonial Agrícola	S. Tomé e Príncipe	
Combustíveis do Lobito (FINA)	Angola	Angola
Comercial Ultramarina (Sociedade)	Guiné	
Comércio e Construções	Angola	
Diamantes de Angola	Angola	Angola
Hidro Eléctrica Revué	Moçambique	Moçambique
Ilha do Príncipe	São Tomé e Príncipe	
Moçambique	Moçambique	Moçambique
Navegação (Nacional de)	Angola + Moçambique	Angola + Moçambique
Navegação Colonial	Angola + Moçambique	Angola + Moçambique
Roça Aliança	São Tomé e Príncipe	
Roça Plateau e Milagrosa	São Tomé e Príncipe	
Seles	Angola	
Sena Sugar	Moçambique	
Sonefe	Angola + Moçambique	Angola + Moçambique
Turismo de Moçambique	Moçambique	
Zambézia	Moçambique	Moçambique

Unknown or doughtful localion

105

Dec/1973		
Name of Company	Listed at BVL	Overseas Index
Águas de Montemor	Moçambique	
Agrícola Bela Vista	São Tomé e Príncipe	
Agrícola de Cassequel	Angola	Angola
Agrícola do Encoge Micula	Angola	
Agrícola de Fernando Poó	Ilha de Fernando Poó	
Agrícola do Incomati	Moçambique	Moçambique
Agrícola das Neves	São Tomé e Príncipe	
Agrícola Ribeira Palma	São Tomé e Príncipe	
Agrícola Ultramarina	São Tomé e Príncipe	
Agricultura S. Tomé e Príncipe	São Tomé e Príncipe	
Açúcar de Angola	Angola	Angola
Algodões de Angola (Cotonang)	Angola	Angola
Angolana de Agricultura	Angola	Angola
Asfaltos de Angola	Angola	
Boror	Moçambique	
Boror Comercial	Moçambique	
Colonial do Buzi	Moçambique	Moçambique
Cabinda	Angola	Angola
Colonial Agrícola	S. Tomé e Príncipe	
Combustíveis do Lobito (FINA)	Angola	Angola
Comercial Ultramarina (Sociedade)	Guiné	
Comércio e Construções	Angola	
Diamantes de Angola	Angola	Angola
Geral de Angola	Angola	
Hidro Eléctrica Revué	Moçambique	Moçambique
Ilha do Príncipe	São Tomé e Príncipe	
Moçambique	Moçambique	Moçambique
Navegação (Nacional de)	Angola + Moçambique	Angola + Moçambique
Navegação Colonial	Angola + Moçambique	Angola + Moçambique
Roça Aliança	São Tomé e Príncipe	
Roça Plateau e Milagrosa	São Tomé e Príncipe	
Seles	Angola	
Sena Sugar	Moçambique	
Sonefe	Angola + Moçambique	Angola + Moçambique
Turismo de Moçambique	Moçambique	
Zambézia	Moçambique	Moçambique

Unknown or doughtful localion

106

Apr/1974		
Name of Company	Listed at BVL	Overseas Index
Águas de Montemor	Moçambique	
Agrícola Bela Vista	São Tomé e Príncipe	
Agrícola de Cassequel	Angola	Angola
Agrícola do Encoge Micula	Angola	
Agrícola de Fernando Poó	Ilha de Fernando Poó	
Agrícola do Incomati	Moçambique	Moçambique
Agrícola das Neves	São Tomé e Príncipe	
Agrícola Ribeira Palma	São Tomé e Príncipe	
Agrícola Ultramarina	São Tomé e Príncipe	
Agricultura S. Tomé e Príncipe	São Tomé e Príncipe	
Açúcar de Angola	Angola	Angola
Algodões de Angola (Cotonang)	Angola	Angola
Angolana de Agricultura	Angola	
Asfaltos de Angola	Angola	
Boror	Moçambique	
Boror Comercial	Moçambique	
Colonial do Buzi	Moçambique	Moçambique
Cabinda	Angola	Angola
Colonial Agrícola	S. Tomé e Príncipe	
Fina - Combustíveis do Lobito	Angola	Angola
Comercial Ultramarina (Sociedade)	Guiné	
Comércio e Construções	Angola	
Comércio de Moçambique	Moçambique	Moçambique
Diamantes de Angola	Angola	
Geral de Angola	Angola	
Hidro Eléctrica Revué	Moçambique	
Ilha do Príncipe	São Tomé e Príncipe	
Moçambique	Moçambique	
Navegação (Nacional de)	Angola + Moçambique	Angola + Moçambique
Navegação Colonial	Angola + Moçambique	
Roça Aliança	São Tomé e Príncipe	
Roça Plateau e Milagrosa	São Tomé e Príncipe	
Seles	Angola	
Sena Sugar	Moçambique	
Sonefe	Angola + Moçambique	Angola + Moçambique
Turismo de Moçambique	Moçambique	
Zambézia	Moçambique	Moçambique

Unknown or doughtful localion

107

Chapter 4
PORTUGUESE MACROECONOMIC PERFORMANCE AND THE BVL EQUITY INDEX

Introduction

Financial markets deserve a considerable attention because of their central role in fuelling the economic development of nations, and also because they provide decisive information for economic decision-making in market-oriented economies.

A long-run view on the twentieth century can only conclude that it was a dramatic time for Europe because (at least) of the two long and bloody wars that determined the European markets and financial flows.

In spite of that, the post-second World War period in Portugal was a very successful time for businesses, as a whole, with the exception of the revolutionary years (1974-1976). This explains the positive economic growth rate performance witnessed during those post-war years. Later on, joining Europe in 1986 brought another boost to the domestic performance until the end of the millennium. By contrast, the new millennium is showing a stagnant character in many European countries, and the Portuguese economy also presents a very sluggish economic growth (Figure 1).

As indicators of saving and investment decisions, in this chapter the capital market and the Stock Exchange are surveyed to discover the importance of the many political events that unfolded in Portugal during the twentieth century (Annex 2 describes the duration of Portuguese governments). The collected data show that the Stock Exchange variables are now decisive for examining the effects of political events on the behaviour of financial markets.[1]

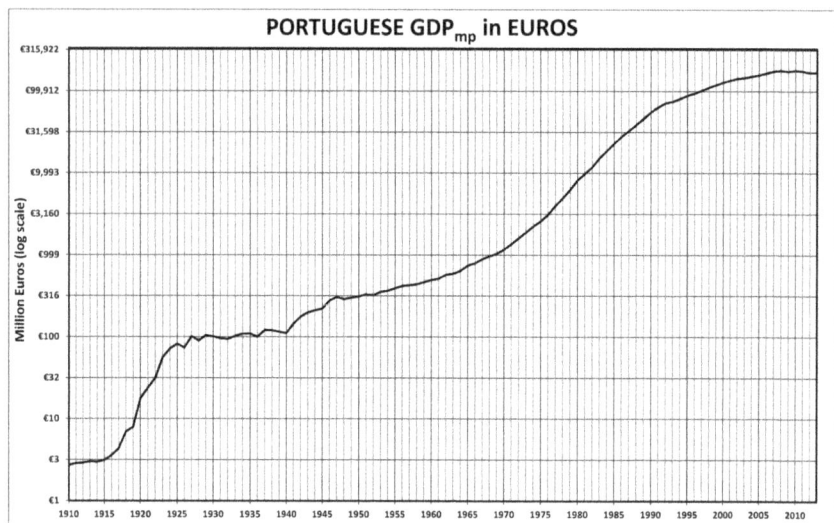

Figure 1 — Evolution of the Portuguese GDP$_{mp}$ expressed in Euros

1. The 45 short-term governments during the 16 years of the 1st Republic

In Portugal, the early years of the twentieth century until the outbreak of WWI were very difficult times. The replacement in 1910 of the traditional monarchic regime that ruled the country since the beginning of the nation in the twelfth century by a Republican

---

[1] See Cornell 1999: 2-4.

regime is but one consequence of the economic, financial, and social difficulties surfacing in that period.

After the murder of the King and the Crown Prince in1908, the subsequent government together with the new (young) king Manuel still made a political attempt to secure the survival of the exhausted monarchy. But all financial markets were then completely closed to the Portuguese government due to the government bankruptcy declared in 1892.

As mentioned in Chapter 2, while negotiations with the foreign lenders led to a 1902 public debt conversion, short-run Treasury needs had to be funded domestically only, either by monetary expansion from the central bank — Bank of Portugal — or via loans extended by *Caixa Geral dos Depósitos* , a local governmental commercial bank.

Some funding could still be collected abroad thanks to special contracts of a Portuguese banker *Henri Burnay*, but this source did not last long as he passed away in 1906. Remittances from Brazilian emigrants also provided some capital inflows to the Portuguese economy.

Contrasting with Portugal, the early years of the twentieth century were very prosperous times for most of our European partners, as well as for the New World. For countries belonging to the gold--standard regime in the core regions of the world — which was not the case of Portugal as it had left this "club" in 1891 — the monetary context was favourable to international business, to foreign direct investment (FDI), and to improving financial interconnections.

Free capital movements (including repatriation of profits and dividends) and fixed exchange rates provided an excellent business background, with no exchange-rate volatility. A European financial civilisation circled the planet, from the UK to Southern Europe, Canada and the USA, from Germany to Eastern European regions and Russia, from continental European countries to Malaysia and the Philippines, and even from the UK and Belgium to Portugal, Angola, and Mozambique.[2] As Keynes (1924) explains,

> *What an extraordinary episode in the economic progress of man that age was which came to an end in August 1914! (...) The inhabitant of London could order by telephone, sipping his morning tea in bed, the various products of the whole earth, in such quantity as he might see fit, and reasonably expect their early delivery upon his doorstep; he could at the same moment and by the same means adventure his wealth in the natural resources and new enterprises of any quarter of the world, and share, without exertion or even trouble, in their prospective fruits and advantages; or he could decide to couple the security of his fortunes with the good faith of the townspeople of any substantial municipality in any continent that fancy or information might recommend.[3]*

But this world financial system broke up in August 1914, when the Austrian Empire declared war on Serbia, and many other European nations decided to support one side or the other in this conflict.[4]

2. WWI and the interruption of Stock Exchange operations

The First World War[5] interrupted prosperity in all European countries. Before WWI, financial affairs belonged primarily to the London City, thanks to the British hegemony over world markets. From the Bank of England, transactions had moved to the street

---

[2] Foreman-Peck, 2001a.

[3] Ibidem, page 11.

[4] Although Spain, Switzerland, Netherlands, Denmark, Norway, and Sweden remained neutral. Hardach, 1987. Bergier, 1983.

[5] WWI began on 28 July 1914 and ended on 11 November 1918.

Change-Alley, with the first building — Capel Court — being made available in 1802 to accommodate a large amount of domestic and foreign financial businesses.[6] The London Stock Exchange (LSE) financial hegemony may be related with its banking system strength, and the character of an island nation with a huge overseas empire.[7] *"The LSE before 1914 was the global stock market: it traded a third of the world's securities and 71 of the world's hundred largest quoted corporations had at least one of their securities listed there".*[8]

The war changed the face of the world, with huge consequences for the Stock Exchanges. The large European empires' traditional hegemony faced newly industrialised allied countries. The extension of the conflict along the lengthy battle line from Belgium to Southern Europe paralysed all normal businesses.[9] All priority was given to hostilities. Universities closed for some periods of time, as did Stock Exchanges, and the conditions for globalisation were disrupted. Submarine warfare almost put an end to Atlantic shipping.[10] The gold-standard suddenly came to an end, as military expenditure in all nations threw convertibility into disarray.

Normal operations and businesses in financial markets were interrupted and financial distress reduced asset prices in foreign markets, and increased transaction costs:[11]

> *In London, the world's foremost financial centre, the week before the outbreak of the First World War saw the breakdown of the markets, culminating with the closure for the first time ever of the London Stock Exchange on Friday 31 July. Outside the Bank*

---

[6] Duguid, 1901, p. 4. Boudon, 1896, 1898. Stringham, 2002.

[7] Sylla, 2009: 234.

[8] Foreman-Peck, Hannah, 2011, p. 5. Antwerp, 1913.

[9] Hardach, 1987. Blakey, 2010.

[10] Rousseau and Sylla, 2003.

[11] Amihud; Mendelson, 1986.

of England a long anxious queue waited to change bank notes for gold sovereigns. Bankers believed that a run on the banks was underway, threatening the collapse of the banking system — all with the nation on the eve of war".[12]

Closures were intended to avoid traders from simultaneously selling-off their inventories of shares (in the context of liquidity urgent need) and gave origin to a diffuse street market. The London Exchange reopened by the end of the following year. In New York, plunging share prices obliged authorities to close the Exchange on July, 31, to reopen only on December 12, *"the longest period of time that the Exchange has not operated".[13]*

The Portuguese government also suspended all operations in the Lisbon and Porto Exchanges — on Cash and on Derivatives — by the Decree nº 797 (25 August 1914), but re-established the (only) Cash market by *"Portaria"* nr. 240 (30 September 1914);[14] the cash market was therefore closed for only two months, but the operations on Derivatives resumed in both cities only much later, on 1 November 1924, following a specific *"Portaria"* (nr. 4206, dated 22 September 1924). In practice the Lisbon Stock Exchange closed during the 1914 summer: there are no daily Bulletins from Wednesday 5 August 1914 to 23 September 1914.

For Portugal, unfortunately, financial equilibrium and economic growth were still being pursued after the 1910 Republican revolution when the WWI broke out, but that purpose had then to be conducted out of the gold-standard and still in the shadow of the 1892 bankruptcy.

---

[12] Roberts, 2013, https://itunes.apple.com/br/book/saving-city-great-financial/id784312364?mt=11.

[13] Hafer and Hein, 2007: XIX.

[14] *"Portaria"* is the Portuguese name of second level governmental diplomas usually used to regulate in detail general principles affirmed by superior Decrees.

Actually, by improving tax collection, the Portuguese public accounts even reached an equilibrium in 1912-13, but again turned red soon after reflecting the high military expenditures necessary to send and maintain troops in the battlefields of Flanders, (from 1917 on) and to reinforce troops (from 1914 on) in two other battlefield scenarios — southern Angola and northern Mozambique — due to their borders with German territories (then called Namibia and Tanzania). This military effort required a loan of £22 million obtained from the allied UK.[15]

This conflict exhausted all nations, all armies, and all families, and by the end of the conflict, Europe was a continent in ruins. Fighting had ravaged not only the battlefields but also national economies. Destruction, death, and annihilation were the image of the face of Europe. London, Paris, Frankfurt, and all the other Stock Exchanges saw a dramatic reduction in their volume of operations.[16] From then on, the great financial centre was New York, on the other side of the Atlantic.[17]

The following decades were still difficult times[18] and in Portugal the twenties were severe years.[19] Treasury difficulties, frequent rotation of government teams (45 governments in 16 years!), and a highly unstable military environment were three related factors (Annex 2). The Portuguese currency (the *Escudo*) introduced in 1911 with the new republican regime depreciated almost 33 times (from around 4.77/£ in October 1910 to 155.54/£ in July 1924),[20] making it vastly more difficult to service the foreign debt.

---

[15] From this authorized amount Portugal used £19.084 million. Valério, 2001.

[16] Aldcroft, 1987.

[17] Michie, 1987.

[18] Milward, 1984, 1987.

[19] For the difficulties in listed firms of the milling sector, see Ferreira, s.d. http://ler.letras.up.pt/uploads/ficheiros/5294.pdf.

[20] Source: Mata, 1987.

According to the Treaty of Versailles Portugal was entitled to receive War reparations, but there was great uncertainty about these payments, because of Germany's inability to accomplish these commitments under its hyper-inflationary conditions of the period. The 1931 Hoover Moratorium and the 1932 Lausanne Conference put an end to any German War reparations, but also cancelled the payment of War loans that depended on them.[21] In Portugal this was compounded with the short-lived and weak governments during those years (Annex 2).[22] In Lisbon, the equity index was quite sluggish.

3. The Great Depression

After 1924 it was possible to announce an effective control of the financial and monetary problems in Portugal, and the implementation of the Dawes Plan also brought hopeful perspectives about the German War reparations. The positive results of financial improvements are clear in the Lisbon Stock Exchange general share index until the Great Depression, as figure 2 shows.

This Portuguese post-war recovery in the second half of the 1920s was very short lived — lasted only until 1924 — and that led on 28 May 1926 to a domestic military coup. In fact, that recovery was not enough to avoid that 1st Republic, installed in 1910, from being ousted by a victorious military junta that created a new political regime that lasted until April 1974.

---

[21] Until 1931 Portugal paid £950,000 of the British War loan (which was scheduled to be paid by 1988, amounting to £29,935 million, with interest).

[22] After 1922 the governments' average duration was less than one year.

HISTORICAL EVOLUTION OF LISBON STOCK EXCHANGE GENERAL EQUITY INDEX
Jan/1900 to Dec/1929. Natural Logs and Weekly Sampling (Wednesdays)

Figure 2 — The Lisbon Stock Exchange share index from 1900 to
the Great Depression

In the beginning of this new regime, and following the international trends then current in many parts of Europe, it openly declared the adoption of a dictatorship under the control of the military forces. Later, in 1933, with a new political Constitution, the regime changed into a simple muscled system with periodic legislative and presidential elections, but all constructed under a single political movement — called *"União Nacional"*, a "movement", not a political party — led by Salazar.

In the meantime, the Great Depression (1929-1933) spread around the globe. In Portugal it drew attention to the need of a separate housing for the Commodity Exchange (*"Bolsa de Mercadorias"*), although physical and organisationally very close to the Stock Exchange, as many tropical goods were produced in the overseas territories but traded in Lisbon.

Figure 3 illustrates how the Lisbon Stock Exchange share index can be used to measure the size of the Great Depression effects upon the Portuguese economy.

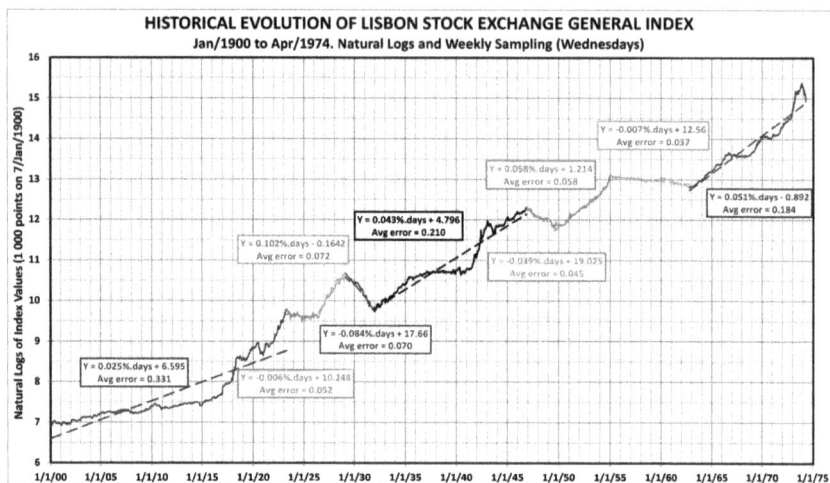

HISTORICAL EVOLUTION OF LISBON STOCK EXCHANGE GENERAL INDEX
Jan/1900 to Apr/1974. Natural Logs and Weekly Sampling (Wednesdays)

Figure 3 — Economic cycles impacting the Lisbon Exchange market as expressed by the share index

Although the tipping point to the Great Depression in the US economy was 24 October 1929, the Portuguese index inverts its positive trend on 13 February 1929, that is eight months in advance: it switches from an impressive average return of +38.2% p.a. to a losing trend of 29.7% p.a. as Table 1 shows.

BVL GENERAL INDEX

Cycles			$\mu_{B\&S\,model}$
	Begin	End	
Jan/00-Apr/23	03/01/1900	18/04/1923	**9.81%**
Apr/23-Jun/26	18/04/1923	02/06/1926	**-0.86%**
Jun/26-Feb/29	02/06/1926	13/02/1929	**38.19%**
Feb/29-Dec/31	13/02/1929	09/12/1931	**-29.74%**
Dec/31-Nov/46	09/12/1931	06/11/1946	**16.46%**
Nov/46-Aug/49	06/11/1946	03/08/1949	**-13.98%**
Aug/49-Jan/55	03/08/1949	05/01/1955	**21.56%**
Jan/55-Oct/62	05/01/1955	17/10/1962	**-2.30%**
Oct/62-Apr/74	17/10/1962	24/04/1974	**19.45%**
1900 - 1974	*03/01/1900*	*24/04/1974*	***11.52%***

Table 1 — Breaking points of the Lisbon General Index and the annualised returns along each cycle

This discovery confirms that in the European countries the chronology of the Great Depression precedes the American crisis: turning points occurred in April 1929 in Germany, June 1929 in the UK, December 1929 in Belgium and Italy, and March 1930 in France. According to Ritschl and Sarferaz (2009), the crisis propagation spread from Germany *"via the banking channel"*.

The Great Depression contagion effects were much longer and more severe on the corporations having businesses in overseas territories. The local maximum turning-point for the Lisbon Stock Exchange index for those corporations having businesses in overseas territories occurred earlier, on 28 September 1928 and the recovery also began later, after the local minimum turning-point of 17 February 1932.

The explanation of these differences in timing has to do with the dramatic price decline of most tropical goods. Portugal, a small producer in a global perspective, could not influence prices through supply management, and was a price-taker.

Between the 24 and 29 October 1929, the NYSE lost a third of its market capitalisation. Not only were the contagion effects quite generalized, but also were reflected in production, employment, and prices. The historiography of all economic activities of the period recognises that *"stock market indexes constituted a better reflection of macroeconomic fundamentals in any given country"*.[23] Measuring the contagion effects on European Stock Exchanges from the American plunge is an important contribution for any national economy.

4. WWII and the subsequent Marshall Plan

Portugal was able to preserve a neutral position during the Second World War, and after the end of the war promoted so successfully its economic growth with the help of its empire that it was able to catch-up to the other Western European countries by the beginning of the 1970s. This successful performance may help to explain the extreme longevity of the political regime.

Portugal´s neutrality may stem from the bad and still living memories of the earlier participation in the bloody 1914-18 conflict, but that neutrality was achieved through a difficult and precarious balancing act between the two sides in conflict. On the one hand, there was the old and traditional Alliance with the UK, while on the other the authoritarian character of Salazar's government contained some ideological sympathy toward the other belligerent side, in particular, Italy and Mussolini. Portuguese society, and consequently, Portuguese sympathies, were sharply polarized during the war. There

---

[23] Hekimian, 2013: 2. Bozerian, 1959. Eichengreen, 1993.

were cleavages in the government, in the army, and in the upper classes — some supporting the Allies, and others the Germans.

If Spain had entered WWII, Portugal would have certainly allied itself with Germany, and thus, Salazar was keen on maintaining Spanish neutrality — something that also alarmed Great Britain.[24] As German Panzer units in occupied France were poised on the Spanish border in the Pyrenees, in December 1940, the UK promised assistance to Portugal should the Portuguese government need to withdraw from Lisbon to the Azores islands in the middle of the Atlantic. The other danger was an Allied occupation of the Portuguese Atlantic islands for strategic military purposes. To protect the country against this possibility, the Portuguese government sought to placate the Germans. An important consequence of the need to balance both side's requirements was the blind eye the government turned to the smuggling of tungsten ores for military purposes to the UK and to Germany against receiving crucial supplies — e.g., steel and pharmaceuticals — along with large amounts of gold. Although an Allied blockade against both Spain and Portugal lasted from 1940 to 1942, the international equilibrium was quite complex, and the Portuguese diplomacy struggled to deal with this dilemma. In 1941, when Germany decided to divert its attention to Eastern Europe, the possibility of a German invasion of Iberia disappeared.

Wartime events are recognized as having strongly influenced European stock markets. The behaviour of stock exchange indexes and capital returns is even considered as an innovative way of assessing the importance of political events in modern societies.[25] In London, for example, *"bondholders recognized the risks posed by Hitler's programme. Bond prices (...) appear to have anticipated the overflow of Hitler and the post-war settlement of foreign bondhold-*

---

[24] Mata, 2010. Berge, 2011.
[25] Walderström; Frey, 2002. Frey; Kucher, 2000: 468-496.

ers' claims".[26] The influence of macroeconomic risk on security returns is a central issue today in financial economics, as well as in financial history.

Portugal's neutrality provided everyday life normality to production and businesses, but also explains the elevated inflows of refugees, who moved large amounts of capital into Portugal. Calouste Gulbenkian's wealth is the most well-known case, but many Jews chose Lisbon as a passage point to reach the USA, or as a place to stay. As German troops were losing the battle of Stalingrad (fought from July 17, 1942 to February 2, 1943), threats from a possible German invasion of Iberia (the only non-occupied European region) almost disappeared and Salazar definitively took sides with the Allies, and the risky extra-profits from tungsten disappeared. And when German troops began being transferred from the East to Italy because of the Allied disembarkment in Sicily it became possible to start foreseeing a German and Japanese defeat.

In spite of the Allied victory, by 1945 all European belligerent countries were exhausted and ravaged by war destructions.

Due to a Russian veto on 4 September 1946, Portugal was refused as member of the newly created United Nations organisation.[27] Criticism of the political regime and the Minister of the Economy because of shortages in the market, led to a failed military putsch on 10 October 1946, with Salazar distributing an official note to the press describing these events from the government's perspective. An inquiry was enacted, and many people arrested on political charges. The Lisbon Stock Exchange index registers a local maximum on 06 November 1946.

---

[26] Brown Jr.; Burdekin, 2002: 665. Appelbaum, 2014.

[27] Portugal joined the United Nations Organisation only on 14 December 1955. Castaño, 2006.

When the Marshall aid plan was offered on 5 June 1947, the initial thought of Salazar's government was to approve that American help for the European reconstruction following the war devastation (ERP- European Recovery Program). In this way, the Portuguese government could secure an international role and prestige by participating in the ERP meetings. With this in mind, the French--British invitation to the July 1947 Conference of Paris to discuss the reconstruction was promptly accepted. The curious fact is that Portugal first presented its position to the United States in terms similar to Switzerland's, that is, refusing the American aid and offering instead to help other countries. It was a singular position that Salazar pushed for at a meeting of the Board of Ministers on the 27 January 1948.

A new period of difficulties followed immediately, the result of sharp international criticism and pressure against the two Iberian political regimes, and also because of local bad weather and poor harvests. The year of 1948 was also an economically disastrous year for Portugal, which was followed by three years of adverse weather conditions, poor crops, low exports, higher imports, hardship in meeting the demand for new equipment for industrialisation, all of which worsened the balance of payments (resulting in a dollar shortage). The 3 August 1949 may be chosen as a local minimum for the index at the Lisbon Stock Exchange.

Optimism increased when the OEEC report of 1 September 1949 announced the Marshal aid sharing amongst the European partners for the 1949/50 year. Funding and technical support became available from 1949 to 1953. Portugal had not yet published any regular national accounting data. The Marshall Plan and the European Economic Conference of Paris on 12 July 1949 was thus a strong motivator to produce data and close the gap regarding the foundations of statistical indicators for macroeconomic variables, in order to share the Marshall aid with the other European partners. GDP estimations were soon made available for 1953 and retrospectively to 1948 by the Portuguese National Institute of Statistics.

In many European nations, even in wealthy nations such as France, Germany, and Italy, *"the polity did not support capital markets in the immediate post-war decades"*.[28] The same can be said about Salazar's government, although nationalisations did not occur in Portugal immediately after the war, as in those countries,[29] but state capital acquired significant slices of many companies in a number of sectors in industries that were more capital intensive (e.g., electricity, water provision, transports, and communications). The Lisbon Stock Exchange equity index confirms this positive mood of businesses during those years, as Figure 4 shows.[30]

At a second moment, indicative planning — *"Planos de Fomento"*[31] — in the form of lists of public investment planned for several years, was also implemented.[32] The government's discretionary power of allocating scarce Marshall funding to alternative aims, choosing the industrial actors, trusting in certain companies that were elected for achieving the government's targets and purposes, was an important factor in the consolidation and development of private groups.

> I was Secretary-general of the *"Banco de Fomento Nacional"*, ...
> I ended as Director of that bank which was charged with the

---

[28] Roe, 2006: 462. Arkes, 1972. Borchardt, 1991.

[29] "In Paris, the nationalisation of the railways, the Banque de France, and after World War Two that of the electricity, coal, gas, banking and insurance industries, deprived the stock markets from many of their biggest listed securities". Le Bris, Hautcoeur, 2008. Valério, 2004.

[30] See also Crédit Suisse Sourcebook, 2014: 149.

[31] Development and investment plans. The first plan covered the six years from 1953 to 1958; the second from 1959 to 1964, and the third from 1967 to 1973. There was a bridge plan for the period 1965 to 1966. Neves, 1994.

[32] Portuguese indicative planning was much less sophisticated than indicative planning in other European countries at the time. See Klausen, 1998: 45, 47, 101, 102, 108, 114-16, 149, 178, 195, 199, 251, 253, 255, 258.

responsibility of managing the funds from the Marshall Plan. And it was me who, as deputy manager of its Legal Department, negotiated all the contracts from 1952 on, in Washington. I closed all those contracts. The corporations that received them were joint stock companies, but there was no trading of such shares in the Lisbon Exchange in spite of being listed. Companies in Portugal only exploded in trading in the second half of the 1960s.[33]

In fact, accepting Marshall aid was a watershed event in leading Portugal toward the European post-war negotiations and international openness, in general. Co-operation with the government and a strategy of growth that included cross-participation with other firms provided safety and more robust opportunities, because individual aggressive competitiveness behaviour only pays off when the expected benefit exceeds the expected cost, which is a difficult condition to match when dimension is small.[34] Subsidies were also very important, because they supported production expansion and other business dimension issues, and were important for facing risk and market competition, in both domestic and international markets.

In Europe in general, the Marshall Plan and the start of the unification of Europe in 1952 with CECA — Coal and Steel European Commission paved the way to considerable co-operation amongst European partners and brought Portugal into close contact with global stock markets. The period between the Marshall Plan (1947) and accession to EFTA (1960) may be envisioned as the first

---

[33] We thank Dr. *José Luís Sapateiro* for this interview kindly conceded to us on November, 3, 2009, at the head office of the construction company *"Mota Engil"* at Linda-a-Velha, Carnaxide.

[34] Mata, 2010. De Long et al., 1993. Ellis, 1950. Gimbel, 1976. Ritschl, 2004. Sousa, 1948.

moment of managerial capitalism in Portugal.[35] This was the opportunity for experiencing rates of growth that were higher than ever in the past, paving the way to an exceptional performance during the 1960s.

The post-war period was the most successful growth period in Portugal's history. It allowed the country to catch up with the developed European countries.[36] It is recognised as the take-off of a sustained economic growth from 2-5% annual rates in the 1940s and 1950s to 5-7% annual rates in the 1960s, following Portugal's participation in the European economic integration process. A genuine economic modernisation and urbanization occurred from the end of the Second World War [37] until the moment when the first oil shock (end of 1973) halted a long period (30 years) with a compounding 6% annual growth rate, and played a decisive role in installing a new political regime in Portugal.[38]

The period witnessed the formation of conglomerates through firms' affiliation under the government development policy. Additionally, this economic policy may have been a critical survival mechanism for small firms by allowing them to gain benefits from homeland and overseas markets in a wild and inhospitable international business environment. Most important were the controls by family owned conglomerates of pyramids of firms through ownership ties and cross-shareholding.

---

[35] Mata, (2009). http://dipeco.economia.unimib.it/impreseestoria/ENG/issues/38_2009.html. Amatori, 2007.

[36] Baptista et al., 1997.

[37] Amaral, 2003. Maddison, 2001.

[38] Amaral, 2003. Cunha, 2007.

Security markets and economic growth went hand in hand in this period until suddenly interrupted by the Carnation revolution in 1974 and the subsequent political turmoil.[39]

> The 1970s Stock Exchange boom (that began at the end of the sixties) was a fruit of the economic growth and Salazar's policy.[40]

5. Portuguese membership in NATO

Although the military character of the political regime was overcome in 1933 when a Constitution was approved by referendum, its authoritarian flavour was preserved until 1974. That regime was based on a single political movement and on *António de Oliveira Salazar* as an all-powerful prime minister. In fact, he remained in that position for 36 years, from 1932 to 1968, being replaced by a more liberal prime minister, *Marcelo Caetano*, only in 1968, when he became physically disabled in that Summer, forcing the President of the Republic to nominate another person.

Following the defeat of Germany and Italy in WWII, the Portuguese regime could have been ousted by the victors, but the fact that the Cold War immediately began in Europe, together with the geographical position of Portugal in the Iberian Peninsula and also in many strategically located territories in Africa and in the far East, advised the western powers — mainly the US and UK, but also France and others — to support Salazar to avoid additional

---

[39] The CUF (Mello family), the Sommer group (Champalimaud family), the Fonsecas & Burnay, and the Espírito Santo. Martins, 1975: 21-65.

[40] Interview kindly conceded to us by *Dr. José Luís Sapateiro*, author of the 1991 Securities Code, on November, 3, 2009, at Mota Engil headquarters at Linda--a-Velha, Carnaxide.

troubles in such an important rear area of Europe — the Iberian Peninsula — and also to maintain their access to military bases in African eastern and western coasts, where Portugal had some of its main overseas territories, should an emergency occur within the cold war.

Nonetheless, the end of WWII also brought the loss of colonial power and massive decolonisation. In particular, Britain lost colonial India on 14 August 1947, and that triggered the emergence of a large wedge between the Portuguese and British positions on colonial issues. Salazar did not want to lose control over Portugal's possessions even if some of them attracted less interest from other powers. The loss of even one would be a precedent for all the others.[41]

The strategy for stability within the dynamic context of the 1940s called for establishing an important role for Portugal in the Atlantic world. The Portuguese government wished for its voice to be heard, and the triple agreement on the military bases in the Azores Islands was achieved in May 1946 accepting the American rights for 18 months — the official ceremony took place on 2 June 1946.[42]

The Portuguese alignment in the Cold War context was clear in joining NATO (on 4 April 1949), and the National Assembly ratified the entrance decision of the North Atlantic Pact on 28 July 1949. The Marshall Plan also represented a very important step in the definition of Portugal's long-run alliance with the US, and NATO, and overall European integration. Mind that the Soviet Union rejected

---

[41] Portugal would preserve her possessions on the Indian subcontinent until 18 December 1961, as well as large territories in Africa until 1974-75.

[42] As the Portuguese government feared American hegemony over the world, the terms for the agreement with the US were also very difficult and cautiously disguised as negotiations with a private American Company for construction of an airport on *Santa Maria* island. The agreement with the US, including facilities at the British-used military bases at *Lages*, was signed only in February 1948.

the Marshall plan on political grounds, stressing its position on the socialist side of that cold war (Eichengreen, 1992).

6. The Portuguese 5th Empire until 1974 and the Bandung conference in 1955

A turning point occurred in the beginning of 1955. The date of 6 January 1955 may be elected as the maximum for the Lisbon Stock Exchange index. On one hand, the Marshall Plan funds were exhausted in 1954, and on the other, the global winds of decolonisation were reinforced by the Bandung Conference — held in Indonesia from 18 to 24 April 1955 — where Asian leaders asked for economic development, free from colonial influence. Expectations on the future of colonial businesses were dark.[43]

The Bandung Conference alerted the western powers to the rising number of countries around the globe making up the newly created Third Movement, which was born in that same conference. Self-interests of those western powers soon led them to change their official views on Portugal in order to avoid losing their influence upon — and their commercial connections with — those new ex--colony countries.

In this arena, Portugal was challenged by the smallness of the motherland — physically, economically, and demographically — compared to the vastness of its overseas empire,[44] which were the vestiges of the role of Portugal in the Discoveries during the 1400s and 1500s. Additionally, the post-war decolonisation

---

[43] In spite of the 9 July 1957 agreement with the Cabinda Gulf Oil C° to explore oil.

[44] Which included the Atlantic islands of Cape Verde and *São Tomé e Príncipe*, large territories in Africa — Guinea-Bissau, Angola, and Mozambique — and other small Asian territories (in India, Macau, and Timor).

experiences of other European empires affected these African Portuguese territories, as they gave examples to establish local movements to fight for independence and offered sanctuaries to guerrilla movements around them. The year of 1960 is a historical milestone[45] in this respect, as a number of British and French territories gained independence in that year and because marks a frontier between a rather peaceful period and a decade in which problems started in all the remaining territories.

Domestically, the opposition to Salazar was reinforced, and proposed general Humberto Delgado to the Presidential election of 1958, after he had declared on 10 May (1958) that he would dismiss Salazar. His victory did not materialise, but the regime continued in a position of permanent alert.

7. The beginning of the end in 1961: Goa, Angola, and the internal political events

1961 was a very difficult one for Portugal from a political standpoint:

- at the end of January-early February *Henrique Galvão* assaulted the elegant cruiser Santa Maria as a protest against the political regime;
- on March 15 white farmers and their employees from the southern tribes of Angola were massacred in northern provinces of the territory, starting a guerrilla war that lasted until 1974;

---

[45] Perhaps the independence of the Belgian Congo in June 30, 1960 is the most significant event to define that milestone.

- in March-April 1961 the Minister of Defense, *General Botelho Moniz*, tried, but failed to oust the prime minister Salazar; apparently this is connected to the fact that the political decision to defend the overseas territories was pivotal for businesses, as it required massive public spending with multiplier effects on the economic activity; military fighting required large transportation of troops for the two domestic shipping companies (*Companhia Nacional de Navegação* and *Companhia Colonial de Navegação*) to the distant overseas territories, equipment production, and extensive imports of war material;
- in December 1961, the Portuguese army suffered an important defeat in the so called *"Portuguese State of India"* when the Republic of India invaded and took by force the three tiny territories of *Goa, Damão,* and *Diu,* controlled by Portugal since the 1500s in that subcontinent;
- in that same year, another military coup was attempted on December 31 without success.

The turning point may be located on 17 October 1962, the local minimum of the Lisbon Stock Exchange equity index.

In 1963 a similar guerrilla war started in Guinea-Bissau[46] and in 1964 in Mozambique,[47] both of them also seeking their independences.

Optimism within the Portuguese army to fight the war and support the empire was very clear when the government decided to

---

[46] The guerrilla war in Guinea-Bissau began on 23 January 1963 with some actions in the Tite region.

[47] The guerrilla war in Mozambique began on 25 September 1964 with an attack to the administrative post of Chai located in the northern district of *Cabo Delgado*.

create two new University studies in Angola and Mozambique (Decree-Law nr. 44530, of 21 August 1962).

The next years allowed the country to catch up to the developed European countries.[48] They are recognized as the take-off of a sustained economic growth. From a level of GDP annual growth rates during the 1940s and 1950s in the interval of 2% to 5%, they jumped to 5% to 7% in the 1960s and early 1970s, following Portugal's participation in the European economic integration process.

However, the Portuguese population slowly moved from full support of that military response in Africa to increasingly rejecting it, having their sons conscripted to fight those three wars year after year. In March 1973 a critical event occurred in the Guinea-Bissau war front, when, for the very first time, a Portuguese Air Force plane was shot down by the local guerrillas with a missile supplied by the URSS.[49] The fact that this incident wiped out completely the air superiority of the Portuguese Army in the fighting areas of that territory alarmed the Portuguese military forces for whom the humiliating defeat suffered in India a few years earlier was still very much alive in their memories.[50]

The Carnation Revolution started with a simple military coup executed during the night from 24 to 25 April 1974, by the so-called *"Armed Forces Movement"*. It basically ousted the very old regime to

---

[48] Baptista, Dina; Martins, Carlos; Pinheiro, Maximiano; Reis, Jaime *New Estimates for Portugal's GDP 1910-1958* (Lisboa: Banco de Portugal, 1997).

[49] The first missile *"Strela"* (also known as SAM-7) was seen by a couple of Fiats G-91 fighters, piloted by LtCl Brito and Lt Pessoa, when patrolling the northern border with Senegal, near *Campada — S. Domingos*, on 20 March 1973.

[50] Recall that the defeat of the French Army in *Dien Bien Phu* in Vietnam in 1954 also had significant consequences upon the political regime in France, and the return of De Gaulle to power in 1959 can be traced back to that defeat. His newly formed cabinet was approved by the National Assembly on 1 June 1958, but subsequently he was elected President of the French Republic and of the African and Malagasy Community on 21 December 1958 by indirect suffrage. He was inaugurated on 8 January 1959.

enthrone a democratic one that could avoid a second military disaster in Guinea-Bissau, where the guerrilla pressure was strongest.

It is much easier to oust someone from power than to implant a newly structured system with a proper long-term strategy. After so many years of a right-wing regime in the country, and under the pressure of the leftist-oriented guerrilla movements in Angola, Mozambique, and Guinea-Bissau, it is understandable that the country would initially swing to the left of the political spectrum before stabilising in a more centrist position.

8. Participation in EFTA

Portugal joined EFTA - European Free Trade Association when she signed the Stockholm Convention on 4 January 1960. As the United Kingdom was also an imperial power wishing to preserve the usual imperial preferences, joining a Free Trade Zone rather than a Trade Union was a shared preference for these two countries.[51] Both countries led the movement to create the European Free Trade Association in 1959, in which Portugal negotiated a special statute in Annex G of the final convention to guarantee a slower abolition of customs protection, particularly for "emergent industries". The European partners were wealthier and economically stronger, and so the Portuguese firms benefited for an interim period from protection in the international markets through tariffs and entry barriers.[52]

Joining the European Free Trade Association was also a commitment to the European integration, which still protected the national economy from the adoption of a common external tariff, but which

---

[51] Hogan, 1987.

[52] "*Condicionamento Industrial*". See Brito, 2004. Andresen-Leitão, 2003. Confraria, 1992.

already opened the national market to the industrial competition coming from the EFTA partners, while a managerial revolution was sweeping the largest firms. At the same time Portugal built another free trade zone, including the homeland and the overseas territories under Portuguese sovereignty, to pursue the alternative long-run geopolitical strategy of an Iberian-African-Brazilian Atlantic community that survived the end of the Second World War.

The instruments for this successful path toward the European economic integration were the business groups, within related or unrelated diversified business, to facilitate their growth in a small less-developed country such as Portugal in the 1940s and 1950s.[53] According to the Reports to the Technical Commission of the European Commission Administration ECA, the hydro-electric power equipment, the chemical industry (particularly, *CUF* factories, *"Amoniaco Português"*, and *"União Fabril do Azoto"*), the cement industries (*ECL* and *CCT*), the paper sector (*"Companhia Portuguesa de Celulose"*), the rail (*CP*), and the oil refining industries (*"Sacor"* and *CPP*), were supported.[54] According to OEEC reports *"the USA provided in the Marshall help a large part of the equipment"* for the refining industry.[55]

9. Portuguese modernisation until 1974

For better or worse, the Marshall Plan was the beginning of re-inforced ties with the US due, on one hand, to the increased trade

---

[53] Rollo, 1994.

[54] Smaller firms also were supported. A good example is electrical machinery (*"Companhia Portuguesa de Fornos Eléctricos"*): reports to the Technical Commission of the European Commission Administration ECA on the use of the direct help, Historical Archive of the Bank of Portugal AHBP, box 67. Ghemawat, Khanna, 1998.

[55] OEEC, 1958: 124. Desai, 2013.

flows lubricated by the increased international financial connections — especially important for Europeans in such a difficult moment — and, on the other hand, due to the geopolitical and cultural connections more intertwined between the two sides of the Atlantic following increased co-operation among partners. Additionally, for Portugal the neutrality maintained during WWII afforded new export opportunities, attracted war refugees with their wealth, technical background and cultural attitudes, and provided capital inflows, all of which brought prosperity to the country and established the foundations for a golden age of economic growth from the 1950s until the early 1970s. Annual equity returns in the 1940s and 1950s have been predominantly positive and attractive (Judt, 2005. Laíns, 2004).

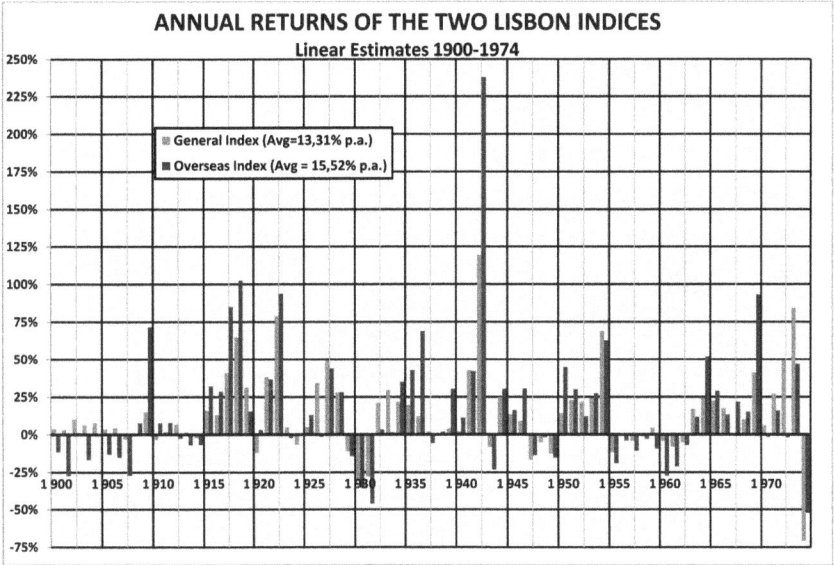

ANNUAL RETURNS OF THE TWO LISBON INDICES
Linear Estimates 1900-1974

General Index (Avg=13,31% p.a.)
Overseas Index (Avg = 15,52% p.a.)

Figure 4 — Average annual returns for the Equity market at the Lisbon Exchange

Then, thanks to EFTA, Portugal also converged to her partners in terms of the legal framework regulating commercial enterprises, including the issuing of shares and bonds to the market.[56] In the agriculture sector Decree-Law 49184 of 11 August 1969 — also influenced by EFTA membership — created the legal background for group agricultural associations.

The performance of the Lisbon Stock Exchange boomed. The annual average real equity total return was 7.9% for investors over the 1960-70 hold period, 9.4% over the 1950-70 hold period, 7.6% in the 1940-70 hold period.[57] This confirms the positive trend of businesses in the late sixties-early seventies, which may be considered as a boom.

This was a very prosperous period and mergers and crossed-capital participations brought strength to several economic groups. Listing also flourished and corporations strongly increased their equity. In many companies ownership became separated from control and corporate governance improved significantly.[58] Although the use of firms' reserves and provisions in funding capital growth was still predominant, and the role of bank loans for venture capital firms was very common, this period witnessed substantial issuance of share capital in the stock market.

Decree-Law 1/72 (3 January 1972) was the first to regulate the profession of official auditors ("Revisores Oficiais de Contas"), their chamber, and the auditing societies ("Sociedades de Revisão"), in order to guarantee transparent accounting and clear appraisal of corporations' financial situations. As important legal standardisations were emerging in the European Economic Community, and the Portuguese

---

[56] Decree 44652 of 27 October 1962 and in the new Civil Code published on 25 November 1966.

[57] Crédit Suisse, Sourcebook 2014: 149.

[58] van der Wee, 1986. Hirschman, 1998. On the criteria for historians to discover this separation, see Hilt, 2008: 652.

regulation on mergers still dating from the old 1888 Commercial Code was considered to be insufficient, in spite of Portugal's participation in the EFTA trade zone and not in the European customs union, Decree-Law 598/73 (8 November 1973) adopted the European laws in advance (*avant la lettre*).[59]

Recognising that overall the framework regulating the listing of companies in Stock Exchanges and the very operation of those organisations was still very much determined by the 1888 Commercial Code, the government published Decree-Law 8/74 (14 January 1974) as a simplified Securities Code intended to introduce the first update to that legal environment around the securities market. In fact, in the preamble of that Decree-Law, the legislator expressly writes that "*a real barrier to spectacular growth*" existed.

Strongly influenced by *José Luís Sapateiro* — then State Secretary of Finance — it opened the possibility of issuing securities without government permission along with the possibility of creating new and autonomous Exchanges in any Portuguese city where the volume, frequency, and expectations of transactions might require the presence of such a market. When asked about the importance of the above firms' freedom to issue their securities enshrined in Decree-Law 8/74, he did not hesitate to explain:

> Before, to issue new securities the authorisation of the "*Inspecção Geral de Crédito e Seguros*"[60] was necessary. After this 1974 "Code", any corporation could issue securities in the market. You may ask why: there is no reason for freedom of issuance not to exist.[61]

---

[59] Duarte, 2008: 55, quoting Ventura, 1972.

[60] A kind of supervisor for Banks, Insurer and the Market included in the Ministry of Finance.

[61] Interview kindly conceded to us by Dr. José Luís Sapateiro, author of the 1991 Securities Code, on 3 November 2009, at Mota Engil, Linda-a-Velha, Carnaxide.

A possible explanation for the survival from the 1901 regulation of the need of previous authorisation from the *"Inspecção Geral de Crédito e Seguros"* for a firm to issue any type of securities may be found in the policy of *"Condicionamento Industrial"*,[62] but *Dr. José Luís Sapateiro*, has a different opinion:

> My philosophy was: whenever there is a trading order, it's necessary to assure that the operation goes on according to the interests of the issuer of that order.[63]

It imposed many information disclosure duties on the corporations listed on the stock market, particularly regarding their listing. Shareholder protection, fixed fees, and strong enforcement were key features.[64] They should result in larger stock market capitalisation, initial public offerings (IPOs), and a greater number of publicly traded companies.[65] The same decree also regulated brokerage activities and recognised the need to evolve to institutionalised intermediaries, but maintained the banks out of this intermediation and kept the figure of the duly authorised individual stockbrokers.

The decree was suddenly rendered useless by the 1974 military revolution as the market was frozen and the Exchanges suspended

---

[62] The government imposed conditions to any initiative to start a new business to avoid oversupply and company failures. This policy was born in the context of the Great Depression to avoid pernicious competition. Firms needed the Finance Minister's authorisation to create new industrial activities or even to expand the installed capacity and equity increases indicating a possible expansion of the business should also be authorized. Mata, 2003.

[63] Interview kindly conceded to us by Dr. José Luís Sapateiro, author of the 1991 Securities Code, on 3 November 2009, at Mota Engil, Linda-a-Velha, Carnaxide.

[64] Penalties for disrespectful behaviour were also established (articles 53, 133 and 134, of the Decree-Law 8/74, official newspaper *Diário do Governo*, I Série, n.º 11, 14 January 1974, p. 42-(12) and (22).

[65] La Porta, Lopez-de-Silanes, Shleifer and Vishny, 1997. La Porta, Lopez-de--Silanes, Shleifer, and Vishny, 1998, 1999.

their operations. It regained its central role after the Lisbon Exchange reopened for bond trading in January 1976 (especially after March 1977 when the operations were extended to all other types of securities). It was superseded in 1991 by the 1st comprehensive Securities Code built under Dr. Sapateiro's guidance.

10. The Carnation Revolution and the suspension of Stock market operations

Portugal experienced a military coup (that became known as the Carnation Revolution) on 25 April 1974 with strategic and structural consequences for the domestic economy and the nation (and therefore also for the domestic Stock Exchange). A number of reasons underpin this historical turning point.

Since 1961, Salazar's political regime faced three overseas battlefields simultaneously, in Angola, Mozambique, and Guinea-Bissau, and the corresponding war effort was painful for the Portuguese society. Probably as a consequence of such wars, the Monetary Union with the overseas territories, at work since 1963, could not succeed and experienced large outflows of capital associated with lack of confidence.

Portuguese weaknesses became clear when the first oil shock (1973) disrupted all recent favourable trends and when, following American aircraft use of the Portuguese military base in the Azores to help Israel in the Yom Kippur War (6-23 October 1973), Portugal suffered immediate retaliations from the Arab oil producers. In particular, the government's announcement of oil consumption restrictions from November 7 of that same year showed that the political regime was really unable to cope with the simultaneous effects of soaring energy costs and the draining expenses of the overseas wars.

28 November 1973 marks the Lisbon Stock Exchange local maximum in terms of the equity index, a signal of profound changes approaching Portugal. A first military putsch on 16 March 1974 failed, but constituted a rehearsal for the new one on 25 April 1974, which was very successful, putting an end to four decades of a long-surviving political regime (at least, from the constitutional approval in 1933).

Besides the exhaustion of economic resources to support troops overseas in three theatres of war, there was a more pressing force under way: the imminent military defeat of the Portuguese army in Guinea-Bissau, which reminded many of its members of the government behaviour in 1961 when India took Goa *"manu military"* and the government blamed the armed forces for that loss. Also leftist ideologies had made inroads especially in the universities, where youth were being motivated to "new" ideals of freedom, democracy, and socialism subsequently voiced to their families and the rest of the population. The abundance of carnation flowers in the market in April and some casual events on the day led the press to nickname the revolution with the name of that flower.

Trading operations were "suspended" in the Lisbon and Oporto Exchanges from 25 April 1974 on. When asked about the revolution effects, *Manuel Ricciardi*, official broker of the Lisbon Stock Exchange since the 1950s and its Chairman for many years commented:

> The April 25 revolution was not a surprise, properly. (...) Many rumours circulated on the possibility of replacing the political regime and on the dissatisfaction of the army. The March 16 [coup] had also taken place, so it was not a real surprise. The April 25 revolution did not close the Stock Exchange. The financial authorities, particularly *Dr. Silva Lopes* and *Professor Jacinto Nunes* [then Governor of the Central Bank], decided that in order

to avoid excesses of volatility typical of such circumstances, Exchange operations should immediately be suspended, to be retaken at any moment further on. However, political events led the country to many street demonstrations, great economic and political turbulence, and the Stock Exchange activity could not restart soon, particularly because property rights began being disrespected. Land occupations for collective units of production, home occupations, and mainly nationalisation of many big corporations in many sectors, brought the need of keeping the Stock Exchange closed.[66]

11. The 1974/75 Nationalisations

At a time when the Soviet Union still played an important role within the context of the Cold War, the socialist ideals of the new political regime soon translated into a policy of decolonisation, nationalisations, and land reform. All of these political structural breaks occurred simultaneously and suddenly. Central planning mechanisms were very fashionable as an alternative to market equilibrium, while decolonisation represented the end of five centuries of expertise in controlling vast empires.[67]

Agrarian reform was undertaken, especially in southern Portugal, the only region where medium-large property was dominant. The abolition of the economic corporatism philosophy coming from the previous political regime, and the institutionalisation of political

---

[66] Interview kindly conceded to us at his son's brokerage office, at *Rua do Comércio*. We evoke here the memory of his great contribution to the Lisbon Stock Exchange.

[67] Smith (1985) identifies three Portuguese colonial empires, the first one based on Asia until the late sixteenth century, a second one based on Brazil, and the last one on Africa. Smith (1979).

parties and trade unions drove domestic politics for a while, and gave a socialist political blueprint to the 1976 new political Constitution. Radical left-wing policies propelled by the Portuguese Communist Party (then the only party with an internal organisation experienced by many years of coveted operations under the former regime) supported land expropriations in 1975 to be placed in the hands of local farm workers.

At the same time, the new regime promoted the nationalisation of many economic sectors that were considered to be vital instruments for government control (Annex 1). In the beginning decisions were taken quietly and paying indemnities to the previous owners. In fact, the first nationalisations were decided in September 1974, and aimed only at the three issuing banks that divided the whole territory:

- *Banco de Portugal*, the sole issuer for the European part of the territory, through Decree-Law 452/74, of 13 September 1974, with effect from September 15 on,
- *Banco de Angola*, issuer for Angola (only), although operating also as a commercial bank in Europe, through Decree-Law 450/74, of 13 September 1974, with effect from September 15 on,
- *Banco Nacional Ultramarino*, common issuer for all overseas territories (except Angola) where it also operated as a commercial bank, through Decree-Law 451/74, of 13 September 1974, with effect from September 15 on.

All those banks were private companies — even listed on the Lisbon Stock Exchange — although with a strong presence of the national government in their managerial bodies.

However, in March 1975 a split within the military forces in the government temporarily gave an upper hand to the leftists in the political arena and these, on 16 March, took a sudden decision to nationalise a number of economic sectors in the country, but now without any indemnities being announced (only many years later some compensation was awarded to the owners, but much below market values).

So, Banking and Insurance were nationalised in March 1975. Electricity production and its distribution, iron and steel production, oil refining and distribution, basic petrochemical, shipbuilding and ship repair sectors, cement, tobacco, and paper (cellulose) were nationalised in April 1975.[68] Most of the transports followed in line, particularly rail and large road firms, maritime and air transport, communication sectors, and urban and suburban mass transports in the two metropolitan areas of Lisbon and Porto. In late 1975 and in 1976 fishing and the media were added to the list of nationalised firms, which *"created the largest public enterprise sector that ever existed in the Portuguese economy"* frightening many entrepreneurs, who left Portugal for Brazil and turned their business to other endeavours.[69]

Table 2 is based on Annex 1 and compares by industrial sectors the market value of the portfolio of shares listed on Lisbon on the last trading day before the Carnation revolution with the market value of the remaining companies still surviving in the beginning of 1978 after the nationalisations, bankruptcies of many of them, and the closure of most overseas firms by the new left-wing governments of the newly independent territories.

---

[68] Decree-Law 203-C/75 of 15 April 1975.
[69] Nunes, et al., 2006. Cunha, 1999. Vilar, 1998. Osório, 1999.

Company Listed in BVL	Estimated Capitalisation (in PTE) on			
	24.04.1974		Jan/1978	
	Number	Value (PTE)	Number	Value (PTE)
Insurance	25	26 342 900 000$	0	0$
of which new cias in 1978			0	0$
Banks	17	98 976 930 000$	0	0$
of which new cias in 1978			0	0$
Electrical Utilities	9	11 543 895 984$	0	0$
of which new cias in 1978			0	0$
Water Utilities	4	1 604 655 000$	4	805 500 000$
of which new cias in 1978			0	0$
Spinning & Wool	4	79 500 000$	2	32 500 000$
of which new cias in 1978			0	0$
Overseas	34	8 440 171 000$	0	0$
of which new cias in 1978			0	0$
Other Sectors	61	84 077 225 225$	29	2 486 835 333$
of which new cias in 1978			4	131 000 000$
TOTAL	154	231 065 277 209$	35	3 324 835 333$

Table 2 — Estimated Capitalisation values before and after the
Carnation Revolution

This was a dramatic hit as it is estimated that average loss per investor was about 98.6% of the initial wealth (before considering the indemnities that were paid later on). Many families suffered a total loss of their shareholding positions, and some lost their entire life savings.

I had applied all my 22 years of savings in Stock Exchange securities. I've lost everything. (I was later given about one 1,000 *contos* of indemnities). I moved to Brazil having only 60 *contos* in my pocket, taking with me my whole family. This was all I had. [70]

[70] Interview kindly conceded to us by *Dr. José Luís Sapateiro*, author of the 1991 Securities Code, on November, 3, 2009, at Mota Engil, Linda-a-Velha, Carnaxide

The portfolio that the Government accumulated with these nationalisations (even after some privatisations initiated in 1989) was very large (Figure 5). The financial sector and transports were the largest fields of the economy in the government portfolio.

PUBLIC PORTFOLIO BY SECTORES

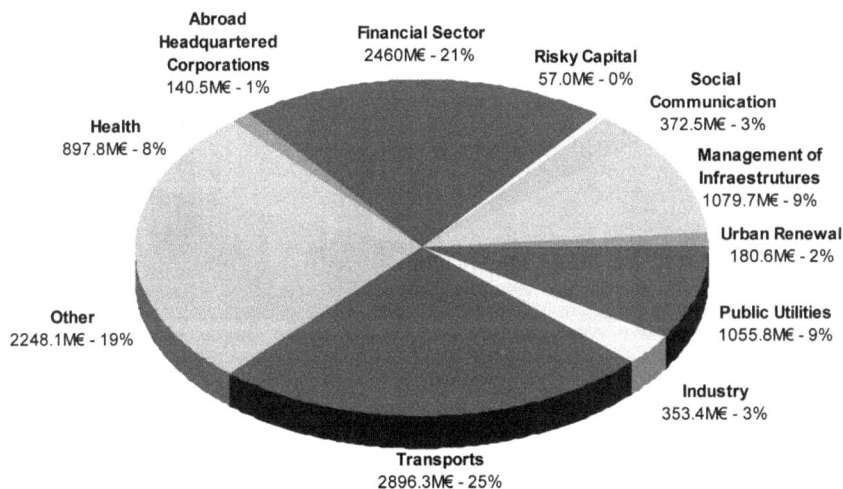

Figure 5 — Portfolio of Companies in the hands of the Portuguese Government after the nationalisations

Source: Direcção-Geral de Estudos e Previsão (1999) *Privatizações e Regulação: A experiência Portuguesa,* Lisboa: Ministério das Finanças.

Nationalisations were extremely detrimental for the Lisbon Stock Exchange and it took many years to recover from such hard impacts.

The revolution stopped everything (...). The Exchange was dead, and only came back to life in 1976 but then only for debt securities (mainly T-Bonds) and only in 1977 reopened for share trading, while foreign Stock Exchanges exploded their markets. It was a lost opportunity.[71]

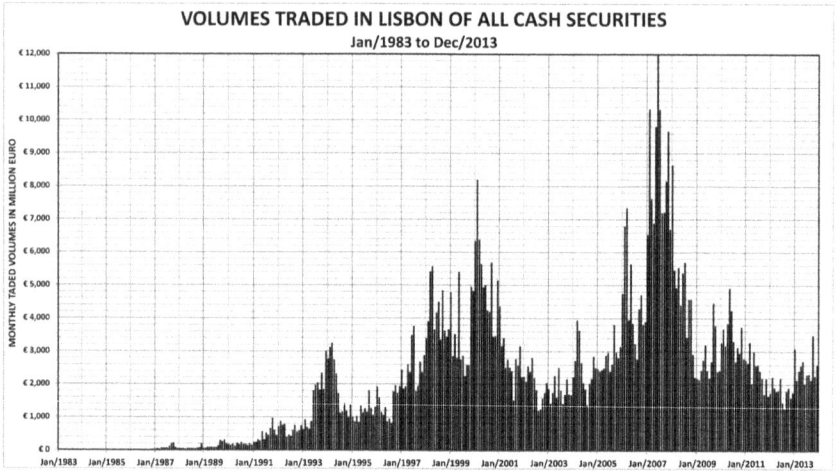

VOLUMES TRADED IN LISBON OF ALL CASH SECURITIES
Jan/1983 to Dec/2013

Figure 6 — Monthly trading volumes (million euros) in the Lisbon Stock Exchange (all securities)

That recovery period can be divided into three phases using trading volume (for shares, bonds, and all other types of securities) and the share index as guiding indicators (Figure 6):

a)   a very sluggish evolution from the re-opening in March/1977 — only two listed firms had their shares traded on March 7, the very first day with effective executions — until joining Europe in 1986; this might be called the re-opening phase;

b)   because the amount of securities in circulation was very limited then, excess demand made quotations skyrocket

---

[71] Interview kindly conceded to us by *Dr. José Luís Sapateiro.*

until October 1987 (nothing to do with the simultaneous crisis in the international markets) when a peak was attained after a number of days in a row with 5% daily gains; excess speculation and operative limitations of the market triggered a crash on 19 October;

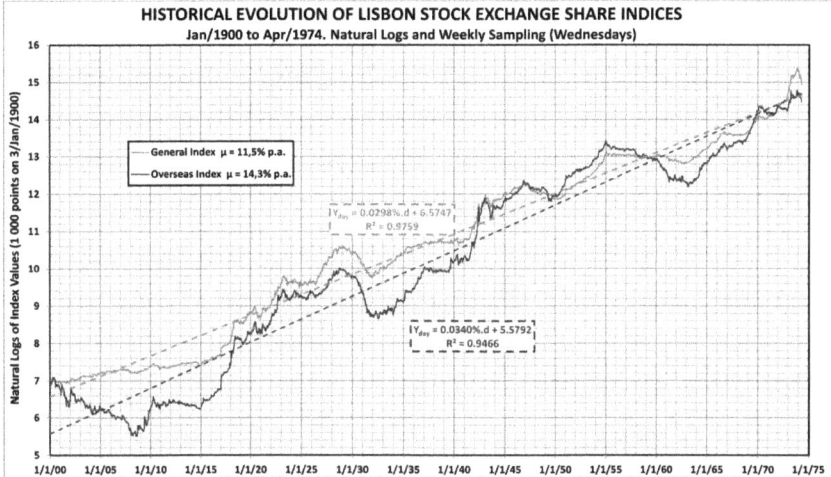

Figure 7 — Extra return from overseas companies as shown by those firms listed on the Lisbon Stock Exchange

c) in 1989 a diversified, long, and visible privatisation programme took off but the simple perception that a new policy was in place with the new government profoundly changed the mind of the man in the street, and so investment in shares suddenly became fashionable; from then on, the succession of Exchange sessions where parts of the capital of many previously nationalized companies were sold to private investors not only started to off-set the heavy losses stemming from the October 1987 crisis (minimum level of the BVL equity index in January 1993), but also triggered an explosion in trading volumes in the

Exchange markets and share quotations, both effects resulting from the low prices offered by the government in the initial sessions of privatisations — providing easy and rapid capital gains to the common investor — together with the restored involvement of domestic and foreign investors in the market (Figure 7).

One cannot forget that each time the government launched a new operation to sell part of a company the media and the propaganda attached to the event had a lasting effect upon the common investor and attracted non-residents.

| Year | Number of Operations | Revenue obtained (€000) | | | | | | Average Revenue per Operation |
		State	I. P. E.	Quimigal	R. N. I. P.	Other Entities	Total Revenue	
1987	4	0	4,665	118	0	0	4,783	1,196
1988	4	0	9,046	14	0	0	9,060	2,265
1989	16	247,673	20,023	20,114	0	105,573	393,383	24,586
1990	19	692,795	76,189	30,435	0	46,395	845,814	44,517
1991	23	525,841	27,740	73,070	0	249,120	875,771	38,077
1992	24	1,068,155	41,091	1,603	22,469	430,650	1,563,968	65,165
1993	26	298,655	58,215	3,411	38,152	2,655	401,088	15,426
1994	20	461,729	11,890	3,948	16,756	444,021	938,344	46,917
1995	35	666,050	81,949	6,017	50,100	1,010,124	1,814,240	51,835
1996	14	2,240,934	128,368	200	0	45,714	2,415,216	172,515
1997	11	4,291,185	28,105	0	0	5,265	4,324,555	393,141
1998	8	3,852,545	676	0	0	0	3,853,221	481,653
1999	8	1,549,964	0	2,993	0	54,988	1,607,945	200,993
2000	10	2,919,912	129,687	0	0	294,867	3,344,466	334,447
2001	3	410,567	0	0	0	145,001	555,568	185,189
2002	3	0	260,359	0	0	0	260,359	86,786
2003	2	45,292	0	0	0	8,262	53,554	26,777
2004	2	832,363	0	0	0	0	832,363	275,291
2005	2	403,200	0	0	0	0	403,200	201,600
2006	3	1,505,409	0	0	0	0	1,505,409	501,803
Total	237	22,012,269	878,003	141,923	127,477	2,842,635	26,002,307	109,714

Legend: I.P.E. stands for "Instituto das Participações do Estado", Quimigal means the public corporation resulting from the nationalisation of the former CUF, and R.N.I.P. stands for "Rodoviária Nacional.

Table 3 — Monetary summary of the most important period of privatisations in Portugal

Table 3 describes privatisations. As a whole, from 1987 to 2006, privatisations involved 164 firms, in 239 operations, producing almost € 26 bn. The 2008 crisis, however, led the index to levels that are much below the lower limit of the one standard deviation confidence interval, as the asset pricing and rewards declined sharply (GAFEEP, 1995).

12. Sudden and Simultaneous Independence of all Overseas Territories

The political event of April 1974 also introduced a radical shift in the strategic evolution of the domestic economy: a country that for around five centuries[72] had based its survival on an extended overseas empire, in the single year of 1975 lost all territories in Africa.[73] This fact forced it to turn its eyes to the European integration movement initiated in Rome in 1957. In fact, Portugal joined the then European Economic Community in 1986, an event also with profound consequences for all of its domestic firms and the resident financial sector.

Additionally and because all local governments in the newly independent territories followed a leftist orientation, all overseas companies listed on the Lisbon Stock Exchange were either nationalised by these African governments or stopped their businesses due to poor political and economic conditions in their operating areas. This explains why no single overseas company remained listed after the Lisbon Exchange resumed operations in equities in 1977.

As stated in the last chapter, on average, the behaviour of the overseas firms listed on the Lisbon Stock Exchange was quite success-

---

[72] The year 1415 is traditionally taken as the initial date because the city of Ceuta in the Gibraltar straits was conquered in that year. Marques, 1987.

[73] During 1975 all overseas territories were granted their independence except for Macau — where China requested some additional time to regain that territory — and East Timor — which was invaded by Indonesia in 1975, but later (2002) also obtained its independence after a referendum in 2000.

ful (profitable) during the decades following the Great Depression[74] although, this extra return came at the cost of more volatility. These results for the overseas businesses are not so different from Grossman (2014) findings:

> *... total returns for domestic and overseas equities listed on the London Stock Exchange during 1869-1928. Indices are presented for Africa, Asia, Australia (including New Zealand), Europe, Latin America, North America (as well as for the UK) and for the finance, transportation, raw materials, and utilities sectors in each region. Returns and volatility were typically highest in emerging regions and the raw materials sector. Dividend yields were similar across regions and differences in total returns were due largely to disparities in capital gains.*[75]

However, the overseas index for the Lisbon market shows different turning points in comparison to the general index[76] suggesting that different factors were impacting the operations of such distant companies. Table 4 compares the different periods between breaks along the window 1900-1974 for the overseas firms with those for the overall market of the Lisbon Exchange.

---

[74] See Chapter 3 Section 13 for a comparison between the evolution for 74 years of the overseas share index and the general index.

[75] Grossman, 2014, http://repec.wesleyan.edu/

[76] Which is calculated with all companies listed on Lisbon Exchange, therefore mainly influenced by the economy of the European part of Portugal.

BVL GENERAL INDEX   BVL OVERSEAS INDEX

Cycles				Cycles			
Begin	End	$\mu_{B\&S\,model}$		Begin	End	$\mu_{B\&S\,model}$	
Jan/00-Apr/23	03/01/1900	18/04/1923	9.81%	Jan/00-Jul/08	03/01/1900	08/07/1908	-11.19%
Apr/23-Jun/26	18/04/1923	02/06/1926	-0.86%	Jul/08-Apr/10	08/07/1908	06/04/1910	54.10%
Jun/26-Feb/29	02/06/1926	13/02/1929	38.19%	Apr/10-Oct/14	06/04/1910	28/10/1914	-0.20%
Feb/29-Dec/31	13/02/1929	09/12/1931	-29.74%	Oct/14-Sep/29	28/10/1914	26/09/1928	27.62%
Dec/31-Nov/46	09/12/1931	06/11/1946	16.46%	Sep/29-Jul/32	26/09/1928	20/07/1932	-39.61%
Nov/46-Aug/49	06/11/1946	03/08/1949	-13.98%	Jul/32-Jan/55	20/07/1932	05/01/1955	21.76%
Aug/49-Jan/55	03/08/1949	05/01/1955	21.56%	Jan/55-Mar/63	05/01/1955	06/03/1963	-12.78%
Jan/55-Oct/62	05/01/1955	17/10/1962	-2.30%	Mar/63-Apr/74	06/03/1963	24/04/1974	23.23%
Oct/62-Apr/74	17/10/1962	24/04/1974	19.45%	1900 - 1974	03/01/1900	24/04/1974	14.31%
1900 - 1974	03/01/1900	24/04/1974	11.52%				

Table 4 — Breaking points of the Lisbon BVL and Overseas Indices
and the annualised returns along each cycle

13. Political Instability

Following examples seen elsewhere in Europe, the political regime
initiated in 1926 understood political parties as an outdated model
to govern a country in the best interests of its people, and therefore
authorised only a single "movement" called *"União Nacional"*.[77] All
other parties were banned in Portugal during the near half century
of that regime. This created a vacuum in the political culture of the
majority of the Portuguese population, the only exception being the
Communist Party, which managed to survive during all those years
even if with very few members. But it maintained an active school of
political education and, during the later years before 1974, focused
its efforts on the university population because of their central role
in the armed forces sent to fight in Africa and as potential leaders
of the Portuguese society in the years ahead.

Immediately after the fall of the old regime, many parties were
legalised covering a wide spectrum from left to right, but only the

---

[77] In February 1970 renamed *"ANP — Acção Nacional Popular"*.

communists were really prepared and with ideas and tested models to mobilise populations and the civil forces.

The first government after the military coup was selected by the armed forces but lasted only a few months — from 16 May 1974 to 18 July 1974 — when a second government was empowered. This political and governmental instability so clearly indicated was the main characteristic of the new regime until July 1976,[78] when the first elected government finally took power. But even this democratically elected regime did not bring immediate stability to the political arena. Consider that the current[79] XXI Constitutional Government, which was empowered in 2015 is led by the 16th different Prime Minister since 1976, which attests to the variability that remains in Portuguese politics following the 1974 coup (Annex 2).[80]

Coupling this political instability with the burden attached to the return of between 700 to 800 thousand[81] former settlers living in the Portuguese African territories during 1974 and 1975 (Table 5), the domestic economy soon entered into recession with a severe imbalance between exports and imports.

---

[78] There were 6 successive "provisional" governments.

[79] This text was up-dated in January 2017.

[80] See in Annex 2 the complete list of all the six Provisional Governments appointed by the military after April 1974, and the 21 Elected (or Constitutional) Governments that have ruled the country since 1976, with an indication of the name of the Prime Minister of each of the 27 successive governments.

[81] These figures should be compared with the resident population in Portugal: around 9.3 million inhabitants. In any case it is difficult to estimate the real number of returnees from Africa in 1974/75 as many subsequently emigrated to Brazil, Venezuela, and other American countries, and others moved to some European countries (France, Germany, etc.) with large Portuguese communities that had been growing since the mid-1960s.

Resident Population Estimated on 31 December of each year

1970	1971	1972	1973	1074	1975	1976	1977	1978	1979
8,663,252	8,624,260	8,636,600	8,629,600	8,879,130	9,307,810	9,403,810	9,507,540	9,608,960	9,713,570

Table 5 — The sudden influx to Portugal of settlers fleeing mainly from Angola and Mozambique

Source: *Pordata* — Base de Dados de Portugal Contemporâneo

In spite of this significant increase of the resident population and the very bad spirit of the new comers after being forced to leave behind their accumulated wealth and standard of living the country was able to accommodate all these newcomers, which, incidentally, added new "blood" to a society less accustomed to starting new projects from scratch.

14. Two IMF Stand-by Agreements. The 2011 MOU with the "troika"

After five defaults during the nineteenth century — the last in 1892 — Portugal maintained government and external accounts balanced for more than half a century, and so lost the habit of facing constraints in its external finances front. But the imbalances triggered by the economic and political events unfolding after 1974 soon forced her to call upon the International Monetary Fund (IMF) for guidance and financial assistance in order to resolve serious balance of payment crises at two different moments during the twentieth century (1978-1979 and 1983-1985).

In 1978 Portugal faced her first risk of default in the century.[82] A succession of external annual deficits immediately following the

---

[82] For a big picture on defaults, see Reinhart, 2008.

1974 revolution completely depleted the foreign reserves accumulated in the Central Bank, forcing the government to sign a first stand-by agreement with IMF in 1978 to obtain an emergency loan in return for a number of domestic economic measures intended to restore the external equilibrium of the country.

This first IMF programme was very successfully implemented, but soon the country returned to her historical trend of importing more than selling abroad and in 1983 a second stand-by agreement with IMF was necessary for very similar purposes and accompanied by similar economic measures. Once again this economic programme was executed so perfectly that it was even referred to internationally as a case study.

As this second foreign intervention was completed, a new (centre-right) government was elected in 1985 that remained in power for ten years in a row, giving to the country the very first period of political stability following the Carnation Revolution (Annex 2). This stability permitted the implementation of a number of economic measures to improve productivity and growth. At the same time, negotiations were initiated in Brussels aimed at joining the then European Economic Community (EEC).

Unfortunately Portugal then allowed considerable slippage in state-managed public works and inflated public wages in parallel with persistent and lasting recruitment policies that boosted the number of redundant public servants. Risky credit, public debt creation, and European structural and cohesion funds were mismanaged across almost four decades. With the 2008 global crisis disrupting the markets and the world economy, Portugal was one of the first and most affected economies to succumb and so, in the first half of 2011, Portugal requested a €78 billion IMF-EU bailout package in a bid to stabilise its public finances. The Portuguese government headed managed to implement measures to improve the State's financial situation and the country started to be seen as moving on the right track but those measures also led to a strong increase of the unemployment rate to over 15 per cent in the second quarter 2012. The stock market could not remain isolated from this domestic and international environments.[83]

15. EEC Accession in 1986. The single currency

The treaty to join the EEC was signed in June 1985 and Portugal became a full member of the European community in January 1986.

Along the very long history of the country — initiated in 1143[84] — and after two strategic swings in its strategic development

- first, in 1415, when the conquest of Ceuta in northern Africa marks the beginning of the overseas expansion
- second, in 1975, when the retreat from Africa marks the end of the Empire and the return to the original territory in the Iberian Peninsula,

this accession to the EEC constitutes a new shift in the Portuguese strategic orientation: no longer toward the sea and the overseas expansion, but toward Europe and its innovative integration movement. Most political parties supported these decisions to the north

---

[83] Berkowitz, 2012.

[84] Normally the Treaty of Zamora signed on 5 October 1143 by Afonso VII, then king of Leon and Castile, and by Afonso of Portugal — from then on King Afonso I — is considered the birth date of this country as it recognised its independence from Leon.

and to integration with other countries, and for a number of political and economic reasons:

- gain political stability
- maintain independence from the traditionally hegemonic Spanish neighbour
- access to large markets in rich economies
- acceleration of modernisation — culturally and economically
- participation in the integration process underway in Europe

  access to budgetary funds provided by the European Commission.

During the first years of membership — until 2000 — the country seems to have profited very well from those advantages, but this cannot be separated from the fact that there was a single prime minister during most of that same period. As a matter of fact, the 1995 Parliamentary elections led to a new party to power — socialist — and to a new prime minister, but until 2000 nothing changed significantly from that positive trend.

In terms of the domestic capital market, the period from 1989 to 2000 saw the return of a number of firms to private hands, especially in the financial and utility sectors. Most of those companies were sold back to investors through a number of public offers executed through the Stock Exchanges (Lisbon and Porto) to increase transparency of the process and to promote the Exchange market in order to establish a "popular domestic capitalism".

In the beginning the Portuguese Political Constitution (even after the 1982 revision that made it more market oriented and less "socialist") authorised selling only up to 49% of the share capital of any nationalised company, but with the revision of 1992, the entire share capital could be sold to private investors. This and the intention to test the market after so many years of reprobation of capital markets led to the policy of privatising most large companies in small tranches according to the capacity available to absorb all shares at the best prices.

In January 1999 Portugal joined the first wave of member states (11 countries) that launched the Euro within the European Community. This fact and the economic and legal measures taken to prepare the country for the monetary transition had a very positive effect upon the Exchange market as the country borders grew more transparent to the free movement of all forms of capital in and out of the country.

16. Privatisations

A full democratic regime could be achieved in Portugal only after land property rights were re-instated, the 1974/75 nationalised corporations were re-privatised, and the Lisbon and Porto Stock Exchanges were re-opened. This return to a perspective of plain respect for property rights was in line with the decision to join Europe (taken in the 1970s), an event that occurred only in 1986 due to the lengthy Spanish similar request.

However, only in the 1990s, after the 1989 revision of the 1976 Constitution, could Portugal pursue a full policy of privatisation of most nationalized sectors as well as return land properties to their former owners. Figure 8 presents the evolution of privatisations during the most significant period after 1974.

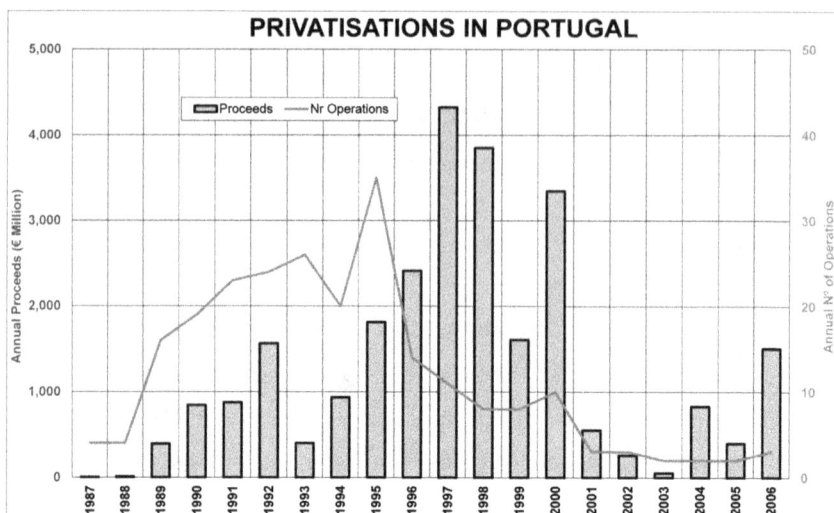

PRIVATISATIONS IN PORTUGAL

Figure 8 — Evolution of privatisations during the most significant
period after 1974

In any case, the first steps into privatisation were initially limited
by the obligation of the State to retain the majority of capital:[85] the
Decree-Law 406/83 (19 November 1983), based on Law 11/83 (16
August 1983) defined the limits between public and private sectors,
paving the way to future privatisations, and the Decree-Law 449/88
(10 December 1988) redefined those limits after many operative proceedings introduced in June 1988. With the constitutional revision
of 1992, the entire share capital could be sold to private investors.

As Figure 8 shows, only in 1989 did large privatisation operations start in earnest, particularly in the insurance and banking
sectors. [86] It is worth mentioning that the option for the execution
of most of the largest transfers of property in the two Portuguese

---

[85] This explains initial limits to sell off only up to 49% of the share capital.

[86] Actually, the first companies returned to private hands in 1987, but were
minor firms. Large and important companies started being privatised only in 1989.
The first was the sale of only 49% of the share capital of *Banco Totta & Açores* on
10 July 1989. Direcção Geral de Estudos e Previsão, 1999.

Stock Exchanges guaranteed great transparency and acceptability to those operations, therefore contributing to their domestic and international acceptance.

This change and the intention to test the market after so many years of reprobation of Capital Markets led to the policy of selling most large companies according to the capacity available to absorb all shares at the best prices.

Curiously, and against all expectations, Portugal was able to re--establish a capital market and develop a modern and efficient Stock Exchange in a very short amount of time (around 15 years after the 1977 opening to share trading in Lisbon), with a success that may be measured by the fact that it was able to join the innovative experience of the Euronext group of Exchanges immediately in 2002 and ahead of many other cases.

The equity index for the Lisbon Exchange demonstrates that the mere prospect of integration into Europe in 1986 and into the euro zone in 1999 had significant impacts upon this market by legitimising the character of the Portuguese political regime and therefore decreasing the required capital risk premium — the index starts climbing as soon as both moves were internalised before those two dates (Figure 9).[87]

However, when the market reopened after the Carnation Revolution, the quotations were below average, a fact that one would expect after the turmoil associated with that political, social, and economic revolution. Early intense recovery followed the international examples in which investors tended to demand above average returns to re-enter the market after a period of very heavy losses as a means to precisely recover from such losses. The fact that this

---

[87] For the differentiated effects in France, Germany, Italy, and Spain of the introduction of the single currency upon stock market's volatility, see Billio et al., 2001. Giannetti, 2006. Peroni, 2009.

recovery did not last long can be connected to our two domestic economic crises — in 1979 and 1983 — which could only be tackled after standby agreements were signed with IMF.

Figure 9 — Impact upon Lisbon quotations of the main steps in the process of integration of Portugal in Europe: 1986 accession to EEC and 1999 participation in the launch of the Euro

With all the Exchange operations to return companies to private hands, the whole decade of the 1990s was very successful for investors, in spite of the initial negative trend of the index after October 1987. But the market fall was dampened by these first privatisations (minimum of BVL Index observed on 13 January 1993) and soon returned to a positive — very positive — upward trend.

Confidence in the potential for Portuguese growth was then very high based on a number of indicators, above all the fact that the Portuguese standard of living of the 1990s had risen to about 50 per cent above the 1970s level. Also, the organisation in Lisbon of a World Exhibition — from 22 May to 30 September 1998 — with an extensive and innovative renewal of a large area in the eastern region of the city of Lisbon, together with the construction of a (second) bridge across the Tagus river in the capital region, testified to the victory of the latest Portuguese economic performance. A local maximum of the Lisbon Stock Exchange index occurred on 8 March 2000.[88]

At the same time, several economic groups flourished during this period, some of which had already been important during the Salazar regime (*"Companhia União Fabril"*, *"Champalimaud"* cement and iron group, and the *"Espírito Santo"* family financial group), but others were recent additions to the domestic economy — *Amorim*, SONAE, and *"Banco Comercial Português"* groups. As all of these had been born after the revolution, they were less touched by the effects of that event and flourished along with democracy.[89]

It is interesting to note that after the 2000 peak the index no longer seems to show the high returns of the past. In spite of the still brief experience accumulated after that date, this attenuation may be due to the fact that the domestic companies are now more interconnected with the external market, a hypothesis that is supported by the increased widening of the Portuguese commercial balance with its European partners and via them with the world. That is, the perceived risk may now be less and also the attraction of diversification may have also diminished.

Privatisations may have played an important role in this overture to the international market, as they were designed to attract non--resident investors due to lack of enough domestic capital to buy all those firms, but the foreign investors brought with them financial expertise, and added an extra demand that reduced the returns required by the whole market.

---

[88] The burst of the international *dot.com* bubble had already hit Portugal along with other open economies.

[89] For the groups that were important before 1974, see Martins, 1975.

17. The new Millennium

Although not immune to the *dot.com* burst of 8 March 2000, there seems to have occurred a change of "mood" in the trending behaviour of the Lisbon Exchange share index:

a) while the market showed a significant positive trend from January 1978 until that break point — annual average return of +29.9% — it seems to have changed to a much lower average return (-2.92%) thereafter (Table 6);

b) this was accompanied by a visible reduction in the volatility around that trend — average deviation from the central line of 0.211 to 0.079 in the end.

BVL GENERAL INDEX

Jan/78-Oct/80	04/01/1978	22/10/1980	1 022	0.148%	0.296	**60.57%**	
Oct/80-Feb/83	22/10/1980	09/02/1983	840	-0.056%	0.032	**-18.86%**	
Feb/83-Oct/87	09/02/1983	07/10/1987	1 701	0.219%	0.376	**84.62%**	29.9%
Oct/87-Jan/93	07/10/1987	13/01/1993	1 925	-0.027%	0.153	**-5.66%**	
Oct/93-Mar/00	13/01/1993	08/03/2000	2 611	0.062%	0.170	**24.06%**	
Mar/00-Oct/02	08/03/2000	02/10/2002	938	-0.067%	0.059	**-22.62%**	
Oct/02-Jul/07	02/10/2002	18/07/2007	1 750	0.056%	0.058	**20.83%**	-2.92%
Jul/07-Mar/09	18/07/2007	04/03/2009	595	-0.146%	0.083	**-48.85%**	
Mar/09-Dec/13	04/03/2009	02/01/2014	1 765	-0.007%	0.108	**-0.52%**	
1978 - 2013	*04/01/1978*	*02/01/2014*	*13 147*	0.040%	*0.837*	*17.49%*	

Table 6 — Time segmentation of the BVL Index behaviour after 1978 with indication of slopes as proxies for daily returns

A number of reasons may be playing a role in this structural change:

• participation in the European integration process has internationalised the Portuguese economy as well as the companies listed in Lisbon; and the use of a common currency after January 1999 certainly reduced the forex risk faced by non-resident investors in domestic securities;

- in February 2002 the Lisbon Exchange joined the Euronext project and that opened the local market to additional, experienced, and well capitalised intermediaries having capacity and ability to dampen price oscillations;

- from the moment (before its effective adoption) the Euro became internalised in the minds of all interested parties, inflation rates fell in Portugal; as low inflation is normally accompanied by less uncertainty about its future levels, interest rates and volatility premium could adjust to lower levels: less volatility drags down smaller *premia*;

- adoption of European rules — especially economic ones — and Directives and Regulations added a new layer of certitude to the domestic economy; the limit to the annual budget deficit of 3% together with the 60% ceiling on the public debt are two important examples. Also important was the adoption of international accounting standards by all listed firms.

A different reason for the index behaviour may be Portugal's sluggish economic growth from the beginning of the new millennium. Economists discuss the reasons for this disappointing performance a great deal, some blaming the Euro, as the excessive initial con--version rate adopted made the Portuguese products very expensive (and non- competitive) abroad, reducing the international competitiveness of the Portuguese economy. So, investors may be anticipating lower future returns for their investments in Portuguese firms — a supply-side explanation.

Of course the sample from the 2000s is still short and the crisis that has been unfolding since the Summer of 2007 may be dragging down the overall trends in this period. In fact, it makes no sense for the market to offer a negative long-term average return (about -3% per year) as that would never attract investors in risky assets like shares. Another indicator of this transitory influence is the expanded volatility observed after 2007, which does not square with the arguments in favour of more stability brought from abroad.

ANNEX 1
SHRINKING OF BVL´S MARKET
BETWEEN 1974 AND 1978

Companies Listed on the Lisbon Stock Exchange	Estimated Capitalisation on 24.Apr.1974	Jan.1978
Insrance		
Alentejo	336 000 000$	
Atlas	777 500 000$	
Bonança	1 188 000 000$	
Comércio e Indústria	1 600 000 000$	
Douro	341 250 000$	
Européa	321 250 000$	
Garantia	750 000 000$	
Império	5 460 000 000$	
Lusitana	237 750 000$	
Madeirense	168 500 000$	
Metropole	275 500 000$	
Mundial	1 504 000 000$	
Mutualidade	1 190 000 000$	
Nacional	735 625 000$	
Nauticus	228 150 000$	
Pátria	641 250 000$	
Portugal Previdente	326 250 000$	
Portuguesa de Seguros	466 000 000$	
Prudência	500 000$	
Sagres	465 625 000$	
Soberana	333 000 000$	
Tagus	326 750 000$	
Tranquilidade	4 120 000 000$	
Ultramarina	2 000 000 000$	
União	2 550 000 000$	
Banks		
Agricultura	3 524 500 000$	
Alentejo (portador)	3 840 000 000$	
Algarva	1 790 000 000$	
Angola (portador)	2 401 250 000$	
Borges & Irmão	3 220 000 000$	
Crédito Predial	3 952 000 000$	
Espírito Santo e Comercial Lisboa	10 670 000 000$	
Fernandes Magalhães	2 327 500 000$	
Fomento Nacional	7 050 000 000$	
Fonsecas & Burnay	8 377 530 000$	
Intercontinental	3 607 500 000$	
Nacional Ultramarino (cupão)	5 962 500 000$	
Pinto de Magalhães	3 444 000 000$	
Portugal	1 700 000 000$	
Português do Atlântico	12 030 150 000$	
Sotto Mayor	17 340 000 000$	
Totta & Açores	7 740 000 000$	
Electrical Utilities		
Aliança Eléctrica do Sul	28 600 000$	
Eléctrica das Beiras	261 750 000$	
Compania Portuguesa de Electricidade	6 174 420 000$	
Companhia Norte Portugal (chenop)	1 204 000 000$	
Gás e Electricidade	1 604 245 984$	
Hidro Eléctrica Alto Alentejo	880 880 000$	
Insular de Electricidade	60 000 000$	
Serra da Estrela	330 000 000$	
União Eléctrica Portuguesa	1 000 000 000$	
Water Utilities		
Curia	285 750 000$	48 000 000$
Luso (Tit-100)	487 305 000$	416 500 000$
Lisboa (portador)	192 000 000$	120 000 000$
Vidago, Melgaço e Pedras Salgadas	639 600 000$	221 000 000$
Spinning & Wool		
Fábrica de Fiação de Tomar	6 000 000$	
Fábrica de Fiação de Torres Novas	67 800 000$	27 000 000$
Lanifícios de Arrentela	200 000$	
Oriental	5 500 000$	5 500 000$
Other Sectors		
Cafés Reunidos	4 500 000$	4 500 000$
Central de Cervejas	3 850 000 000$	
Chá Oriental	5 000 000$	
Compal	164 160 000$	96 000 000$
Industrial Aliança	250 000 000$	100 000 000$
Moagem Lisbonense	3 000 000$	10 500 000$
Padarias	5 000 000$	4 750 000$
Portugal e Colónias	1 448 000 000$	176 000 000$
Celulose do Guadiana	354 000 000$	
Cimentos de Leiria	11 050 000 000$	
Cimentos do Tejo	8 802 000 000$	
F. Ramada	374 000 000$	76 000 000$
Fornos Eléctricos	860 000 000$	107 500 000$
JOTOCAR		21 000 000$
Portuguesa de Celulose	2 308 500 000$	
Siderurgia Nacional	11 904 860 050$	

Companies Listed on the Lisbon Stock Exchange	Estimated Capitalisation on 24.Apr.1974	Jan.1978
Other Sectors (cont.)		
SOCEL	1 762 500 000$	
CIDLA	940 000 000$	
União Fabril	7 210 000 000$	
Intar	293 333 700$	
Nitratos de Portugal	270 000 000$	
Petroquímica	747 000 000$	
Sacor	6 105 000 000$	
Tabacos de Portugal	172 000 000$	
Tabaqueira	2 540 000 000$	
União Fabril do Azoto	438 750 000$	
União Fabril Farmacêutica	81 000 000$	16 200 000$
Pesca Lusitânia		30 000 000$
Artística	6 000 000$	
Cerâmica Lusitana	5 250 000$	5 250 000$
EFACEC	558 000 000$	253 125 000$
EMPOR	1 240 000 000$	36 000 000$
REGISCONTA		20 000 000$
Estoril (caminhos de ferro)	20 000 000$	
Estoril Plage	2 444 475$	
Fábrica Portugal	45 000 000$	45 000 000$
Gases e Produtos Químicos	20 000 000$	30 000 000$
Grão-Pará	487 230 000$	
Grão-Pará Portuguesa	336 000 000$	
Lisnave	5 775 000 000$	935 000 000$
Metalurgica Casal		60 000 000$
Livraria Bertrand	0$	1 000 000$
MABOR	1 750 000 000$	140 000 000$
MATUR	103 250 000$	
Nacional de Publicidade	150 000 000$	
Navegação Nacional	1 500 750 000$	
Navegação (Colónia)	420 000 000$	
Novinco	10 500 000$	30 000 000$
Portuguesa de Pesca	101 875 000$	
Portugueses (C.P.)	18 350 000$	
Prestamista Portuguesa	31 500 000$	6 000 000$
Primeiro de Janeiro	500 000$	7 500 000$
Recreios Lisbonense	200 000$	400 000$
Ribatejana	5 000 000$	5 040 000$
SALVOR	345 000 000$	
SETENAVE	4 365 000 000$	
TAP	1 452 000 000$	
Tauromáquica Lisbonense	14 400 000$	10 272 000$
Turística da Penina	282 500 000$	50 000 000$
Vinhas do Alto Douro	172 000$	
Rádio Marconi - Portador	2 231 000 000$	209 798 333$
Overseas Companies		
Águas de Montemor	35 000 000$	
Agrícola de Bela Vista	3 780 000$	
Agrícola de Cassequel	302 750 000$	
Agrícola de Encoge Micula	5 000 000$	
Agrícola do Fernando Póo	2 500 000$	
Agrícola de Incomati	150 750 000$	
Agrícola das Neves	13 520 000$	
Agrícola Ribeira Palma	500 000$	
Agrícola Ultramarina	18 396 000$	
Agricultura de S. Tomé e Príncipe	41 200 000$	
Açúcar de Angola	299 250 000$	
Algodões de Angola	108 000 000$	
Angolana de Agricultura	178 750 000$	
Asfaltos de Angola	5 250 000$	
Boror	205 000 000$	
Boror - Comercial	60 000 000$	
Buzi	181 500 000$	
Cabinda	79 800 000$	
Colonial Agrícola	1 000 000$	
Fina	410 000 000$	
Comercial Ultramarina	3 000 000$	
Comércio de Construções	3 200 000$	
Diamante de Angola	4 584 500 000$	
Geral de Angola	65 000 000$	
Hidro Eléctrica do Revué	133 750 000$	
Ilha do Príncipe	63 000 000$	
Moçambique	270 000 000$	
Roça Aliança	300 000$	
Roça. Plateau Milagrosa	3 000 000$	
Seles	7 000 000$	
Sena Sugar - Ordinárias	921 375 000$	
Sonefe - Portador	222 500 000$	
Turismo de Moçambique	7 000 000$	
Zambézia	54 600 000$	

ANNEX 2
GOVERNMENTS

General remarks:

The governments shown as being coalition governments included Ministers from most of the main parties. The governments shown as being non-party governments were formed from outside the framework of parties, being based on the political support of the King or the President of the Republic. The parties shown in brackets as forming part of the political base of some governments did not participate in the government, but gave it their support in Parliament for some time.

Date	Head of Government	Political base	Notes
24/Sep/1834	Pedro Sousa Holstein (Duke of Palmela)	conservatives	
28/Apr/1835	Vitório Andrade Barbosa (Count of Linhares)	conservatives	
27/May/1835	João Oliveira Daun (Marquis of Saldanha)	moderate conservatives + moderate progressists	
18/Nov/1835	José Jorge Loureiro	moderate conservatives + moderate progressists	
20/Apr/1836	António Severim Noronha (Duque of Terceira)	conservatives	
10/Sep/1836	José Carneiro Sousa (Count of Lumiares)	progressists	Government formed as a result of a revolutionary movement (September Revolution).
3/Nov/1836	José Portugal Castro (Marquis of Valença)	conservatives	Government formed as a result of a coup d'état (Belenzada).
5/Nov/1836	Bernardo Sá Nogueira (Viscount of Sá da Bandeira)	progressists	Government formed as a result of the defeat of the Belenzada.
1/Jun/1837	António Dias de Oliveira	progressists	
10/Aug/1837	Bernardo Sá Nogueira (Viscount of Sá da Bandeira)	progressists	
18/Apr/1839	Rodrigo Pinto Pizarro (Baron of Ribeira de Sabrosa)	progressists	
26/Nov/1839	José Travassos Valdez (Count of Bonfim)	orderly conservatives	
9/Jun/1841	Joaquim António de Aguiar	orderly conservatives	

Date	Head of Government	Political base	Notes
7/Feb/1842	Pedro Sousa Holstein (Duke of Palmela)	orderly conservatives	
9/Feb/1842	António Severim Noronha (Duke of Terceira)	radical conservatives	Government formed as a result of a revolutionary movement (Carnival Revolution)
20/May/1846	Pedro Sousa Holstein (Duke of Palmela)	progressists + orderly conservatives	Government formed as a result of a popular rebellion (Maria da Fonte).
6/Oct/1846	João Oliveira Daun (Marquis of Saldanha)	radical conservatives	Government formed as a result of a coup d'état (Emboscada).
28/Apr/1847	No President of Council was appointed for this government.	radical conservatives	Between Oct/1846 and Jun/1847 some regions of mainland Portugal we recon trolled by a progressist government based in Porto and led by Francisco Silva Pereira (Count of Antas).
18/Dec/1847	João Oliveira Daun (Duke of Saldanha)	radical conservatives	
18/Jun/1849	António Costa Cabral (Count of Tomar)	radical conservatives	
26/Apr/1851	António Severim Noronha (Duke of Terceira)	radical conservatives	
1/May/1851	João Oliveira Daun (Duke of Saldanha)	Regenerator Party	Government formed as a result of a revolutionary movement (Regeneração).
6/Jun/1856	Nuno Moura Barreto (Marquis of Loulé)	Historic Progressist Party	
16/Mar/1859	António Severim Noronha (Duke of Terceira)	Regenerator Party	
1/May/1860	Joaquim António Aguiar	Regenerator Party	Joaquim António Aguiar became head of government on the death of the Duke of Terceira.
4/Jul/1860	Nuno Moura Barreto (Marquis of Loulé)	Historic Progressist Party	
17/Apr/1865	Bernardo Sá Nogueira (Marquis of Sá da Bandeira)	Historic Progressist Party	
4/Sep/1865	Joaquim António Aguiar	Regenerator Party + Historic Progressist Party	
4/Jan/1868	António José Ávila (Count of de Ávila)	Reformist Party + Conservative Party	Government formed as a result of a popular rebellion (Janeirinha).
22/Jul/1868	Bernardo Sá Nogueira (Marquis of Sá da Bandeira)	Conservative Party + Reformist Party	
11/Aug/1869	Nuno Moura Barreto (Duke of Loulé)	Historic Progressist Party	
19/May/1870	João Oliveira Daun (Duke of Saldanha)	Military, later future Constituent Party	Government formed as a result of a revolutionary movement (Saldanhada)

Date	Head of Government	Political base	Notes
29/Aug/1870	Bernardo Sá Nogueira (Marquis of Sá da Bandeira)	coalition (excluding Constituent Party)	
29/Oct/1870	António José Ávila (Marquis of Ávila e Bolama)	Conservative Party + Reformist Party later Conservative Party (+ Regenerator Party)	
13/Sep/1871	Fontes Pereira de Melo	Regenerator Party (+ Conservative Party + Constituent Party)	
5/Mar/1877	António José Ávila (Duke of Ávila)	Conservative Party (+ Regenerator Party)	
29/Jan/1878	Fontes Pereira de Melo	Regenerator Party	
1/Jun/1879	Anselmo José Braamcamp	Progressist Party	
25/Mar/1881	António Rodrigues Sampaio	Regenerator Party	
14/Nov/1881	Fontes Pereira de Melo	Regenerator Party	
24/Oct/1883	Fontes Pereira de Melo	Regenerator Party	
20/Feb/1886	José Luciano de Castro	Progressist Party	
14/Jan/1890	António Serpa Pimentel	Regenerator Party	
14/Oct/1890	João Crisóstomo Sousa	non-party	
25/May/1891	João Crisóstomo Sousa	non-party	
17/Jan/1892	José Dias Ferreira	non-party	
27/May/1892	José Dias Ferreira	non-party	
22/Feb/1893	Ernesto Hintze Ribeiro	Regenerator Party	Dictatorship, i.e. the Chamber of Deputies and the elective part of the Chamber of Peers were dissolved and no elections were called, between Nov/1894 and Jan/1896.
7/Feb/1897	José Luciano de Castro	Progressist Party	
18/Aug/1898	José Luciano de Castro	Progressist Party	
25/Jun/1900	Ernesto Hintze Ribeiro	Regenerator Party	
28/Feb/1903	Ernesto Hintze Ribeiro	Regenerator Party	
20/Oct/1904	José Luciano de Castro	Progressist Party	
27/Dec/1905	José Luciano de Castro	Progressist Party	
20/Mar/1906	Ernesto Hintze Ribeiro	Regenerator Party	
19/May/1906	João Franco Castelo Branco	Liberal-Regenerator Party	
2/May/1907	João Franco Castelo Branco	Liberal-Regenerator Party	Dictatorship, i.e. the Chamber of Deputies was dissolved and no elections were called.
4/Feb/1908	Francisco Ferreira do Amaral	Progressist Party + Regenerator Party	
25/Dec/1908	Artur Campos Henriques	Progressist Party + dissidents regenerators	

Date	Head of Government	Political base	Notes
11/Apr/1909	Sebastião Sousa Teles	Progressist Party + dissidents regenerators	
14/May/1909	Venceslau Lima	Progressist Party + dissidents regenerators	
22/Dec/1909	Francisco Veiga Beirão	Progressist Party + dissidents regenerators	
26/Jun/1910	António Teixeira de Sousa	Regenerator Party	
5/Oct/1910	Teófilo Braga	Republican Party	Provisional government formed as a result of the republican revolution of 5 October 1910.
3/Sep/1911	João Chagas	coalition	
12/Dec/1911	Augusto Vasconcelos	coalition	
16/Jun/1912	Duarte Leite	coalition	
9/Jan/1913	Afonso Costa	Democratic Party (+ Unionist Party)	
9/Feb/1914	Bernardino Machado	Democratic Party	
23/Jun/1914	Bernardino Machado	Democratic Party	
12/Dec/1914	Azevedo Coutinho	Democratic Party	
25/Jan/1915	Pimenta de Castro	Military + Evolutionist Party + Unionist Party	Government formed as a result of a *coup d'état* (Movimento das Espadas)
17/May/1915	José de Castro	Democratic Party	Government formed as a result of a revolutionary movement. On 15/May/1915 João Chagas was appointed head of government, but he was physically incapacitated and unable to take power.
18/Jun/1915	José de Castro	Democratic Party	
29/Nov/1915	Afonso Costa	Democratic Party	
15/Mar/1916	António José de Almeida	Democratic Party + Evolutionist Party	
25/Apr/1917	Afonso Costa	Democratic Party (+ Evolutionist Party)	
11/Dec/1917	Sidónio Pais	Military + Unionist Party later National Republican Party	Government formed as a result of a revolutionary movement (December Revolution).
14/Dec/1918	Canto e Castro	National Republican Party	Canto e Castro became head of government as a result of the assassination of Sidónio Pais.
16/Dec/1918	Tamagnini Barbosa	National Republican Party	Between 19/Jan and 13/Feb/1919, some regions of the north of mainland Portugal were controlled by a monarchist government based in Porto and presided over by Henrique Paiva Couceiro.

Date	Head of Government	Political base	Notes
27/Jan/1919	José Relvas	coalition (including National Republican Party)	Between 19/Jan and 13/Feb/1919, some regions of the north of mainland Portugal were controlled by a monarchist government based in Porto and presided over by Henrique Paiva Couceiro.
30/Mar/1919	Domingos Pereira	coalition (excluding National Republican Party	
29/Jun/1919	Sá Cardoso	Democratic Party	On 15/Jan/1920, a Liberal Party government led by Fernandes Costa was appointed. Due to a rebellion, this government did not take office.
21/Jan/1920	Domingos Pereira	Democratic Party	
8/Mar/1920	António Maria Baptista	Democratic Party	
6/Jun/1920	Ramos Preto	Democratic Party	Ramos Preto became head of government on the death of António Maria Baptista.
26/Jun/1920	António Maria da Silva	Democratic Party + Popular Party	
19/Jul/1920	António Granjo	Liberal Party + Reconstituent Party	
20/Nov/1920	Álvaro de Castro	Reconstituent Party + Popular Party	
30/Nov/1920	Liberato Pinto	Democratic Party + Reconstituent Party + Popular Party	
2/Mar/1921	Bernardino Machado	Democratic Party + Reconstituent Party	
23/May/1923	Barros Queirós	Liberal Party	Government formed as a result of a revolutionary movement.
30/Aug/1921	António Granjo	Liberal Party	
19/Oct/1921	Manuel Maria Coelho	Radical Party	Government formed as a result of a revolutionary movement (Oct Revolution)
5/Nov/1921	Maia Pinto	Radical Party	
16/Dec/1921	Cunha Leal	coalition (excluding Radical Party)	
6/Feb/1922	António Maria da Silva	Democratic Party	
15/Nov/1923	Ginestal Machado	Nacionalist Party	
18/Dec/1923	Álvaro de Castro	Reconstituent Party + Democratic Party	
6 July 1924	Rodrigues Gaspar	Democratic Party	
22/Nov/1924	Domingues dos Santos	Democratic Party	
15/Feb/1925	Vitorino Guimarães	Democratic Party	

Date	Head of Government	Political base	Notes
1 July 1925	António Maria da Silva	Democratic Party	
1/Aug/1925	Domingos Pereira	Democratic Party	
17/Dec/1926	António Maria da Silva	Democratic Party	
30/May/1926	Mendes Cabeçadas	Military	Government formed as a result of a revolutionary movement (28/May).
19/Jun/1926	Gomes da Costa	Military	Government formed as a result of a *coup d'état*.
9/Jul/1926	Óscar Carmona	Military	Government formed as a result of a *coup d'état*.
18/Apr/1928	Vicente de Freitas	Military	
8/Jul/1929	Ivens Ferraz	Military	
21/Jan/1930	Domingos Oliveira	Military	During part of 1931, the region of Madeira was controlled by a democratic government based in Funchal and presided over by Adalberto Sousa Dias.
5/Jul/1932	António de Oliveira Salazar	Military	
11/Apr/1933	António de Oliveira Salazar	União Nacional	Government formed as a result of the approval of the 1933 Constitution.
18/Jan/1936	Oliveira Salazar	União Nacional	
27/Sep/1968	Marcelo Cetano	UN later ANP	Government formed as a result of the physical incapacity of Oliveira Salazar.
25/Apr/1974	António Spínola	Military	Responsibility for government taken over by the Junta of National Salvation as a result of a revolutionary movement (25/April).
15/May/1974	Palma Carlos	PPD + PS + PCP	1st provisional government.
17/Jul/1974	Vasco Gonçalves	Military + PPD + PS + PCP	2nd provisional government.
30/Sep/1974	Vasco Gonçalves	Military + PPD + PS + PCP	3rd provisional government formed as a result of a revolutionary movement (28/September).
26/Mar/1975	Vasco Gonçalves	Military + PPD + PS + PCP	4th provisional government formed as a result of a revolutionary movement (11/March).
8/Aug/1975	Vasco Gonçalves	Military	5th provisional government.
19/Sep/1975	Pinheiro de Azevedo	Military + PPD + PS + PCP	6th provisional government.

Date	Head of Government	Political base	Notes
23/Jun/1976	Almeida Costa	Military + PPD + PS + PCP	Almeida Costa became head of government as a result of the physical incapacity of Pinheiro de Azevedo.
23/Jul/1976	Mário Soares	PS	1st constitutional government formed as a result of the 1976 elections for the first constitutional legislature.
23/Jan/1978	Mário Soares	PS + CDS	2nd constitutional government formed as a result of the rejection of a motion of confidence in the 1st constitutional government by the Assembly of the Republic.
29/Aug/1978	Nobre da Costa	non-party	3rd constitutional government formed as a result of the CDS leaving the 2nd constitutional government.
22/Nov/1978	Mota Pinto	non-party	4th constitutional government formed as a result of the rejection of the programme of the 3rd constitutional government by the Assembly of the Republic.
31/Jul/1979	Lurdes Pintassilgo	non-party	5th constitutional government formed as a result of the approval of a motion of a lack of confidence in the 4th constitutional government by the Assembly of the Republic.
4/Dec/1980	Sá Carneiro	Democratic Alliance (= PSD + CDS + PPM)	6th constitutional government formed as a result of the 1979 elections held for the completion of the first constitutional legislature (elections brought forward).
4/Dec/1980	Freitas do Amaral	Democratic Alliance (= PSD + CDS + PPM)	Freitas do Amaral became head of government on the death of Sá Carneiro.
9/Jan/1981	Pinto Balsemão	Democratic Alliance (= PSD + CDS + PPM)	7th constitutional government formed as a result of the 1980 elections for the 2nd constitutional legislature.
4/Sep/1982	Pinto Balsemão	Democratic Alliance (= PSD + CDS + PPM)	8th constitutional government formed as a result of the CDS leaving the 7th constitutional government.

Date	Head of Government	Political base	Notes
9/Jun/1983	Mário Soares	PS + PSD	9th constitutional government formed as a result of the 1983 elections for the 3rd constitutional legislature (elections brought forward due to the split in the Democratic Alliance).

Date	Head of Government	Political base	Notes
6/Nov/1985	Cavaco Silva	PSD (+ PRD)	10th constitutional government formed as a result of the 1985 elections for the 4th constitutional legislature (elections brought forward due to the PSD leaving the 9th constitutional government).
17/Aug/1987	Cavaco Silva	PSD	11th constitutional government formed as a result of the 1987 elections for the 5th constitutional legislature (elections brought forward due to the approval of a motion of censure in the 10th constitutional government by the Assembly of the Republic).
4/Dec/1991	Cavaco Silva	PSD	12th constitutional government formed as a result of the 1991 elections for the 6th constitutional legislature.
28/Oct/1995	António Guterres	PS	13th constitutional government formed as a result of the 1995 elections for the 7th constitutional legislature.
25/Oc/1999	António Guterres	PS	14th constitutional government formed as a result of the 1999 elections for the 8th constitutional legislature.
6/Apr/2002	José Manuel Durão Barroso	PSD + PP	15th constitutional government formed as a result of the 2002 elections for the 9th constitutional legislature (elections brought forward due to the resignation of the former prime-minister).
17/Jul/2004	Pedro Santana Lopes	PSD + PP	16th constitutional government formed as a result of the resignation of the former prime-minister (who became President of the European Commission).

Date	Head of Government	Political base	Notes
12/Mar/2005	José Sócrates (Pinto de Sousa)	PS	17th constitutional government formed as a result of the 2005 elections for the 10th constitutional legislature (elections brought forward due to the dissolution of the Assembly of Republic by the President).
26/Oct/2009	José Sócrates (Pinto de Sousa)	PS	18th constitutional government formed as a result of the 2009 elections for the 11th constitutional legislature.
21/Jun/2011	Pedro Passos Coelho	PSD + PP	19th constitutional government formed as a result of the 2011 elections for the 12th constitutional legislature (elections brought forward due to the resignation of the former prime-minister).
30/Oct/2015	Pedro Passos Coelho	PSD + PP	20th constitutional government formed as a result of the 2015 elections for the 13th legislature.
26/Nov/2015	António Costa	PS	21th constitutional government formed as a result of the rejection of the programme of the 20th constitutional government by the Assembly of the Republic.

Source — Nuno Valério (ed.), Portuguese Historical Statistics, Estatísticas Históricas Portuguesas, Lisbon, INE, 2001.

AD — Aliança Democrática [Democratic Alliance] (= PSD + CDS + PPM)
ANP — Ação Nacional Popular [National Popular Action] (former UN)
CDS — Centro Democrático e Social [Democratic and Social Centre] (later PP)
PCP — Partido Comunista Português [Portuguese Communist Party]
PP — Partido Popular [Popular Party] (former CDS)
PPD — Partido Popular Democrático [Popular Democratic Party] (later PSD)
PPM — Partido Popular Monárquico [Popular Monarchic Party]
PRD — Partido Renovador Democrático [Democratic Renewal Party]
PS — Partido Socialista [Socialist Party]
PSD — Partido Social-Democrático [Social-Democratic Party] (former PPD)
UN — União Nacional [National Union] (later ANP)

CHAPTER 5

STOCK MARKETS IN PORTUGAL.

ORGANISATIONAL FEATURES

Introduction

During the twentieth century, Portugal maintained centralised securities markets only in Lisbon and in the northern town of Porto.

In Lisbon, the Exchange was a natural response to the country´s
needs stemming from the overseas voyages initiated in the beginning of the fifteenth century, with the purpose of organising the
trading of commodities (spices being imported from India and elsewhere), and also to accumulate the necessary financial means to
fund and cover the risks of those sailing voyages. Officially, the
Lisbon Exchange is considered to have been institutionalised only in
January 1769, because in November 1755 a massive earthquake that
destroyed the city forced the transformation of the rather informal
market that functioned downtown in the open air at the *"Rua Nova
dos Mercadores"*[1] into a regulated institution established inside a
specially constructed room included in the newly rebuilt (eastside)
tower of a building designed to accommodate most of the government departments of the time (Figure 1).

---

[1] Also known as *"Rua dos Ferros"* due to a separate area implanted in a larger
part of that street where a metallic fence segregated a small space — the "trading
floor" — to allow traders to conduct their bargaining with some isolation from the
surrounding crowds. Freire, 1789.

It is interesting to summarise the evolution of the legal status of the Exchanges in Portugal during the twentieth century. The 1889 Commercial Code[2] maintained the private character of all Exchanges and their control by the local Commercial Associations of the towns in which they were headquartered. They were closer to private clubs of brokers than to private commercial companies.

Figure 1 — The Ministry of Finance building on the east side of the *"Praça do Comércio"* near the river with the tower where the Lisbon Exchange was installed from 1769 until 1994.

Between 1889 and 1974, these markets remained regulated by the same legal infrastructure based on that Code, but the rapid expansion of the activity in the Exchanges from the end of the 1960s

---

[2] This is the second Commercial Code published in 1888 to be used from January 1889 on. The first one was issued in 1834.

forced the government to publish an interim Code in January 1974. This legislation determined the nationalisation of the two Exchanges, which from then on remained simply as autonomous departments of the Ministry of Finance.

In 1991, a comprehensive updating of the whole legal environment transformed the Exchanges into semi-private not-for-profit Civil Associations run by the community of local brokers and banks, although the government kept a strong voice in strategic issues. Only in 2000 did the merged BVLP institution (joining the Lisbon and Porto markets) acquire a full commercial and for-profit character, whose initial shareholders were the previous members of the two organised markets.

1. Origins of the Lisbon Exchange. Earliest Legal Features and Regulations

Examining the legal features of our stock market throughout Portugal's history is of interest. As for other European countries, the term Stock Market designates the principle for the organisation of the institutional market, as well as the registration of the operations, the institution itself, and the physical location (the house) where negotiation and trading operations occurred.[3]

As summarised above, there is much evidence that during the fifteenth century, a rudimentary form of market already existed in Lisbon, closely linked to the Portuguese Discoveries at their peak. This was in response to two main financial problems: mobilizing the large amounts of money necessary to finance the fleets and voyages, and dealing with the premium of the insurance contracts to cover

---

[3] Braudel, 1979, tome 2: 78.

the associated risks.[4] These are financial activities that characterize cosmopolitan capital cities of Europe in the next centuries.[5]

Lisbon pioneered the experience of world trade, shipping, and maritime insurance, thanks to the international trade routes connecting the city to the Americas, Africa, India, and beyond. Since then the role of the Portuguese trade and financial market in the global network of financial operations has been reflected in the special legal rules and settings that framed the Lisbon Bourse.[6] It is even possible to say that this framework became a market-maker, due to the concentration on local specialities throughout the 1500s, although, in the following century, it lost that prominence.[7]

Gathering the business of medieval maritime insurance into a common Bourse in Bruges, Porto, and Lisbon, has led some historians to argue for the medieval origin of the Lisbon Stock-Exchange.[8] However, these *gildes* were different institutions, which certainly helped to develop training and expertise in maritime business, but cannot be identified as the same continuous institution over time.

The vigorous Brazilian trade in the eighteenth century re-instated Lisbon to a world-market position, in part due to the monopolist companies that were engaged in colonial commodities traffic. Networked professionals and cosmopolitan traders[9] gathered then in a new trading room, built after the catastrophic 1755 earthquake, although no formal investment analysts and trust companies were yet available. Trading in these markets was under the surveillance

---

[4] Santarém, 1552, 1961, is a treatise on insurance regulation. See also Amzalak, 1958.

[5] Justino, 1994: 1-5.

[6] Neal, 1990: 3.

[7] Neal, 1990: 131.

[8] Barbosa, 1874, quoting Fernão Lopes. Ulrich, 1906: 85-88.

[9] Stockbrokers, bankers, company promoters, accountants, lawyers, information providers, directors, and security marketing specialists

of the local municipal authorities, and operations on letters of exchange under Crown regulations, while government payments to/from abroad were channelled to bill brokers or forex[10] intermediaries district by district throughout the country.[11]

The Lisbon Bourse also developed the professional expertise for managing contracts, and the presence of brokers (*"corretores"* in Portuguese) is documented in archival sources on municipal regulations from the fourteenth century for urban provisioning businesses, and for maritime businesses thereafter.[12] In fact, the law of 23 August 1342 compiled the rules for the exercise of that profession, and defined tabular data for the value of the listing fees and trading commissions (*"corretagens"*). This legal framework represents the first known attempt to control transaction costs, along with provisions for market transparency.

By the end of the fifteenth century, the royal law (*Carta Régia*) of 15 February 1492 reduced the number of brokers from 25 to 12, in order to promote the implementation of a policy of profession privileges, at the discretion of the monarch, in order to reward the king's twelve most trusted aristocrats for relevant services provided to the Crown.[13] This means that the profession was highly desired and profitable. Such regulation also means that the profession was honourable in a society based on clear social cleavages resulting from the differentiation between common labourers and the upper strata, which included respectable merchants and traders. Financial business was not considered an unsavoury way of life for the Portuguese nobility.[14] The warrior/merchant (*"cavaleiro-*

---

[10] Forex: short name for foreign exchange market

[11] Justino, 1994: 31.

[12] Justino, 1994: 11, quoting Oliveira 1891: 92-94.

[13] Justino, 1994: 13.

[14] Godinho, 1980.

-*mercador*") was a very elegant gentlemanly condition that united military activities in Portugal or overseas with benefits and profits, a distantly noble posture of life.

The elevated esteem of the brokerage profession was clearly expressed in a law dated from 11 November 1491 that stipulates that brokers should take a leading position in the rank-structured file in Lisbon's annual *Corpus Christi* procession, which traditionally meandered from the Cathedral throughout the main streets of the capital city.[15]

Initially, all the revenues from listing fees and commissions on financial businesses were pooled together in a purse (*"bolsa"* in Portuguese), and shared equally among all brokers, according to the 1458 resolution of the municipal Senate.[16] As some brokers were more agile than others in dealing and negotiating the operations, two years later some of them complained to the King about that forced equality, but the equal division of the revenues prevailed, and a new law of 15 July 1473 consecrated that principle and even forbade competition amongst them.[17] These facts suggest that the government saw the existence of the Bourse and the services it provided to trade and long-distance markets as a public good whose dominant role was to fuel the implementation of a geopolitical project for the nation.

The original 1485 Regulation (*"Regimento de 1485"*) also required that all operations be recorded in a single ledger as a corporation, by a clerk (*"escrivão"*), so that the equal division amongst the brokers of the profits collected by the receiver (*"recebedor"*), could be honest, in spite of recognising that some of them had a larger portfolio of clients and operations than the others.[18] This means that a division

---

[15] Ulrich, 1906: 102.

[16] Justino, 1994: 22.

[17] Justino, 1994: 22.

[18] Justino, 1994: 25-26.

of labour within the corporation created specialised tasks amongst the brokers. Penalties collected for disrespectful behaviour were also registered in the book, as well as some common costs of the corporation (such as the funeral expenditures upon the death of a broker).

The importance of market trust and confidence was a decisive feature, but it did not prevent the authorisation for sub-establishment, which was consecrated in the royal law ("*Carta Régia*") of 20 August 1500. This meant that the brokerage function belonged to someone, who could now delegate the practice of his function to a specialised clerk under his responsibility, as the Regulation Book for the profession ("*Livro do Regimento dos Corretores*") clearly shows, in registering four cases of individual brokers whose names are followed by another name.[19]

This regulation reveals that the profession required technical abilities that only trained people could provide, was very honourable from a social perspective, in great demand due to the high revenues it could provide to the entitled person, and very conspicuous with the political authorities in order to provide financial help to them at a central and local (municipal) governmental level, a requirement to be met for the appointment.

To implement market transparency and maximise rewards for the regulatory authority, in 1500 it became routine for the municipal Senate to award those broker positions to the highest bidder, thereby discontinuing the aristocratic requirement for applicants, because the condition of trader and merchant could also lead to a personal noble title ("*enobrecimento*") to attain the merchant/warrior status of "*mercador-cavaleiro*".[20]

---

[19] Justino, 1994: 13, quoting the *Livro do Regimento dos Corretores*, Lisbon Municipal Archive, follium 31 V°.

[20] Justino, 1994: 15.

It also happened that political authorities inspected the business of letters of exchange to apply penalties for usurious behaviour, but overlooked those penalties against the opportunity of obtaining loans for the king and the government. For example, in January 1443 the government bought armaments in Bruges with the credit granted by local merchants and paid for with letters of exchange issued by Lisbon traders and merchants who lent the necessary funds to the central government.[21]

Brokers ("*corretores*") could deal in maritime transportation freight, insurance premia, credit, letters of exchange and foreign currency, international trade, and lending to government. Domestic public debt (short-run floating debt and long-run redeemable public debt) also became a financial business in the Lisbon stock market, because the Crown developed entrepreneurial merchant (retail) activity in the Cape route shipping (Figure 3). As the public revenue was not enough to manage the huge colonial empire that the government dared to build, the participation of the central state in the maritime shipping provided funding for new undertakings.[22]

In the seventeenth century complaints against the "impure blood" of some individuals approved for the position of broker were coupled with the compulsory character of their intervention in all transactions, as they should encourage businesses rather than hinder them. However, the royal law of 28 October 1718 defended their business assistance as an important social mission to assure safety and confidence, and already refers to their meetings in a house close to the main downtown Lisbon location. The complaints may reveal a decrease of the relative importance of the Lisbon Exchange-market in the European context, as other countries developed powerful

---

[21] Justino, 1994: 33, 34.
[22] Godinho, 1971. Laíns, 1998.

trade companies as assertive and successful business organisations, and European shipping.

Fortunately, in the middle of the 1700s, King Joseph appointed *Marquis de Pombal* as Prime Minister of the Kingdom. Indeed the very destructive earthquake that struck Lisbon and the southern part of the country in 1755 allowed him to tackle the huge problems created by that catastrophe in the capital of the kingdom (earthquake, extensive fire and a tsunami), especially determining the rebuilding of a significant part of downtown Lisbon (Figure 2).

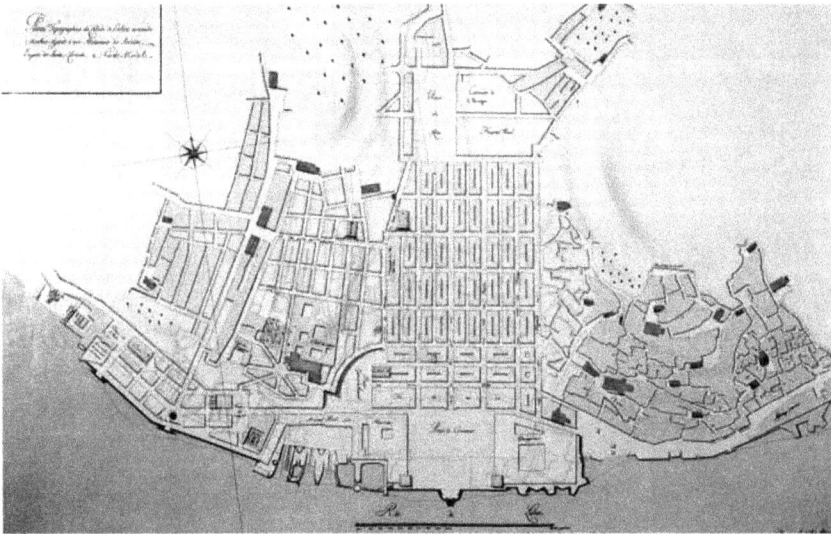

Figure 2 — Map of the reconstruction plan of downtown Lisbon by Eugénio dos Santos. On the right hand side of the main square (by the river) stands the Ministry of Finance building, whose tower at the left lower corner housed the Stock Exchange in the ground floor from 1769 until 1994.

Destruction, disruption of trade, social turmoil, and de-regulation of economic life led a group of important traders and merchants of Lisbon to ask the government for the use of a collective donation to rebuild the customs house and the Bourse as a physical place for negotiation, dealing, and financial operations.

Prime Minister Pombal also founded the first three (very large) limited-liability corporations in Portugal, funded by shares, which reinforced the need to construct a proper place to headquarter the Lisbon Stock Exchange within the Ministry of Finance, itself rehoused in the eastern side of the (also rebuilt) central square near the river. In fact, economic functions propel stock markets, and stock markets develop when large capital is required for larger enterprises.[23]

Figure 3 — The Lisbon open-air Stock Market at *Rua Nova dos Mercadores* (*Zona dos Ferros*), according to a painting from the early seventeenth century. Source: http://artuk.org/ discover/artworks/town-scene-in-lisbon-148320 Kelmscott Manor Collection - Society of Antiquaries of London. "This image can be used for non-commercial research or private study purposes, and other exceptions to copyright permitted under the Copyright, Designs and Patents Act 1988, as amended and revised."

[23] Roe, 2006: 1.

He also decreed rules for the market to function properly on a daily schedule: the decree of 2 January 1756 granted that collective donation, the decree of 28 May created its rules as a disguised tax, and the decree of 16 January 1758 ordered the reconstruction of the Stock Exchange house (the Bourse, Figure 4).

Figure 4 — The famous door of the Lisbon Exchange with the identification above

With all these institutional aspects and the three limited-liability corporations[24] bringing new business for the stock market, some authors defined this moment as the formal birth of the Lisbon Stock Exchange. This is the reason to consider 1 January 1769, as the inaugural date for the Lisbon Stock Exchange.[25] The issue of bonds with the character of Letters of Exchange may be considered as the first loan of modern Public Debt, according to the decree of 29 October 1796. Increased by the authorisation of the law of 13 March 1797, public debt was also a new financial business, and a very successful one in the conversion of earlier issued public loans. Military expenditures, aggravated by the risk of Napoleonic invasion (beginning of the 1800s), obliged the Exchequer to seek financial innovation, particularly the issuing of paper money in the stock market, according to the law of 13 July 1797.

These two features point to corporate finance and bonds as criteria for defining the existence of a real Stock Exchange market.[26] From this perspective the formal birth of the Lisbon Stock Exchange (January 1769) is contemporaneous with today's largest global Exchange, the New York Stock Exchange, whose Board was established on 17 May 1792 (Figures 5 and 6), in the Buttonwood Agreement, signed by 24 brokers under a tree[27] at Wall Street (see Chapter 3, p. 43.

And it is interesting to note that they all committed "to not buy or sell from this day for any person whatsoever, any kind of Public

---

[24] The *"Companhia de Grão Pará e Maranhão"* was created by the law of 6 June 1755, the *"Companhia Geral da Agricultura e das Vinhas do Alto Douro"* by the law of 10 September 1756, and the *"Companhia de Pernambuco e Paraíba"* by the law of 13 August 1759.

[25] Justino, 1994.

[26] Brealey, R.; Stuart M., 2009.

[27] Meeting usually in a coffee house and having a long trading experience. Perkins, 1999.

Stock at a less rate than one quarter per cent Commission on the Specie value and that we will give preference to each other in our Negotiations".[28] The purpose was also public debt trading, after the depletion of the new nation's treasury. Agreeing on minimum commission fees is a practice that prevails everywhere until today.[29]

Three more things helped to modernise the financial sector in Portugal. The first was the book regulating the brokers' profession (*"Livro do Regimento dos Corretores"*, 28 February 1825). It mentions, for the first time, twelve brokers in Lisbon and eight in Porto. It was a very liberal system of regulation. The municipality of Lisbon lost the right of decision in the provision of these positions in the capital city, as from then on only technical abilities were required, independent of social conditions at birth. Each broker should be remunerated according to his own operation, and the revenue from listing fees and commissions was no longer pooled together. Moreover, traders were not obliged to use the brokers' intervention, something that had been in practice for two decades.

The second modernisation event was the birth of the first bank in Portugal (the *Bank of Lisbon*), authorised by the law of 31 December 1821.

The third was the first Commercial Code of 18 September 1833, authored by José Ferreira Borges, who recognises his inspiration in the Prussian, Flemish, and French similar codes. Once again it gives a corporation character to Stock Exchanges, each one with only one chamber.[30] This important legal framework for all commercial activities provided detailed rules which were concentrated in the Code

---

[28] Among the 24 names, two of them were Sephardic Jews of Portuguese and Caribbean origin, respectively: *Benjamin Seixas* (1747-1817), and *Isaac Gomez* (1768--1831). (The NYSE statutes date from 8 March 1817). NYSE Archive, *The Buttonwood Agreement, 1792*.

[29] Sylla, 1997, 2006.

[30] Ulrich, 1906: 111. Borges, 1833, 1856.

Title II, which sought to prevent de-regulation provoking volatility[31]. The subsequent regulation book for brokers that was approved by the decree of 16 January 1837, fixed the amounts for each kind of operation, and allowed varying rewards for the brokers.

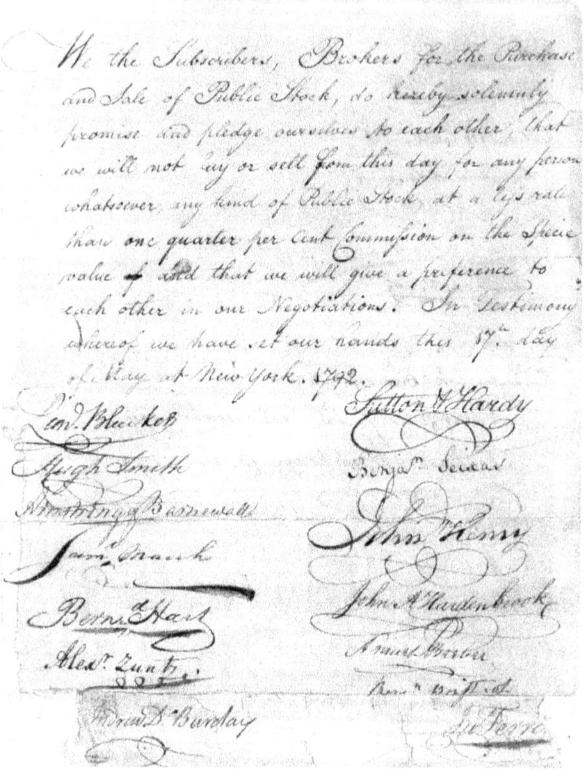

Figure 5 — First page of the Buttonwood Agreement signed in New York on May 17, 1792. On the right column, the second signature is of "Benjamin Seixas", a Sephardic Jew of Portuguese origin

---

[31] A different perspective prevailed in Spain, where *Pedro Sainz de Andino*, the 1829 Code's author, avoided including any regulations on Stock Markets, choosing to devote to this new market a separate law, of September 10th, 1831, because it could be adjusted independently of the Commercial Code. According to some interpretations, this reflects a strong need of a Stock Exchange in Madrid to trade public debt necessary to support the construction of a state bureaucracy, but at the same time a big hesitation about the success of an official market strongly regulated by government. See Cagigal, 2009, page 41. Galvarriato, 1935.

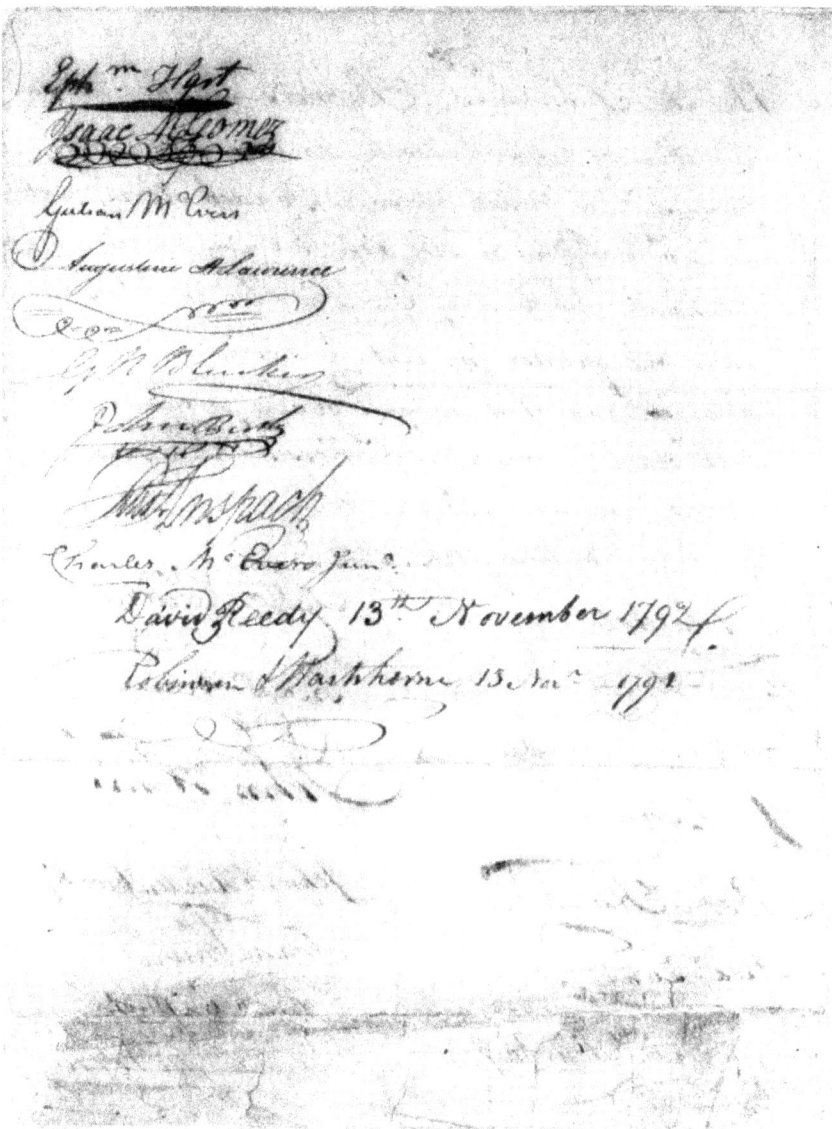

Figure 6 — Second page of the Buttonwood Agreement signed in New York on May 17, 1792. The second signature is of "Isaac Gomez", a Sephardic Jew with Caribbean origin

Public debt had become an important constituent of the operations in the Stock Exchange, as new debt was issued throughout the

Portuguese 1832-34 civil war[32]. Specialisation amongst the brokers was recommended for Lisbon (dividing them into bill brokers, exchange brokers, ship brokers, stock brokers, insurance brokers, and custom-house brokers) but not for Porto, meaning that the dimensions of the two markets were very different[33]. A chamber for their meetings was also provided in Lisbon, adjacent to the trading floor, while in Porto, only later did the law of 19 June 1841 provided a building (the old convent of São Francisco) to the city Bourse.

A general conversion of all public debt (into a single 3% consolidated loan), authorized by the Decree of 18 December 1852 simplified the operations on bonds and created confidence in a central state. The railway-construction fever from the mid-1850s on, also fuelled additional Exchange operations, and the law of 22 June 1867 liberalised the creation of domestic corporations, which were required to use the label of "limited liability" in their name, and regulated the entrance of foreign companies to operate in Portugal.[34] These needed to apply for government authorisation (from the Ministry of Public Works, Commerce, and Industry), after submitting their statutes and pledging to abide by the Portuguese law and courts. Foreign companies were coming more and more into sectors such as mining, insurance, and engineering (which included railway construction, urban gas illumination, and water provision to urban centres). Listings in Lisbon and Porto burgeoned, and corporations were to be audited, according to the same law of 22 June 1867. This

---

[32] In spite of the abolition and withdrawal of the paper money by Decree of 23 July 1834.

[33] The books registering the operations, the exchange rates, and the quotations for bonds, shares, and other securities in Lisbon dating back to 1837 are preserved in the municipal archives. They list corporations and new banks, as well as more and more public debt issued to fund public works and the military expenses of the 1846-47 civil war.

[34] Mata, 1998.

was an important step for Portugal into foreign direct investment (FDI) capital flows and global business.[35]

Global business cycles afflicted the market in periods such as 1875-76, when the 1875 euphoria for Options, Futures, and Warrants gave way to crisis and panic in 1876, particularly for the owners of some bank securities.

Transactions outside the official stock market worried government in the aftermath of that crisis, as may be detected in the law of 7 May 1878. One of the reasons cited for the creation of an additional percentage to the stamp tax in that law was the existence of private Bourses (*bolsins*) where transactions escaped transaction costs (brokers' fees, bank commissions, and taxes). Such a worrying attitude reveals the desire to tax the provision of these services following the government´s public-good vision of the stock market, which was based on the need for a legally-defined environment to provide a seal of trust and confidence to the users in order to avoid poor practice. Predatory pricing is an obvious example. Efficient pricing may result in setting price on a particular platform market side below measures of average variable or marginal cost incurred for customers on that market side.[36] Moreover, information costs, asymmetric information, and moral hazard also underpin marked failures and explain the need for regulation.

2. Bank financing versus Market Instruments

Amongst financial historians a distinction has been recognised between two different kinds of financial systems: the Anglo-American

---

[35] Mata, 2008. Amatori, 2003.

[36] Theories of market leveraging in antitrust, and restrictions in regulation are other areas that the economics of multi-sided platform markets illuminates. Evans, 2003: 238.

financial system organisation combines a Banking system, a Money market and a Securities market; the Continental European financial system organisation is made of a banks' domination "*while the money market and the securities market are relegated to minor, secondary roles*". The extreme case of the Continental European financial system is Germany, it is said.[37] In fact, as in many continental European countries, "*During the period of industrialisation, universal banks played a major role in the (...) economy: they facilitated its 'take--off', they provided loans to the modern industrial firms, and they monitored industrial corporations. Close bank-industry relationships ameliorated liquidity constraints of industrial firms and thereby made investment easier and supported industrial growth*". With the exception of self-financing of investments using retained profits, "*bank loans were only one way to ensure the financing of an industrial enterprise*".[38]

In all cases, Banks have been an important source of funding for corporations and other firms in general. And the Stock Exchange channel requires some financial literacy, but there are more subjective reasons behind that preference for the bank channel:

- a number of nations tend to position Stock Exchanges as true gambling casinos where investors make bets with their small pockets;
- speculation is understood as a negative human behaviour, not as the rational objective of any investor (big or small) of obtaining capital gains (Chateaudun, 1870);
- financial capital is still negatively envisioned in comparison to labour, a position that leads to frequent heavy taxation of savings similar to what burdens consumption;

---

[37] Sylla, 1998: 83.
[38] Burhop; Gelman, 2010: 5.

- in the common culture of the man-in-the-street, finance matters are traditionally absent, probably due to its increasing sophistication and unnatural parlance; the current financial literacy programme launched by the European Union attests precisely to that deficiency.

No wonder that the world in general and the European Union in particular are now "rediscovering" the importance of nurturing Small and Medium Enterprises (SME) and the importance of simplifying the access of those small enterprises to market financing.

In this respect, Portugal is peculiar in comparison with other continental European countries: for a long time the Lisbon Stock Exchange was the financial institution that fulfilled most of the capital needs of large businesses by collecting pocket savings that together could underwrite the requested capital for entrepreneurial activities. The first bank was created only in 1821, the *Bank of Lisbon*, much later than in other countries.

Banking prospered in Portugal during the second half of the nineteenth century when banks became very important financial partners in serving the financial needs of both small firms and large corporations.

Financial crises are particularly disturbing in bank-dominant financial systems.[39] Grossman (2010, p. 74) discovers a macroeconomic relationship between the most well-known historical cyclical banking crises and the boom-bust fluctuations that occurred both before and after the First World War. In Portugal the banking system also faced several episodes of instability throughout the twentieth century. This results in a higher cost of credit intermediation due to the risk premium added in funding firms. *"Cycles of over lending that drive or are accompanied by bubbles in asset markets, such as equity*

---

[39] Reinhart; Rogoff, 2009; Grossman, 2010. Jordà, Schularick, and Taylor, 2011. Schularick, and Taylor, 2012.

and housing, have also shown to increase financial instability", says Campbell, Coyle, and Turner, (2014:5). Recent studies demonstrate a long-run causal relationship between banking instability and the credit-risk premium faced by businesses.[40]

3. The Portuguese Brokerage System

As mentioned before, at least beginning in the 1400s and from the docks near the Lisbon royal palace, fleets were leaving to the Mediterranean Sea and to the Northern European seaports (of France, Flanders, and Britain), but more and more regularly to the Atlantic islands, Africa, and America. In the 1500s they were frequently leaving for India — following Gama's inaugural voyage that opened the Cape sea route to that destination in 1498 — as well as crossing the Atlantic to the New World, thanks to *Columbus* and to *Cabral's* voyages.[41]

A market for the commodities then imported as well as for meeting some financial needs of the Discoveries — fund raising and risk covering — was naturally established in the lower part of the city of Lisbon. All transactions were conducted in the open air in a delimited part of a major downtown street, the *Rua Nova*, which is described in most archival documents as the longest and noblest in the city, as it served many professional establishments making it very busy, and additionally connected the many narrow and tortuous medieval streets to the nearby Royal Palace. Milanese, Genovese, and Florentines performed an important role in this kind of financial business in Lisbon.

At this stage one cannot yet speak of a specialised market, but of a business centre, a market-maker for freight, trade, insurance, and negotiation, as credit and risk must be rewarded. Brokers were

---

[40] Campbell, Coyle and Turner, 2016.
[41] Justino, 1994: 5-10. Ulrich, 1906: 103.

194

traditionally seen as liberal professionals that were authorised and had the monopoly to trade within an Exchange on behalf of their clients. The second Commercial Code defined a number of criteria a broker had to meet before being appointed by the government, and also a number of limitations to their commercial activities. Importantly, they could not have any interest in any transaction other than the commissions they collected from their clients after the execution of an order.

One relevant characteristic of this brokerage activity was the absolute lack of tradition of allowing these intermediaries to be part of a transaction as a means to supplement the liquidity conveyed only by investors to the market. And although banks were required to place their orders for an Exchange trade through the intermediation of a broker, they also never developed any aptitude for making markets in securities. Portuguese banks always invested in shares, and mainly in T-Bonds, but the activity of providing liquidity to shares or bonds was never taken seriously in spite of no legal impediment.

Another characteristic of the Portuguese model is that brokers were understood as necessarily members of an Exchange. There was no such intermediary without being member of one of the two domestic Exchanges. And due to the geographical distance between Lisbon and Porto, there were no overlapping between the memberships of those two Exchanges.

In terms of quantity, their numbers changed according to the evolution of the domestic market, and in this field three periods may be specified (Figure 7):

- until Derivative contracts were "suspended" in both Exchanges in April 1949;
- the following period until the military coup in April 1974;
- the period after the market resumed in 1976/1977.

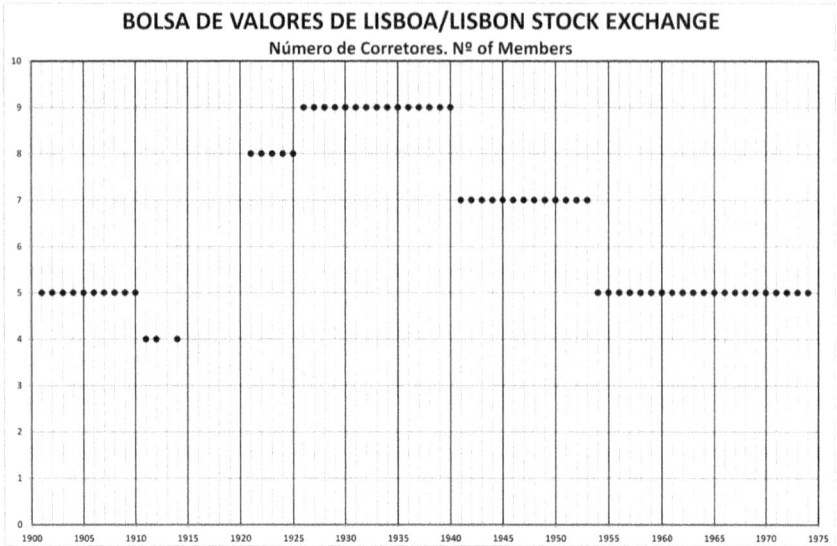

BOLSA DE VALORES DE LISBOA/LISBON STOCK EXCHANGE

Número de Corretores. Nº of Members

Figure 7 — Members of the Lisbon Exchange (personal brokers)

In the beginning of the century the Chamber was composed of five members. After the Republican revolution in October 1910 it decreased to four, but all of them had already been in function during the Monarchy, meaning that there was no political watershed. The profession was considered to be very technical, and experience was required and praised in order to inspire confidence and trust.

In the 1920s, eight members composed the Chamber, increasing to nine after the 1926 revolution and until 1952. As in the case of the Republic, the new political regime of 1926 preserved in functions the same brokers, and added only one more (with the same surname of another). From 1941 to 1953, seven were considered enough for the tasks to be performed, a number that decreased even further to five from 1954 to 1974.

The five brokers remaining at the beginning of 1974 were probably those that resisted the closing of the important derivatives market in 1949, but of these five, only three survived the period of 20 months — from April 1974 to January 1976 — when the Lisbon Exchange was fully[42] closed (Table 1). The extraordinary recovery of the capital market in Portugal after resuming operations in 1976/7 soon gave space to a fourth broker in Lisbon, *José Alberto Taveira Marques* who, in 1986, was the first broker from a new generation to enter this profession.

1974	1976
Fernando Valentim N. Lourenço	Fernando Valentim N. Lourenço/ Pedro Reis Fernandes Caldeira
Eduardo V. Roquette Ricciardi	Eduardo V. Roquette Ricciardi
António Jacinto Medeiros	
Abílio Agostinho de Sousa	Abílio Agostinho de Sousa
José Casimiro Serrão Franco	

Table 1 — Individual brokers that were members of The Lisbon Stock Exchange before and after "suspension" of trading operations from 1974 to 1976.

---

[42] Mind that from 25 April 1974 until 12 January 1976, all trading remained "*suspended*" in the two Portuguese Exchanges. Then the government authorised the Lisbon Exchange to resume operations in Bonds (public and private) but not in shares, and maintained the Porto Exchange closed until January 1981 (first day of trading, 27th). Share trading in Lisbon was authorised from 28 February 1977, although the first businesses (only 2 companies) only occurred on 4 March 1977.

As to the Porto Stock Exchange (also closed in April 1974), it resumed operations only in January 1981, and with only three personal brokers[43]:

— Maria Cândida Cadeco da Rocha e Silva Sanches
— Adolfo Jorge Pinheiro de Castro e Brito
— João Paulo Martins da Rocha Pinto[44]

In 1986 the government decided to expand the membership of each Exchange to 10 brokers and so, in 1987 and 1988, both markets started operating with 10 intermediaries each without any dual memberships. But soon even 10 seemed too little a figure, and a second concourse was opened to expand again to 20 individual brokers in each location.

Besides their number, the brokers operating in the two Stock Exchanges[45] also changed during the twentieth century in terms of their legal figure. Two periods can be detected:

- until 1988: the profession of broker is both personal and public and the admission to an Exchange takes place through public concourse including an examination by the Stock Exchange and subsequent approval by the Ministry of Finance
- after 1988: all individual brokers had to incorporate their business activities into either a small capital limited liability

---

[43] These three brokers were appointed by ministerial decision ("*Despacho Ministerial*") dated from 19/Dec/1990 according to article 95 of the Decree-Law nr. 8/74, dated from 14/Jan/1974. See the notice ("*Aviso*") published in the Daily Bulletin of the Porto Stock Exchange of 27/Jan/1991.

[44] This broker left the Porto Exchange in August 1984 (last day in the Daily Bulletin is 23 August 1984) replaced by a new broker Angelino Cândido de Sousa Ferreira (first day on 31 August 1984).

[45] Mind that the 1901 Regulation of Brokers activities considered three types of brokers, one of which was for securities trading. Also remember that the Commodities Exchanges had a separate set of brokers.

company that could only broker between clients' interests or into a dealers' society with a larger capital base and taking the form of a joint stock corporation.

In 1988 the government decided[46] to open the possibility to institutionalise the brokerage function through the creation of the figure of a Broker Firm (*"Sociedade Corretora"*) and the figure of a Dealer Firm (*"Sociedade Financeira de Corretagem"*). The first was intended to perform the very same role as the previous individual brokers but now under the limited liability of a corporation with a reduced capital. The second was in fact a broker-dealer firm requiring 10 times more minimum capital[47] since, in addition to simple brokerage, they could also buy and sell securities to and from their own balance sheet. However, both types of firms had to be structured around one or more pre-existing personal brokers.

When banks were for the very first time admitted to membership in 2000, their much larger financial capacity, their countrywide (and overseas) distribution network, and their diversified clientele deviated a large part of the market out of those initial intermediaries except from those that, meanwhile, were taken by banks as it occurred with most of them. The end result is that today in Portugal Exchange orders are mostly channelled via bank branches and only a few institutional but independent brokers remain operational in the local market. Despite this, market making activities remains unexpectedly unattractive to banks and other intermediaries.

It is known with a certain detail the number and names of the personal brokers of the Lisbon Stock Exchange from 1900 to 1974. Table 2 presents the list for the period 1900-1974 of the brokers who

---

[46] Decree-Law nr. 229-I/88, dated from 4 July 1988. Djelic, 1998.

[47] *"Portaria"* nr. 481/88 dated from 22 July 1988: simple Broker Firms were required to have at least PTE50 million and their Dealer counterparts at least PTE500 million of nominal equity capital (*"capital social"*).

were members of the Lisbon Stock Exchange, detailing the names of those who were also Chairman of the Brokers' Chamber (with some lacunae that sources could not cover). Looking at the names it is possible to say that brokerage offered long-term positions and that the Chamber composition was quite stable, giving origin to established practice implementation. The renewal consisted of a new name when someone retired. This may mean that this was a desired job. For example, *José Casimiro Franco* was Chairmen for 23 years (1950-1973) although he belonged to the Chamber since 1936, which means a 38-year professional career.

Manuel Ricciardi explained[48] that the Chamber was a much respected organ because of honnourability behaviour values, having mild and friendly relationships amongst its members, and expertise from the lengthy career-track character of the professional. On the difficulties in achieving the position, *Ricciardi* mentioned having had no difficulties, as he had a good family name in financial circles and the money to pay for the required fee.[49]

Brokerage is an old and male profession. As everywhere, the Portuguese Stock markets were traditionally a male universe, made of financiers, magnates, politicians, and great businessmen. In Portugal, the first exception to the "gender rule" in brokerage occurred at the Porto Stock Exchange (Figure 8).[50]

Maria Cândida Rocha e Silva applied to a public contest for this position in 1980, and was approved, thanks to her professional expertise in her father's family banking house *Casa Carregosa*, a prestigious nineteenth century currency-exchange house (Figures 8 and 9).

---

[48] Interview kindly conceded to us at his son's (Luís Ricciardi) office, at *Rua do Comércio*. We evoke here the memory of his great contribution to the Lisbon Stock Exchange.

[49] Ibid.

[50] See Section 3 above.

Figure 8 — *Maria Cândida Rocha e Silva*, the first female official broker in Portugal (Porto Stock Exchange)[51].

The development of this financial intermediation led in 2009 to the conversion of the brokerage house into a Bank which she runs as President of the Board[52].

---

[51] We are grateful for her authorisation to publish this picture.

[52] Much earlier, in New York, Muriel Siebert (1928-2013) had "made history on 28 December 1967, when she became the first female member of the New York Stock Exchange", going into the membership of the 1,365 all-male Big-Board of NYSE. The connection to financial institutions is a decisive common feature among these women. Curiously, there is a special and strange case of the 1870s' New York Stock Exchange, which also confirms the rule. "The two most symbiotic, and scandalous sisters in American history", the radical, suffragist, spiritualist, and audacious Victoria Woodhull and Tennessee Claflin opened America's first female brokerage firm at Hoffman House, nr. 24 of Broadway Street, on 5 February 1870. MacPherson (2014, 2014a) quotes the New York Herald newspaper describing the inauguration event as quite a revolutionary initiative, to stress "how much they considered women as capable of making a living as a man".

List of Individual Brokers who were Members of the Lisbon Stock Exchange (Chamber´s Chairman in bold)

Books with the "Minutes of Meetings" of the brokers' chamber

1900	1901	1902	1903	1904	1905	1906	1907 (Livro de Actas da Câmara da Sind)
	António Serrão Franco	**António Serrão Franco**	**António Serrão Franco**	**António Serrão Franco**	**António Serrão Franco**	**António Serrão Franco**	**António Serrão Franco**
	José Casimiro Franco	José Casimiro Franco	José Casimiro Franco	José Casimiro Franco	José Casimiro Franco	José Casimiro Franco	José Casimiro Franco
	António da Costa Ivo	Caetano Silva Pestana	António da Costa Ivo	António da Costa Ivo	António da Costa Ivo	António da Costa Ivo	António da Costa Ivo
	Caetano Silva Pestana	Virgílio Marques da Costa	Caetano Silva Pestana	Caetano Silva Pestana	Caetano Silva Pestana	Caetano Silva Pestana	Caetano Silva Pestana
	Virgílio Marques da Costa	António da Costa Ivo	Virgílio Marques da Costa	Virgílio Marques da Costa	Virgílio Marques da Costa	Virgílio Marques da Costa	Virgílio Marques da Costa
0	5	5	5	5	5	5	

Books with the "Minutes of Meetings" of the brokers' chamber

1908	1909	1910	1911	1912	1913	1914	1915
António Serrão Franco	**António Serrão Franco**	**António Serrão Franco**	**António da Costa Ivo**	**António da Costa Ivo**		**António da Costa Ivo**	
José Casimiro Franco	José Casimiro Franco	José Casimiro Franco	José Casimiro Franco	Caetano Silva Pestana		Caetano Silva Pestana	
António da Costa Ivo	António da Costa Ivo	António da Costa Ivo	Caetano Silva Pestana	José Casimiro Franco		José Casimiro Franco	
Caetano Silva Pestana	Caetano Silva Pestana	Caetano Silva Pestana	Virgílio Marques da Costa	Virgílio Marques da Costa		Virgílio Marques da Costa	
Virgílio Marques da Costa	Virgílio Marques da Costa	Virgílio Marques da Costa					
5	5	5	4	4		4	

From the signatures on the Daily Bulletins or the Books with the Minutes of the Meetings

1916	1917	1918	1919	1920	1921	1922	1923
					Virgílio Marques da Costa	**Virgílio Marques da Costa**	**Virgílio Marques da Costa**
					António Maria Pires	António Maria Pires	António Maria Pires
					Mário Gastão Ferreira	Mário Gastão Ferreira	Mário Gastão Ferreira
					Augusto Plácido	Augusto Plácido	José Casimiro Serrão Franco
					Henrique do Carmo Ferreira	José Casimiro Serrão Franco	Alberto Lima
					Alberto Lima	Alberto Lima	Augusto Plácido
					José Casimiro Serrão Franco	Henrique do Carmo Ferreira	Henrique do Carmo Ferreira
					João da Silva Carvalho	João da Silva Carvalho	João da Silva Carvalho
					8	8	8

Signatures on the Bulletins or the Minutes of the Meetings

1924	1925	1926	1927	1928	1929	1930	1931
Virgílio Marques da Costa	**António Maria Pires**	**António Maria Pires**	**Augusto Plácido**	**Augusto Plácido**	**Augusto Plácido**	**Augusto Plácido**	**Mário Gastão Ferreira**
Mário Gastão Ferreira	Mário Gastão Ferreira	Augusto Plácido	Virgílio Marques da Costa	Virgílio Marques da Costa	José Casimiro Serrão Franco	José Casimiro Serrão Franco	José Casimiro Serrão Franco
José Casimiro Serrão Franco	José Casimiro Serrão Franco	João da Silva Carvalho	João da Silva Carvalho	João da Silva Carvalho	António Maria Pires	António Maria Pires	António Maria Pires
António Maria Pires	Henrique de Barros Gomes	Alberto Lima	Mário Gastão Ferreira	Mário Gastão Ferreira	António Carvalho Ivo	António Carvalho Ivo	Henrique de Barros Gomes
João da Silva Carvalho	Alberto Lima	Virgílio Marques da Costa	António Serrão Franco	António Serrão Franco	Mário Gastão Ferreira	Mário Gastão Ferreira	António Carvalho Ivo
Augusto Plácido	João da Silva Carvalho	Mário Gastão Ferreira	Alberto Lima	Alberto Lima	João da Silva Carvalho	João da Silva Carvalho	António Casanovas Augustone
Henrique do Carmo Ferreira	Augusto Plácido	José Casimiro Serrão Franco	António Maria Pires	António Maria Pires	Alberto Lima	Alberto Lima	João da Silva Carvalho
Alberto Lima	Virgílio Marques da Costa	Henrique do Carmo Ferreira	José Casimiro Serrão Franco	José Casimiro Serrão Franco	António Casanovas Augustone	António Casanovas Augustone	Manuel da Silva Carvalho
	Alberto Lima	António Serrão Franco	Henrique do Carmo Ferreira	Henrique do Carmo Ferreira			Alberto Lima
8	9	9	9	9	9	9	9

1932	1933	1934	1935	1936	1937	1938	1939
Mário Gastão Ferreira	**José Casimiro Serrão Franco**	**José Casimiro Serrão Franco**	**José Casimiro Serrão Franco**	**António Maria Pires**	**António Maria Pires**	**Henrique de Barros Gomes**	**António Carvalho Ivo**
José Casimiro Serrão Franco	António Carvalho Ivo	António Carvalho Ivo	António Carvalho Ivo	António Carvalho Ivo	António Carvalho Ivo	António Carvalho Ivo	Henrique de Barros Gomes
António Maria Pires	Henrique de Barros Gomes	João da Silva Carvalho	João da Silva Carvalho	João da Silva Carvalho	João da Silva Carvalho	João da Silva Carvalho	João da Silva Carvalho
Henrique de Barros Gomes	António Carvalho Ivo	Manuel da Silva Carvalho	Manuel da Silva Carvalho	Manuel da Silva Carvalho	Manuel da Silva Carvalho	Manuel da Silva Carvalho	Manuel da Silva Carvalho
António Carvalho Ivo	António Casanovas Augustone	Álvaro Alfredo Machado da Costa	Álvaro Alfredo Machado da Costa	Álvaro Alfredo Machado da Costa	Álvaro Alfredo Machado da Costa	Álvaro Alfredo Machado da Costa	Álvaro Alfredo Machado da Costa
António Casanovas Augustone	João da Silva Carvalho	António Casanovas Augustone	António Casanovas Augustone	António Casanovas Augustone	António Casanovas Augustone	António Casanovas Augustone	António Casanovas Augustone
João da Silva Carvalho	Manuel da Silva Carvalho	José Casimiro Serrão Franco	José Casimiro Serrão Franco	José Casimiro Serrão Franco	José Casimiro Serrão Franco	José Casimiro Serrão Franco	José Casimiro Serrão Franco
Manuel da Silva Carvalho	Mário Gastão Ferreira	Henrique de Barros Gomes	Henrique de Barros Gomes	Henrique de Barros Gomes	Mário Gastão Ferreira	Mário Gastão Ferreira	Mário Gastão Ferreira
Alberto Lima	Alberto Lima	António Maria Pires	António Maria Pires	Mário Gastão Ferreira	Henrique de Barros Gomes	Mário Gastão Ferreira	António Maria Pires
9	9	9	9	9	9	9	9

Table 2 — Appointed brokers (and members) of the Lisbon Exchange

1940
- Antonio Carvalho Ivo
- Henrique de Barros Gomes
- João da Silva Carvalho
- Manuel da Silva Carvalho
- Álvaro Alfredo Machado da Costa
- Antonio Casanovas Augustine
- José Casimiro Serrão Franco
- Antonio Maria Pires
- Mario Gastão Ferreira
- 9

1941
- Antonio Carvalho Ivo
- Henrique de Barros Gomes
- Antonio Casanovas Augustine
- Manuel da Silva Carvalho
- Antonio Carvalho Ivo
- Henrique de Barros Gomes
- José Casimiro Serrão Franco
- Mario Gastão Ferreira
- 7

1942
- Antonio Carvalho Ivo
- Henrique de Barros Gomes
- Antonio Casanovas Augustine
- Manuel da Silva Carvalho
- Antonio Maria Pires
- José Casimiro Serrão Franco
- Mario Gastão Ferreira
- 7

1943
- Antonio Maria Pires
- Henrique de Barros Gomes
- Antonio Carvalho Ivo
- Antonio Casanovas Augustine
- José Casimiro Serrão Franco
- Mario Gastão Ferreira
- Manuel da Silva Carvalho
- 7

1944
- Antonio Maria Pires
- Henrique de Barros Gomes
- Antonio Carvalho Ivo
- Antonio Casanovas Augustine
- José Casimiro Serrão Franco
- Mario Gastão Ferreira
- Manuel da Silva Carvalho
- 7

1945
- Antonio Maria Pires
- Henrique de Barros Gomes
- Antonio Carvalho Ivo
- Antonio Casanovas Augustine
- José Casimiro Serrão Franco
- Mario Gastão Ferreira
- Manuel da Silva Carvalho
- 7

1946
- Antonio Maria Pires
- Henrique de Barros Gomes
- Antonio Carvalho Ivo
- Antonio Casanovas Augustine
- José Casimiro Serrão Franco
- Mario Gastão Ferreira
- Manuel da Silva Carvalho

1947
- Antonio Maria Pires
- Henrique de Barros Gomes
- Antonio Carvalho Ivo
- Antonio Casanovas Augustine
- José Casimiro Serrão Franco
- Mario Gastão Ferreira
- Manuel da Silva Carvalho

1948
- Antonio Maria Pires
- Henrique de Barros Gomes
- Antonio Carvalho Ivo
- Antonio Casanovas Augustine
- José Casimiro Serrão Franco
- Mario Gastão Ferreira
- Manuel da Silva Carvalho
- 7

1949
- Antonio Maria Pires
- Henrique de Barros Gomes
- Mario Gastão Ferreira
- Antonio Casanovas Augustine
- Antonio Carvalho Ivo
- José Casimiro Serrão Franco
- Henrique de Barros Gomes
- Antonio Carvalho Ivo
- 5

1950
- José Casimiro Serrão Franco
- Antonio Maria Pires
- Henrique de Barros Gomes
- Mario Gastão Ferreira
- Antonio Carvalho Ivo
- Antonio Casanovas Augustine
- Manuel da Silva Carvalho
- 7

1951
- José Casimiro Serrão Franco
- Antonio Maria Pires
- Henrique de Barros Gomes
- Mario Gastão Ferreira
- Antonio Carvalho Ivo
- Antonio Casanovas Augustine
- Manuel da Silva Carvalho
- 7

1952
- José Casimiro Serrão Franco
- Antonio Maria Pires
- Henrique de Barros Gomes
- Mario Gastão Ferreira
- Antonio Carvalho Ivo
- Antonio Casanovas Augustine
- Manuel da Silva Carvalho
- 7

1953
- José Casimiro Serrão Franco
- Antonio Maria Pires
- Henrique de Barros Gomes
- Mario Gastão Ferreira
- Antonio Carvalho Ivo
- Antonio Casanovas Augustine
- Manuel da Silva Carvalho
- 7

1954
- José Casimiro Serrão Franco
- Henrique de Barros Gomes
- Antonio Carvalho Ivo
- Manuel da Silva Carvalho
- Antonio Casanovas Augustine
- 5

1955
- José Casimiro Serrão Franco
- Henrique de Barros Gomes
- Antonio Carvalho Ivo
- Manuel da Silva Carvalho
- Antonio Casanovas Augustine
- 5

1956
- José Casimiro Serrão Franco
- Eduardo Roquette Ricciardi
- Manuel da Silva Carvalho
- Henrique de Barros Gomes
- Antonio Carvalho Ivo
- 7

1957
- José Casimiro Serrão Franco
- Eduardo Roquette Ricciardi
- Antonio Carvalho Ivo
- Henrique de Barros Gomes
- Manuel da Silva Carvalho
- 5

1958
- José Casimiro Serrão Franco
- Antonio Carvalho Ivo
- Henrique de Barros Gomes
- Eduardo Roquette Ricciardi
- Manuel da Silva Carvalho
- 5

1959
- José Casimiro Serrão Franco
- Henrique de Barros Gomes
- Fernando Valentim N. Lourenço
- Eduardo Roquette Ricciardi
- Manuel da Silva Carvalho
- 5

1960
- José Casimiro Serrão Franco
- Henrique de Barros Gomes
- Fernando Valentim N. Lourenço
- Eduardo Roquette Ricciardi
- Manuel da Silva Carvalho
- 5

1961
- José Casimiro Serrão Franco
- Henrique de Barros Gomes
- Fernando Valentim N. Lourenço
- Eduardo Roquette Ricciardi
- Manuel da Silva Carvalho
- 5

1962
- José Casimiro Serrão Franco
- Henrique de Barros Gomes
- Fernando Valentim N. Lourenço
- Eduardo Roquette Ricciardi
- Manuel da Silva Carvalho
- 5

1963
- José Casimiro Serrão Franco
- Henrique de Barros Gomes
- Fernando Valentim N. Lourenço
- Eduardo Roquette Ricciardi
- Manuel da Silva Carvalho
- 5

1964
- José Casimiro Serrão Franco
- Henrique de Barros Gomes
- Fernando Valentim N. Lourenço
- Eduardo Roquette Ricciardi
- Manuel da Silva Carvalho
- 5

1965
- José Casimiro Serrão Franco
- Henrique de Barros Gomes
- Fernando Valentim N. Lourenço
- Eduardo Roquette Ricciardi
- Manuel da Silva Carvalho
- 5

1966
- José Casimiro Serrão Franco
- Henrique de Barros Gomes
- Manuel da Silva Carvalho
- Eduardo Roquette Ricciardi
- Manuel da Silva Carvalho
- 5

1967
- José Casimiro Serrão Franco
- Manuel da Silva Carvalho
- Eduardo Roquette Ricciardi
- Fernando Valentim N. Lourenço
- Augusto Mesquita dos Santos
- 5

1968
- José Casimiro Serrão Franco
- Manuel da Silva Carvalho
- Eduardo Roquette Ricciardi
- Fernando Valentim N. Lourenço
- Augusto Mesquita dos Santos
- 5

1969
- José Casimiro Serrão Franco
- Eduardo Roquette Ricciardi
- Fernando Valentim N. Lourenço
- Abílio Agostinho de Sousa
- Manuel da Silva Carvalho
- 5

1970
- José Casimiro Serrão Franco
- Eduardo Roquette Ricciardi
- Fernando Valentim N. Lourenço
- Abílio Agostinho de Sousa
- Manuel da Silva Carvalho
- 5

1971
- José Casimiro Serrão Franco
- Eduardo Roquette Ricciardi
- Fernando Valentim N. Lourenço
- Abílio Agostinho de Sousa
- Manuel da Silva Carvalho
- 5

1972
- José Casimiro Serrão Franco
- Fernando Valentim N. Lourenço
- Antonio Jacinto Medeiros
- Abílio Agostinho de Sousa
- Eduardo Roquette Ricciardi
- 5

1973
- José Casimiro Serrão Franco
- Fernando Valentim N. Lourenço
- Antonio Jacinto Medeiros
- Abílio Agostinho de Sousa
- Eduardo Roquette Ricciardi
- 5

1974
- Fernando Valentim N. Lourenço
- Eduardo Roquette Ricciardi
- Antonio Jacinto Medeiros
- Abílio Agostinho de Sousa
- José Casimiro Serrão Franco
- 5

Sources: generally, the daily Bulletins of Lisbon Stock Exchange; for 1901 to 1912, books with the "Minutes of Meetings" of the brokers' chamber; for 1921 to 1925 both sources.

Figura 9 — The first building where the financial intermediary *L. J. Carregosa* started in Porto

In Lisbon, *Judite Correia* was the first female to open a brokerage firm in Lisbon, founding the *Sociedade Financeira de Corretagem, SOFIN,* in 1990.[53] She had previously been appointed as an individual broker of the Lisbon Stock Exchange by Decision ("*Despacho*") of the Secretary of the Treasury dated from 19 January 1988[54].

---

[53] Following the spirit and the determination of Decree-Law 229-I/88, dated from 4 July 1988, this Dealer firm was founded in 1990 by initiative of *Judite Correia* who was a former individual broker and member of the Lisbon Stock Exchange since February 1988. The legal statutes of this intermediary were published in the Daily Bulletin of this Exchange on 31 December 1990 and Sofin started operating in substitution of *Judite Correia* on 2 January 1991. The initial share capital was PTE 500 million, of which *Judite Correia* controlled 40% giving her the presidency of the Board.

[54] See notice ("*Aviso*") nr. 79/88 in the Daily Bulletin of 23 February 1988.

All these brokers were mere individuals as this profession had always been seen as a "private undertaking" with some similarities to the practices of lawyers. But the development of the domestic market in size, diversity of investors, and sophistication of products and operations soon suggested copying the best practices of more mature and internationalised foreign markets.

A change of scale of operations and of the risks involved pointed to the need to allow institutionalised intermediaries to operate in Portugal and, therefore, the Preamble of the Decree-Law 8/74 (below nicknamed as the "Interim Code" published in Jan/1974) already pointed out the need for more modern organisational brokerage. Article nr. 92 of this diploma even opened the possibility of corporate institutionalisation, but went on keeping the traditional unlimited responsibility of individual brokers. Banks were not yet accepted as potential Exchange members.

Asked about why this law still forbade banks in the brokerage activity, *Dr José Luís Sapateiro*, the Finance Secretary of State in 1974, who wrote this law, commented:

> I was not visionary enough. As for the Banks, my worry was to avoid them commanding the Stock Exchange. Economic and Finance power are very important and could be used by Banks, which I tried to avoid. [55]

Even the first Securities Code enacted in 1991 kept banks somewhat away from this market although it created a strange figure called "non-members" of a Stock Exchange in order to allow them to have a word in the daily and strategic running of the Portuguese

---

[55] Interview kindly conceded to us on 3 November 2009, at Mota Engil, Linda--a-Velha, Carnaxide.

Exchanges but maintaining the brokerage activity in the hands only of non-bank institutions.

Only in 1999, with the revision of that Code, were banks given the privilege of brokerage together with full membership of Stock Exchanges. Two reasons forced this legal authorisation. On one hand, the extraordinary expansion of Mutual Funds and Pension Funds introduced a scale of operations that only banks could cope with in terms of geographical distribution of these products and in terms of the supporting capital. On the other hand, the rebirth of Derivatives Trading in the Porto Exchange in 1996 forced the presence of banks in this very risky business. It therefore no longer made sense to have banks trading derivatives as members of the Derivatives Exchange (at Porto) but not being allowed to trade cash instruments in the Lisbon Stock Exchange.

4. Listing of Securities Issues

The 1889 Commercial Code includes only one and very short article — number 352 — dedicated to the listing procedures applicable to any private issue[56]: the Chamber of Brokers was the decision body and for that purpose it could demand any information and documents deemed necessary for that screening process. In case of rejection of an application for listing, an appeal could be filed with the local Commercial Association Court.

The Regulation written in the wake of that Commercial Code to detail the operational rules of the Exchanges only repeated the

---

[56] Free translation: "*Treasury instruments will be admitted to quotation as soon as recognised as tradable; other securities, only upon decision of the respective Brokers Chamber which can only be positive if it agrees that they are legally issued and sufficiently guaranteed*". Note that it clearly states that any tradable Treasuries were automatically entitled to be admitted to the Exchange market without any screening from its decision body, that Chamber.

same ideas without defining either the minimum documentation to be handed in or the size and quality of the issue or the issuer. Basically the decision on each listing case was left to the Chamber. The unique concern stated in the Law and in the Regulation relates to credit risk, as it explicitly mentions that the Chamber should measure the conditions of reimbursement. In particular, nothing was defined as to the minimum size of an issue, to the minimum age of the issuer, or even to a minimum expected liquidity, probably with the intention of helping to attract small and/or young firms to the Exchange market.

The Interim Code enacted in January 1974 by Decree-Law 8/74 was much more detailed in this respect as it includes articles nr. 34 to 42 with a whole set of minimum conditions to be met for a listing along with a full list of documents to be submitted:

- the issuer must have published at least three Annual Reports before the application, although exceptions were possible
- the minimum estimated capitalisation of PTE 200 million (or an equal threshold for the nominal equity of the share issuer) was required for shares; for bonds the listing mini--mum nominal amount was PTE 100 million
- and a minimum dispersion of 25% of the issued capital was established, or alternatively, 500,000 shares if that guarantees a "regular functioning" of the market.

This sophistication and the level of detailing of the legal framework were further developed with the subsequent first Securities Code — Decree-Law 142-A/91 of 10 April 1991 — and implemented from September 1991 on. Just as examples:

- Art 304 of this Code refers to the conditions demanded for listing Shares: it is divided into 8 sub-articles, some of which with many paragraphs, for a total number of entries of 21;

- for Bonds, listing requirements are detailed in Art 305, and for listing other types of securities and for foreign ones, there are two more articles;
- on top of this there are 11 additional articles on this matter — 310 to 320 — to which an issuer must comply with a number of Regulations issued by the Regulator/Supervisor (CMVM)[57] and by the Exchange proper;
- in particular, the listing Prospectus had (and still has) to be analysed and approved by CMVM, although the listing process and the admission decision remained with the Exchange.

In fact, this 1991 Securities Code was intended not only to update the domestic legislation with the experience accumulated and to incorporate the new set of European Directives applicable because of the participation of Portugal in the EEC from 1986, but it also sought to bind in a single volume both the generalist laws ruling that market and the operational details typical of the subsequent Regulations[58].

Some years later, the fact that at the European level the legislation for the Capital Market had improved in money facets[59] during the 1990s (and beyond), along with the fact that the experience accumulated with this first Securities Code suggested the need for a new,

---

[57] This corresponds to the American SEC or the French AMF and was established in 1991. In 1991 alone, this CMVM published 16 Regulations plus 2 Instructions. Of relevance is Regulation 91/6 with the conditions for admission to the main board of an Exchange, and Regulation 91/7 with the minimum contents of a Prospectus.

[58] This Code summed 687 articles, many of which had a very large number of sub-articles and these also with large numbers of indents.

[59] And had to be translated to the domestic market according to the European Union rules.

updated but "less regulatory minded" version, led to the publication of a second Securities Code in 1999[60] planned to be implemented from March 1, 2000. This new version counts only 421 articles, all of them written much more succinctly making the whole Code a much thinner book than the previous one. Unfortunately, the market still had to complement this piece of law with a set of Regulations issued by CMVM plus those issued by the Exchange and the local Central Securities Depository (CSD).

This second Securities Code also "improved" the requirements on the disclosure of information from any issuer. Not only there is a demand for periodic publication of accounting data with minimum contents, but it is also necessary to disclose immediately any relevant information that may affect market quotations. The transparency inherent in these requirements and the costs involved in that disclosure may be discouraging many potential issuers.

However, these two Securities Codes continue to suffer from a common characteristic: the admission of any issue to trading on any Exchange still places a high hurdle in front of any issuer, and continues to contribute to chase away many issuers, especially those with less experience and/or economic dimension. One cannot forget that a company exists for some economic purpose and that need of business focus makes it difficult and/or expensive to deviate experienced human resources just to fulfil the bureaucratic requirements conceived by legislators.

Transparency is of course of utmost importance for investors and for competitors[61], but the current experience shows that the

---

[60] It is named "*Código dos Valores Mobiliários*" and was published by the Decree-Law nr. 486/99 which is dated from 13 November 1999. http://www.cmvm.pt/en/Legislacao/Nacional_legislation/CodigocodigodosValoresMobiliarios/Pages/DL_486-99_Decreto_Preambular.aspx?v=

[61] But one should balance that objective with the pragmatic truth that "*transparency is clouding away information disclosure!*"

listing requirements are so demanding that many potential issuers prefer to remain closed to the investor community in order to avoid a number of costs and bureaucracies.

Main hurdles faced by companies, especially the smaller ones, are:

a) first, the current legislation targets mainly those companies that already have a track record (typically, three years);

b) second, the amount of laws and regulations involved is extensive, sophisticated, and growing;

c) third, the legislation requires a lot from the issuer in terms of information disclosure;

d) fourth, the whole process of listing and remaining listed is very expensive both in terms of the fees to be paid and the man power necessary to maintain the market informed and fulfil all the legal requirements.

This experience seems to be guiding a number of initiatives being pondered now in several geographies in order to divide the whole Exchange market into very distinct segments in which some will maintain the stringent demands that can easily be fulfilled by large issuers, but other segments are designed basically to facilitate access to a lit[62] market of small and/or young issuers and issues without a proper listing screening, and impose only a minimum standards of age, disclosure, and liquidity (or even not disclosing such detailed and frequent information). The logic is that it is better to have the visibility of an Exchange[63], even if attenuated, than the

---

[62] The word "*lit*" here is intended to compare with a number of alternative solutions recently invented in Europe with the first version of the MEFID Directive that coined the so called MTF — Multilateral Trading Facilities where most of that market information is not publicly disclosed ("*dark markets*"). Knobl, 2005.

[63] From February 1983 on, the Lisbon Exchange market was divided into two segments: the so called "*Official Market*" — the main market — where the larger and "senior" companies could list their shares; and the "*Market without Quotations*",

opacity of OTC markets, provided that the investment community is fully aware of the different qualities of the securities "listed"[64] in each distinct segment.

In fact, the Brussels Stock Exchange followed precisely this view when launching the new *"Expert Market"* on 9 December 2014. The press release[65] sates that *"the new electronic format aims at facilitating the trading of securities that are not admitted to listing on a regulated market by offering broader and more efficient access through Euronext Expert Market members who, over the years, have built expert knowledge in trading non-listed securities. By standardising and automating the post-trade chain, this market will become more transparent and more efficient"*.

5. The Porto Exchange

In the northern part of the country another centralised market was put in place in the city of Porto, probably following the liberal spirit that Napoleon brought to the country in the three invasions of the French army, from 1808 to 1811[66]. The Porto Exchange is the result of an initiative of the local Commercial Association, which

---

created to trade (but not list) some junior companies or the provisional certificates of shares (and bonds) issued by corporations already listed, while their final paper certificates were being printed and distributed among the investors.

[64] Probably some segments do not have a true listing procedure, but simply allow temporary or permanent trading whenever requested by members of the Exchange on behalf of investors or issuers.

[65] Released on 2 December 2014.

[66] Mind that this was also the moment when Spain established its first stock market in Madrid, which opened on 28 January 1811. This was the result of the royal decree of 14 October 1809, when Napoleon's brother, Joseph I, ruled over the country. The regulation of the decree of 20 July 1810 was clearly inspired by the Paris model (see Rojo, 1977; Chevilliard, 1904). The Spanish war for Independence interrupted this market's operations for two decades, and the law of 10 September 1831 is now considered as the legal foundation of the Madrid stock market (see Cagigal, 2009: 41).

applied for the establishment of such a market after its current headquarters building was completed in the middle of the 1800s (Figure 10). Officially, the Porto Stock Exchange — that is for securities — was authorised to operate only in January 1891[67]. Although the Lisbon and Porto Exchanges always competed in the securities business, the origin of the second stems from the needs of the local community of merchants. Wine growers in the region and especially exporters of Port Wine to Britain and elsewhere, were a large wealthy merchant class in need of a place to trade.

Figure 10A — The Stock Exchange Palace in the lower quarters of the Porto town with the main hall inside

---

[67] From 29 January 1891 on.

212

Figure 10B — *«Pátio das Nações»* in The Stock Exchange Palace, Porto.

Though the Porto market was formally converted into a Stock Exchange only in 1891, and traded volumes there were always much smaller than in Lisbon, it is a fact that the presence of that second Exchange was a signal of the city's political influence over the country. As in other countries, the importance of the Exchange market in the second urban centre (Porto) reflects the particular role this city always performed in the Portuguese political scene: Porto was besieged by the liberal army during the 1832-34 civil war, and was also an important source of funding for the liberal government following the victory of the Liberal blueprint in this civil war; all political revolutions that have succeeded in Portugal were first acclaimed in Porto, and the ones that were planned and failed were those that did not receive the support of Porto's people.[68] In the nineteenth-century, Portugal was truly a two-headed country.

---

[68] Mata, 1991.

213

6. Commodities Exchanges in Portugal

Until the implementation in January 1889 of the second Commercial Code[69] — known as *"Código Veiga Beirão"* after the name of its main author — there was no specialisation within the Exchange, that is, trading occurred in both securities and commodities[70]. That Code,[71] and especially the subsequent Regulation of the broker's activity,[72] introduced a certain segmentation that later led to the full migration of the commodities operation to a separated and fully *"governmentalised"* Exchange.

In August 1914, under the constraints brought to the external commerce of the country by the beginning of WWI, the Government decided to institutionalise a Commodity Exchange in Lisbon and another one in the northern town of Porto. But it took a very long time to go from intentions to the actual markets, and only in the 1930s did both Exchanges come into being[73].

---

[69] Published by a Decree dated from 23 August 1888 printed in the Official Gazette (*"Diário do Governo"*), nr. 203 dated from 6 September 1888. Mind that initially only Lisbon had an Exchange.

[70] More in detail, Art. 351 of this second Commercial Code lists all types of goods and services that could be traded in an Exchange:
- treasury securities (domestic and/or foreign)
- shares, corporate bonds and other private credit instruments
- metals
- any type of commodity
- insurance contracts
- contracts for transports
- buildings and any attached rights

[71] Article 82 of the Code suggests some specialisation by forcing Exchanges to include in their official name the type of assets in which they specialise.

[72] Published on 10 October 1901. And its Article 4 divides the brokers into three categories: brokers of securities and forex; brokers of shipping and insurance; brokers of commodities. But its Article 5 allows for a person to broker in all the three categories of assets, provided (Article 6) that he fulfils the particular requirements of each one.

[73] The two Commodities Exchanges of Lisbon and Porto were institutionalised by Decree nr. 784 of 21 August 1914, but were only regulated by Decree nr. 18 002 (20 February 1930), subsequently modified by Decrees nr. 20 584 (30 November

Meanwhile, in May 1925, the Government implemented what was then called an Agriculture Exchange[74] — "*Bolsa Agrícola*" — within the Ministry of Agriculture after merging a number of existing institutions working within that same Ministry. The overall objective was to promote more effectiveness and more efficiency to the whole set of organisations dealing with agriculture subjects in the country.

This institution was extinguished in 1930 when the Government decided to immediately install the Lisbon Commodities Exchange — "*Bolsa de Mercadorias de Lisboa*" — within the Ministry of Commerce and Communications[75]. The first trading day was on 3 July 1931, following a schedule with only two sessions per week (Tuesdays and Fridays) from 11h30 to 12h30 and intermediated by only six brokers. One year later it increased to three sessions per week on Tuesdays, Thursdays and Saturdays. It remained active until 1966.

In the north, the Porto Commodities Exchange came into existence in 1935 not only to regionalise the service offered by its sister in Lisbon — from which it copied the rules and regulations — but also to offer specialised markets in wines due to the importance of the many wine regions in the environs and especially the Douro Valley where the famous Port Wine was (and still is) produced. As in Lisbon, this was fully integrated in the Ministry of Commerce and it also maintained its doors open until 1967[76].

1931), nr. 21 858 (31 October 1932) and nr. 22 702 (19 June 1933). But the Porto Commodities Exchange was only created by the Decree nr. 22 504 (10 May 1933), later supplemented by the Decrees nr. 23 525 (29 January 1934), nr. 24 573 (18 October 1934) and nr. 24 813 (26 December 1934).

[74] See Decrees nr. 10 805 of 28 May 1925 which centralises all services within the Ministry of Agriculture in this Exchange, nr. 10 887 of 8 June 1925 with the internal regulation of the Exchange, and nr. 10 943 of 20 July 1925 with the trading rules.

[75] See Decree nr. 18 002 of 20 February 1930, in which Art 4 leaves for a later date starting a similar Commodities Exchange in Porto. Art 56 extinguishes the Agriculture Exchange.

[76] See the annual budget for the exercise of 1967 of the Ministry of Commerce published in the Official Gazette on 30 December 1966.

7. Derivatives in Portugal

History suggests that markets everywhere started with the simplest trades in which, after the initial bargaining and the final agreement on the price, traders make an "immediate" delivery of the products or services, even if the respective payment slides somewhat into a future date due to sales credit. In simplified wording, a common transaction is agreed in one moment and implemented in the next.

However, nothing forbids two parties from agreeing now on the price of a product and, at the same time, defining that the transfer of property and the (counter) payment will occur only sometime later (some days or even some months ahead).

In fact, there are indications that a few centuries ago Japan already had this type of transaction for rice, exploring the opportunities opened by the normal agro annual cycle where planting and growing occurs always some months before the corresponding harvest. With such delayed delivery contracts growers could enjoy the certainty of pre-selling their crop before the coming harvest season — fixing in advance the quantity, the quality, and the price — and, by the same token, buyers of rice acquire the guarantee of supply for their inputs some time ahead of the actual use of the crop.

In modern times it is customary to localize in Chicago (US) the invention of the first centralised markets to negotiate the so-called "*to-arrive*" contracts, developed to meet grain growers and grain industrialist needs regarding the delivery of certain fixed amounts of specified agriculture commodities at a fixed price. In these Exchanges the object of the negotiation between the two parties is not the physical stuff mentioned in those contracts — the so called underlying asset — but the contracts themselves.

Because these Exchanges do not offer markets for trading shares or bonds, but demand special rules of operation that are typical of Stock Exchanges, they became known as Derivatives Exchanges precisely because they trade on contracts derived from the physical market of the underlying stuff.

At first sight, these new Exchanges seem similar to more traditional Stock Exchanges, but they were actually designed to address some important innovations that deserve mention here:

a) the market values of the contracts negotiated in the trading pits of Derivative Exchanges depend on the quotations of the products underlying those contracts; therefore the underlying cash market and the respective derivative market are intimately connected, meaning that the prices found in one place immediately spill over to the other market;

b) the counterpart risks involved in these Derivative markets are much greater than in the cash markets: while a share negotiated on day D in a Stock Exchange is normally delivered after a few days — today most trades are settled on day D+2 or D+3 — a Derivative contract could be negotiated on one day with the delivery of the underlying asset scheduled for only one year later, therefore requiring the buyer and the seller of that contract to trust each other during that long period;

c) in order to minimise such counterparty risks, Derivatives Exchanges soon developed an auxiliary mechanism to maintain a permanent control on the risk of all trading parties: it is the so called Clearing House connected to the Exchange markets, whereby traders and intermediaries are screened before operating and their level of risk is also permanently checked via a system of margins and a mutual guarantee fund;

d) while Stock Exchanges were created to (simply) let the intermediaries trade those shares and bonds already "invented" and placed in the market by their issuers, Derivatives Exchanges soon discovered that they needed to permanently develop new contracts on the same assets (or on others) but with different features — size, maturity, trading hours, etc. — to better respond to the needs of their constituencies.

In Portugal the securities Exchanges in Lisbon and Porto offered tradability to shares, bonds and to other securities — the "cash" market — but the Lisbon Exchange also offered a derivatives[77] market which is said to be more dynamic than the underlying spot counterpart[78]. Also important in Lisbon was the forex market which, until April 1949, supplied reference quotations to the domestic banks.

In 1949 the government *"closed"* the derivatives segment of the Lisbon Stock Exchange together with the forex market. The last trading day was 7 April 1949.

During the 1990s Portugal finally initiated a process of making its borders much more transparent to trade — including money flows, in and out — and that evolution raised the question of the long-term survival of the two Stock Exchanges of Lisbon and Porto. It also suggested the opportunity to re-offer Futures and Options contracts to the local financial community.

This need to re-launch derivatives contracts explains the agreement that was negotiated in 1994 between northern and southern centralised markets whereby the Porto Exchange closed its cash markets in return for receiving the monopoly to develop a brand new Derivatives Exchange in Portugal, and the Lisbon Exchange gave up its intention to also offer centralised derivatives by receiving in return the entire cash market of Portugal.

---

[77] Today the types of contracts traded in this section would be called Futures and Options but at the time they were simply designated *"fixed term contracts"* and *"contracts with prime"*. Underlying assets were either listed shares or listed bonds.

[78] See Ulrich, 1906, 2011, both by *Imprensa da Universidade de Coimbra*.

In the US, Derivatives Exchanges have been able to maintain some independence from the domestic Stock Exchanges (cash products), but in Europe the consolidation move that merged first the domestic regional Exchanges tended to include also the Derivatives Exchanges. It is not yet clear whether this closer proximity of the two types of markets benefits both sides or, on the contrary, if each one is negatively impacted by the idiosyncrasies of the other market. It is necessary to accumulate more experience, for more years and from more diverse economies, as it may be that the answer depends on the particular country involved. The recent (2012) merger between the Tokyo Stock Exchange — mainly a cash market — and the Osaka Exchange — mainly a derivatives one — will certainly contribute to this enlightening.

8. Clearing and Settlement of Exchange Trades

Our focus to this point on listing and trading is just a partial view of the activities of most Stock Exchanges. In fact, a transaction of any financial instrument always involves two steps:

- negotiation: first, there needs to be a bargaining and an agreement struck between buyer and seller as to the quantity and the price to be executed;
- settlement: subsequently, the buyer needs pay the seller and this seller must deliver the traded product to the buyer.

Actually, these two final operations settle the initial agreement and, in the old days, they involved handing over the paper certificates to the buyer and transferring money bills into the hands of the seller. There are two different settlement operations — the physical transfer of ownership of the securities — Physical Settlement — and the counter transfer of cash — Financial Settlement. It is crucial that they are executed at the same time in order to avoid any finalisation risks[79]. These two operations are part of what is now called the Post-trade activities of an Exchange.

Until 1974, these markets operated in Portugal under a set of rules essentially designed under the 1889 Commercial Code, and remained without any significant changes for about 85 years. Securities existed in paper form and were kept either at home or deposited in the vaults of commercial banks. The tradition was for individual investors to contact a broker with whom they deposited the estimated amount of money to pay for the desired shares or bonds to be purchased, or they left the securities they wished to offer for sale.

The two Portuguese Stock Exchanges[80] basically offered tradability to security issues. Settlement of all trades was made transaction by transaction — called "gross settlement" — and demanded the physical delivery of the certificates object of the previous bargain together with the counter flow of cash for payment. In particular, the settlement of Exchange transactions was first done between brokers and subsequently between each broker and its clients. For small volumes of transactions and few investors this settlement procedure was sufficient and inexpensive to operate.

Also, dividends and coupons were handled by the respective issuer and demanded the personal presence of the investor either in the offices of that particular issuer or in those of a contracted bank or broker.

---

[79] If delivery occurs some "instants" before payment, this cash transfer may not be implemented and the other way round. History has supplied examples where payment did not occur because the transfer agent went bankrupt in between.

[80] Mind that, on the opposite, both Commodities Exchanges were always part of the Portuguese state. Dahlquist, 2012.

Manuel Ricciardi, official broker of the Lisbon Stock Exchange from 1956 to 1999 and a number of years President of its Board, explained that the clients of the Lisbon Stock Exchange were people from business activities, but added that there were also inexperienced (but knowledgeable) individuals who came to buy stock to apply their savings. He mentioned bank employees, public servants, and lawyers as people he had amongst his clients.[81]

However, this was a very inefficient operative model that included many opportunities for errors and prolonged delays between trading and settlement. And the fact that many bond and share issues used certificates aggregating more than one security — e.g. 10 shares or 50 bonds in one certificate — introduced additional problems when the owner intended to sell only part of one such multiple certificate.

> Manuel Ricciardi reported his personal brokerage experience in this period, saying "this was a new experience in my professional life" to express how great was the enthusiasm for stocks in the late sixties-early seventies, because of the rising prices. He added that this was the time when the non-official market increased a great deal: "It was very common to observe private transactions among stock holders in the open-air parking of *Terreiro do Paço*. People opened their cars' luggage space to take out their shares and negotiated among them, out of any official system".[82]

---

[81] Interview kindly conceded to us at his son's (Luís Ricciardi) office, at *Rua do Comércio*. We evoke here the memory of his great contribution to the Lisbon Stock Exchange.

[82] Ibid. It is curious that no teaching on financial issues was provided in undergraduate studies in Economics, at the "*ISCEF-Instituto Superior de Ciências Económicas e Financeiras*" school at this time. Caetano, 2003.

Things started to derail when, in the middle of the 1960s, particularly with the popular enthusiasm discovered in 1972 and 1973 for risky investments, the number of securities traded exploded along with the number of retail investors involved. This revealed the deficiencies of an architecture that had been designed long ago at the end of the 19th century and for a market that was much smaller.

It is in the light of those insufficiencies that an interim and simplified Securities Code[83] was published at the very beginning of 1974 as a first step to remedy such deficiencies. It was this legislation that nationalised the two Portuguese Stock Exchanges by turning them into mere autonomous departments of the domestic Ministry of Finance. It also introduced netting[84] between the trading moment and the settlement finalisation to reduce the amount of paper transfers and cash flows, although this was implemented only after the resumption of operations on the Lisbon Exchange in 1976/77.

Indeed, the leftist military coup in April 1974 interrupted this updating process of the whole system around the Stock Exchanges and their legal environment. Even when political conditions allowed that move a few years afterwards, the priority was then much more to reactivate the Capital Market and the Lisbon Exchange (from 1976 on) than to redesign the whole legal framework. Only at the end of the 1980s, was the time ripe enough to resume that modernisation plan, and the author of that Interim Code was then asked to write a brand new but comprehensive Securities Code which entered into effect during the second half of 1991.

---

[83] Decree-Law nr. 8/74, published on 14 January 1974, to be implemented from 13 April 1974 on.

[84] See Art. nr. 79.

Meanwhile, the government took measures to gradually immobilise all certificates in securities accounts offered to investors by the local banks. In fact, with this immobilisation:

- it was simpler to place orders for trading as banks and brokers required only a declaration from the banks attesting that those securities existed and were "frozen" in those securities accounts;
- settlement could be implemented in a much easier way, either between two accounts in the same bank — if both seller and buyer were clients of the same bank — or transferring inter-banks only the net amounts of securities resulting from many trades in the space of a few days;
- the financial side also benefited from this intense use of banks for very similar reasons.

The final step in this area was taken with:

- first: dematerialisation of all securities, initiated in 1988;[85]
- second: following the publication of the first Securities Code, creation in 1991 of a CSD - Central Securities Depository — called Interbolsa — where every securities issue was registered and which was charged with the netting and the settlement operations following the execution of all Exchange transactions.

In particular, this Code integrated the main market segments of the two Portuguese Exchanges — "*mercado de âmbito nacional*[86]" — and determined the creation of the first nationwide CSD (the

---

[85] Decree-Law nr. 229-D/88 of 4 July 1988.

[86] Nationwide market.

Interbolsa) to be owned in equal parts by the two Exchanges, which were also "semi-privatised". The implementation of this company to execute all those post-trading functions was very much facilitated by the adoption of the electronic trading system *Tradis* borrowed from the Rio de Janeiro Stock Exchange in 1991. In fact, this was a rare case of an integrated computer programme that encompassed both the trading of securities and the netting and settlement of those transactions. In addition this same system also cared for the execution and control of all corporate events that cash instruments periodically undergo, such as payment of dividends and coupons, rights issues, bonus shares, amortisation of debt instruments, etc.

Another important characteristic of the settlement model adopted in Portugal was the use of Central Bank money to settle the financial "leg" of all Exchange transactions: members of the two domestic Exchanges were debited or credited in their cash accounts with the Portuguese Central Bank[87] by the amounts calculated by *Interbolsa* after netting all buy and sell orders executed during each business day. This option for the Central Bank money fully eliminated any potential credit risk associated with the use of a (single) commercial bank.

From that moment on, Portugal adopted the model of an integrated package of services offered by local Exchanges to the domestic market, which is very similar to the one existing in other countries. In fact, and although not universal and not central to the particular

---

[87] Actually, the brokers saw those debits and credit done in their accounts opened in a commercial bank. It was this bank that had their reserve accounts maintained with the Central Bank debited or credited by Interbolsa to implement the financial settlement.

role of a Stock Exchange in a country, many Stock Exchanges today offer an integrated package of services that include:

- **listing**: it is the screening process that restricts the admission to official trading of any interested issue according to a set of conditions designed to give quality, liquidity, and confidence;
- **registration and custody of securities**: even if securities retain the paper form (not dematerialised), investors, issuers, and financial intermediaries can reduce their operating costs if one single national entity — the CSD — registers whatever issue is placed in the market, holds the corresponding certificates, and executes and controls the debits and credits on the securities accounts (under the names of the many investors exposed to each issue) whenever each investor receives or delivers a certain number of shares or bonds;
- **settlement**: from the data sent by the centralised market after two trading orders are matched — what security, how many shares or bonds, the agreed price — someone has to implement the simultaneous transfer of money from buyer to seller and the transfer of ownership from seller to buyer; and if the financial settlement is implemented in the banking system, the two cash accounts must be debited and credited in due time and in correct amounts;
- **netting**: since some investors execute buy and sell orders during one single day — notably the case of brokers who execute a large number of orders received from their clients — it makes sense to net the total amount of payments to be made by each side against the total amount of credits to be received, in order to reduce the money volume changing hands to one single cash flow per day; and similarly for

each individual security where all hand-ins can be netted against all hand-outs;

- **corporate events**: issuers periodically pay dividends and/or coupons to their investors and these distributions can gain efficiency if handled centrally; also capital increases rights issues, and other corporate events can benefit from such an organised and centralised procedure;

- **guarantee (clearing)**: since all markets tend to maintain a small (but not zero) time window between the moment a trade is agreed upon in a Stock Exchange and the day that same transaction is actually settled — typically two to three days — there always exists the risk that one of the parties in a trade may in the meantime default either on the financial side or the securities side; for that reason some markets offer the possibility to all investors of acquiring a guarantee of timely settlement of any agreed trade.

Today Interbolsa offers all these services except that guarantee step which is now outsourced to the Anglo-French LCH-Clearnet firm via a delegation operating next door to the Interbolsa offices.

The participation of Portugal in the European Union also had a consequence regarding the integration of the local Exchange in the consolidation process initiated in 2000, when Paris, Brussels, and Amsterdam merged their Exchanges into a single organisation called Euronext[88]. As it often happens, in terms of post-trading this merging experience also brought some valid lessons: the three domestic CSDs of France, Belgium and Holland were promptly sold to an international organisation called Euroclear according to the idea that Exchanges basically should provide only listing and trading services to their clientele.

---

[88] Portugal entered this Group of Exchanges in February 2002. March, 2005.

However, for a number of reasons, Portugal did not follow this movement and instead kept *Interbolsa* within the package of services offered to the market by the Exchange. The fact is that, after all these years of experience, the advantages of such an integrated offer — from Listing to Custody — are now recognised and so *Interbolsa* has now been converted into the *"knowledge centre"* of post-trading services of the whole Euronext Group.

9. Large versus SME companies in the Exchange

Statistics indicate that the Portuguese model of financing local corporations has in general favoured the banking channel in detriment to direct access to savers[89], even for funding long-term corporate investments. Also it seems that the same predominance has prevailed during most of the twentieth century (if not always). For example, during the 81 years from 1930 to 2010, the number of listed companies varied widely under the influence of economic and political events, but the importance of this source of funding (equity only) in the whole economy has always been small as Table 3 expresses by comparing the year-end global nominal share capital of the listed companies with the Portuguese GDP.

These statistics tend to under-measure the funding capacity provided by this market channel, as they are based on nominal values, not on market quotes. Indeed, experience indicates that most of the time the market-prices of listed shares were considerably above their respective par values, and also, typically, new shares were offered

---

[89] See for example the semi-annual survey conducted by the Portuguese Statistics Office — *"Inquérito de Conjuntura ao Investimento"* — in which resident corporations are questioned about their planned means to finance future investments. As a matter of fact, those surveys routinely report that bonds and shares (listed or not) represent less than 1% of their total funding mechanisms.

by issuers to investors only slightly below their market quotations. Therefore, one can accept that the above numerical estimates — using par values — are clearly pessimistic, and that those companies were able to raise much more funding than what is indicated above. Unfortunately this under-measurement does not change the overall picture due to the low values of the percentage of equity in comparison to GDP. Also, the number of listed companies is small, and more recently only large and medium-large companies are present in the Exchange market. Small firms only exceptionally appear in the list of those with shares admitted to an Exchange.

This "rejection" of small firms can be noticed by segmenting the whole group of listed corporations in:

- the group of "10 largest" firms which almost always accounted for around 50% of the total nominal capital obtained by the entire collection of listed companies;
- therefore, the remaining companies — between 85 and 135 firms — took the remaining 50% share of listed money; that is, around 9 times more (non-large) firms were able to raise funds via this listing in Lisbon.
- Amongst those non-large companies, some tiny companies — called the "10 smallest" — were also accepted in the Exchange during this entire 81-year period, in spite of the fact that all of them together raised less than 1% of the whole aggregate listed.

This suggests that the Exchange market was more favourable to larger companies for raising capital than to smaller ones.

	1930	1935	1940	1945	1950	1955	1960	1965	1970	1973	1977	1980	1985	1990	1995	2000	2005	2010
Total nº of Listed Companies	112	98	104	104	110	123	132	137	136	145	35	25	46	181	169	110	77	69
Banks	*10*	*9*	*8*	*10*	*11*	*11*	*12*	*13*	*12*	*17*								
Insurances	*15*	*15*	*17*	*18*	*17*	*20*	*19*	*20*	*24*	*25*								
Textile industries	*4*	*4*	*5*	*5*	*5*	*5*	*5*	*5*	*5*	*4*								
Railways	*4*	*4*	*4*	*5*	*3*	*3*	*2*											
Utilities								*17*	*12*	*12*								
Others	*46*	*42*	*47*	*45*	*51*	*56*	*60*	*49*	*50*	*53*								
Colonials	*33*	*24*	*23*	*21*	*23*	*28*	*34*	*33*	*33*	*34*								
Total Share Capital Listed on BVL (PTE 000 000), (EUR 000 000)	948	1 031	1 059	1 727	3 251	5 897	9 353	13 318	23 331	35 822	2 661	3 686	37 314	502 249	1471 316	17 990	21 178	31 722
Share of the 10 largest	59.32%	66.02%	59.71%	50.11%	53.25%	50.16%	49.92%	48.55%	54.39%	45.96%	82.31%	84.07%	83.20%	41.90%	42.34%	71.83%	81.39%	78.20%
Share of the 10 smallest	0.18%	0.22%	0.25%	0.21%	0.11%	0.06%	0.04%	0.03%	0.02%	0.01%	1.26%	5.89%	0.85%	0.34%	0.16%	0.09%	0.06%	0.06%
Share of the middle others	40.50%	33.76%	40.04%	49.69%	46.64%	49.78%	50.04%	51.42%	45.59%	54.03%	16.42%	10.04%	15.95%	57.76%	57.50%	28.42%	21.39%	21.74%
Share of the 50 smallest	4.36%	4.84%	3.83%	3.53%	2.99%	1.83%	1.30%	0.85%	1.23%	0.83%	N. A.	N. A.	N. A.	3.79%	2.08%	2.52%	3.80%	7.66%
GDPmp (PTE 000 000), (EUR 000 000)	18 239	19 785	19 990	39 989	56 092	70 572	88 994	135 681	212 358	342 817	722 257	1476 316	4131 014	10 072 063	15 912 873	115 548	127 490	162 163
Total Share Capital in % of GDP	5.20%	5.21%	5.30%	4.32%	5.80%	8.36%	10.51%	9.82%	10.99%	10.45%	0.37%	0.25%	0.90%	4.99%	9.25%	15.57%	16.61%	19.56%

Table 3 — Total number of listed corporations on the Lisbon Stock Exchange, 1930-2010 [90]

Source: Daily Bulletins of the Lisbon Stock Exchange, BVL Historical Archive.

[90] Since the market closed in April 1974, and because this analysis sampled the month of December of every five years, the year of 1974 could not be included.

The period after 1977 is a rather difficult period to analyse, as it covers a sequence of events and their respective transition years. At least the following events should be borne in mind.

When the market for shares[91] resumed in March 1977, only 35 companies were still listed from the previous 145 ones in 1973; nationalisations and the independence of the overseas territories where many firms had their businesses can explain that difference. Until 1985, a succession of political, social, and economic crises (including two stand-by agreements signed by the Portuguese government with the International Monetary Fund (IMF)) distanced companies and investors from the Stock Exchange. Only with the elections held in 1985 that led to the first government of *Prime Minister Cavaco Silva* — who adopted centre-right policies — was a strategic plan for the revitalisation of the domestic capital market established in Portugal.

So successful was that planning that the market over-reacted in a few months and speculation overtook the installed capacity in the economy to satisfy the renewed — but excessive — demand for shares. Quotations grew significantly until October 1987, when that equity bubble burst, and the quotations started a long lasting plunge until January 1993. That fall was progressively attenuated by a number of IPOs that were very well received by local investors.

10. Financial Literacy in Portugal

Finance is usually considered to be a complex science, made up of unsatisfactory explanations to interpret the mystery and volatility of financial markets. Expectations, the mood of the market, as

---

[91] Actually the government authorised the Lisbon Exchange to resume operations (only) in Bonds in January 1976 in order to bring tradability to the increasing volumes of public debt being issued at the time.

well as investment strategies to manage diversified portfolios, are intimidating issues for most people, even today.

The tradition was for the literature available about Corporate Finance and Stock Exchanges to focus almost entirely on legal matters: law, government regulations, shareholders' rights, juridical codes, and legal proceedings. [92] One of the rare texts that sought to explain the economic logic and the intricacies of financial markets is *"Confusion de Confusiones"* written in archaic Portuguese in 1688 by Joseph de la Vega, a Sephardic Jew with possible Portuguese roots who emigrated to Amsterdam after being expelled from the Iberian Peninsula in the Sixteenth Century (Figure 11). Unfortunately this is a very long text written with some moral objectives in mind, but which also dedicates a few dozen pages to explain how people can invest in shares and in options and the risks they face with both of them. The text takes the shape of a trialogue between a merchant, a philosopher, and a shareholder[93] and is considered the first text on such matters, *"intended for the edification of the Jewish community of Amsterdam, largely Portuguese"*.[94]

This means that the dominant perspective until the beginning of the Twentieth Century was descriptive or normative, but not explicative.[95] Only a few books adopted an economic perspective.

Individuals, companies and institutional investors needed financial education. Business operations throughout a century long globalisation process were exposed to great risk. The seventeenth-century Dutch and British East India Companies' trading businesses with

---

[92] Cosack 1905, Gründt 1899, Hayaux 1901, Sayous 1898, Vivant 1902, Fontaine 1905, Moysen 1904, Thaler 1900, Weil 1902, Franchi 1890, Marghieri 1886, Lambert 1902, Lyon-Caen et Renault 1901, Pfleger and Gschwindt 1899, Passos 1905, Say 1854, Scherer 1886, Vidal, 1896, 1901, Guilmard 1904, Guillard 1877, Tedeschi 1897.

[93] Cardoso, 2002.

[94] Neal, 1990: 16.

[95] Bedarride, 1901, Buriat, 1903 are good examples. Proudhon, 1857. Raffalovich, 1900. Supino, 1875, 1898. Regnault, 1863.

Asia required pioneering organisational features of modern tradable shareholding and limited liability that framed new corporate principles.[96] The large expertise that was achieved in the organisation of securities markets, and in distributing high annualised dividends, furthered European financial literacy and stock markets. Identical principles also inspired the eighteenth-century Portuguese-Brazilian trade companies.[97] However, the analytical perspective on the main concepts related with Stock Exchanges is the heritage of nineteenth--century financial erudition.

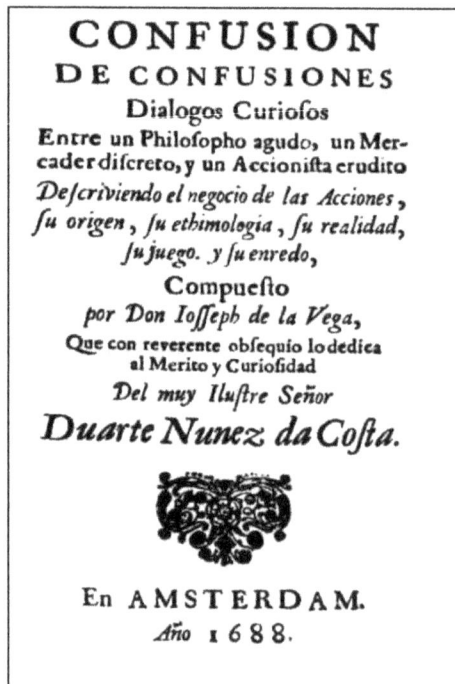

Figure 11 — Original cover of the famous book *"Confusion de Confusiones"*

---

[96] Gederblom, 2013.

[97] Pedreira, 1998.

In the early twentieth century *Ruy Ennes Ulrich* wrote his doctoral dissertation on Stock Exchanges and financial markets, which was published in Coimbra in 1906 by the University Press (Figure 12). Previously, lectures on Finance did not exist at the University of Coimbra[98], but when working toward his PhD in 1906 at the University of Coimbra, he chose Stock Exchanges as his dissertation topic, with the aim of subsequently teaching a course in Finance in the Law School. This textbook mentions a number of important books then available in France, Italy, Spain, Germany, and the UK, intending to show in a simple and pedagogical way how Capital Markets worked, how they were organized, how useful they were for current life, and how they had evolved from past to present (the early 1900s).[99]

Figure 12 — Professor *Ruy Ennes Ulrich* when Chairman of the Portuguese railway company[100]

---

[98] The only University that existed in Portugal in the beginning of that century. Mata, Costa, 2013.

[99] Mata, Costa, Justino, 2011.

[100] We thank the Historical Archive of the Portuguese railway company (CP) the license to reproduce his picture.

Ulrich's textbook is not well known internationally, as it is written in Portuguese, and it is therefore not listed in specialised bibliographies (Figure 13).[101] Note that his goal was to "nationalise" financial knowledge due to lack of alternatives in Portuguese[102]. Also, because it was written as a dissertation in Law, Ulrich's book seems at first glance to be a purely academic work. However, a closer examination reveals that it does not follow a strict juridical approach. He covers both the economic and business aspects of Stock Exchanges, and includes a fair treatment of some organisational features of Stock Exchanges in Portugal and elsewhere in Europe. He also makes an excursion into ways to improve the Lisbon Stock Exchange that would make it more efficient, up-to-date, and competitive with the other European capital-city markets, so that its economic and financial functions could more properly serve the needs of savers, investors, and customers in general.

Everyday life operations are described along with the institutional aspects, while separating the case of operations in securities (such as shares and debt instruments) from the case of commodities (such as foodstuffs, mineral ores, and other goods). On the importance of Stock Exchanges for securities trading, Ulrich says explicitly that *"although it is rare to trade securities outside Exchanges, it is common to sell commodities outside of them"*.[103]

The book reveals refined legal erudition, and most of the issues of law pertaining to the Stock Exchanges of the largest European cities are described. It also provides deep economic and financial analyses. Actually, the nineteenth century had been the period of

---

[101] Almodôvar, Cardoso (1998) .

[102] In any case, his proficiency was not wasted, as he was one of the most sought-after and successful experts in Finance in Portugal, and was later called upon to manage large Portuguese corporations, putting his academic and scientific knowledge to direct practical use.

[103] In Portuguese: *"Sendo raríssima a venda de valores fora da Bolsa, é vulgaríssima a venda de mercadorias fora d'ella"*, page 6.

most rapid industrialisation in many European countries, had ushered in intensified trading networks amongst European nations and the rest of the world, and had witnessed important migration flows of people leaving Europe, in the context of far-reaching globalisation of capital flows amongst capital markets. Large corporations and multinationals were founded, thanks to the principles of limited liability and capital sharing, in the most diversified sectors of economic activity, from industry to transportation, from agriculture to trading, from mining to insurance, prompting the multiplication of regional and global Stock Exchanges for supporting the needs of international business in the Old and New Worlds.

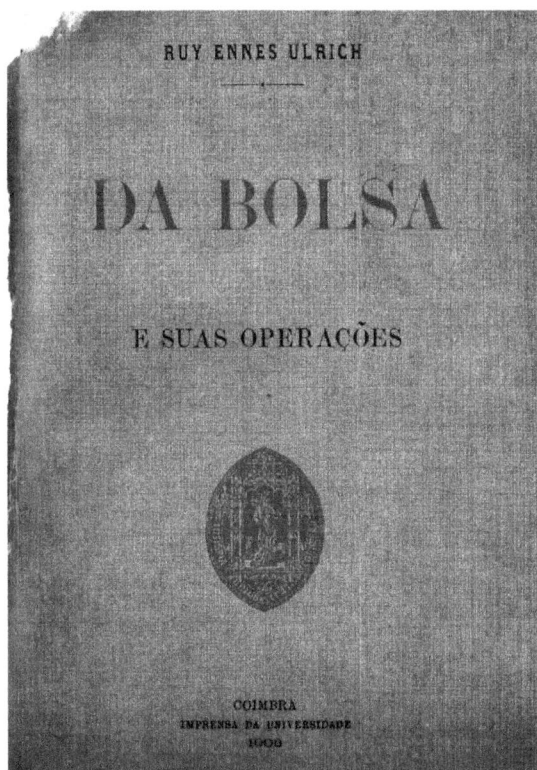

Figure 13 — Cover of Ulrich's 1906 Doctoral Dissertation "*Stock Exchange and its Operations*"

The book devotes special attention to the evolution of markets from Antiquity to the present (1906), discussing the origins and needs leading to their organisation. Beginning with the Portuguese case and expanding to Europe, it covers a long time span and a wide geographical area, in order to make possible some theorising on the role of Stock Exchanges and Capitalism in support of sophisticated modern societies. The book never uses the term *"transaction costs"*, but the author presents all transactions (be they on commodities or on securities) as the top expression of alternative uses for capital (including transfers among shareholders' hands in the vast world of business), in order to remark on the role of the wealth contained in tradable securities and its impact on collective prosperity and economic growth.

Ulrich's book speaks clearly to any educated citizen. Anyone can read it, but it is also deep enough to be classified as a real handbook on Finance. It is, in fact, a masterpiece that deserves to be quoted as top readership on the issues it addresses. In contributing to the spread of financial literacy amongst its readers, this book is an instrument of good practices in itself, and is also an instrument to evoke the responsibility of all partners and agents in the market.

Ulrich's case illustrates that Portugal was not out of the mainstream knowledge on financial markets in the early twentieth century. His book covers all of Portugal's commercial and financial life, and is a textbook of wide practical and educational interest.

Today, the development of the financial industry has been so accelerated after WWII that most countries are now recognising the significant financial illiteracy of their populations. At the same time, many developing countries are currently evolving toward the inception of Stock Exchanges in their own jurisdictions, requiring the education of different constituencies (and over a long period of time) on the workings of those markets and on their traded products. This explains the attention given by many Exchanges to these education activities, to both local parties and foreign entities.

Part of that education translates into a number of books and other forms of documentation covering a broad range of matters connected to the instruments listed, the companies admitted to the market, and to the operations executed by Exchanges. Of course, these written materials also serve the promotional efforts of many dynamic and competitive Exchanges.

11. The Trading Week of the Lisbon Stock Exchange

During most of the twentieth century the Lisbon Stock Exchange operated five days a week, closing on Saturdays, Sundays, all national holidays (civil or religious celebrations) and municipal free days. However, there are four important exceptions:

- in the beginning of the century and until 1919, Saturdays were still a business day and therefore Exchanges operated normally on these days;
- during the regime initiated in 1926 (until 1974) trading occurred also on Saturdays in the years 1932 to 1935;

LISBON STOCK EXCHANGE
Trading Days during the Week

1974	1973	1972	1971	1970	1969	1968	1967	1966	1965	1964
Monday to Friday										
5	5	5	5	5	5	5	5	5	5	5

1963	1962	1961	1960	1959	1958	1957	1956	1955	1954	1953
Monday to Friday										
5	5	5	5	5	5	5	5	5	5	5

1952	1951	1950	1949	1948	1947	1946	1945	1944	1943	1942
Monday to Friday										
5	5	5	5	5	5	5	5	5	5	5

1941	1940	1939	1938	1937	1936	1935**	1934*	1933	1932	1931
Monday to Friday						Monday to Saturday				Md to Fr
5	5	5	5	5	5	6	6	6	6	5

1930	1929	1928	1927	1926	1925	1924	1923	1922	1921	1920
Monday to Friday										
5	5	5	5	5	5	5	5	5	5	5

1919	1918	1917	1916	1915	1914	1913	1912	1911	1910	1909
Monday to Saturday										
6	6	6	6	6	6	6	6	6	6	6

1908	1907	1906	1905	1904	1903	1902	1901	1900
Monday to Saturday								
6	6	6	6	6	6	6	6	6

* Note issued on 30 June 1934: "*by superior authorisation, from July to September there will be no sessions on Saturdays*".
** Last Saturday with session occurred on 14 December 1935
Source: Daily Buletins of Lisbon Stock Exchange

Table 4 — Trading days per week during the first 75 years of the twentieth century

- after resumption of the operations in 1976 in Lisbon (and in 1981 in Porto) the two Exchanges did not trade on Mondays — but were open for all other businesses — in order to have time to do the heavy paperwork still attached to the settlement of the agreed transactions;[104]
- after joining the European Union (1986), the creation of the single currency in 1999 led to a standardisation of the bank

---

[104] The fact that a huge number of trades — from the trading peak in 1972 and 1973 — remained to be settled also explains this four-day trading week: there was still some backlog from that time being tackled.

238

holidays within that Union — the so called TARGET Days[105] — implying that, apart from very few common closing days, all domestic markets (Banks and Exchanges) remain open during all local bank holidays.

Table 4 describes the opening periods.

On the other hand, the Exchanges closed only during two difficult and volatile periods:

- with the beginning of WWI[106], the Government suspended all operations — on cash and derivatives — in the Lisbon and in the Porto Exchanges by the Decree nr. 797, (25 August 1914), but re-established only the cash market by "*Portaria*" nr. 240 (30 September 1914); the cash market was therefore closed for eight weeks only, but the operations on Derivatives resumed in both places only much later, on 1 November 1924, following "*Portaria*" nr. 4206, (22 September 1924);
- due to the Carnation Revolution on 25 April 1974, the Government "suspended" operations in the two Exchanges on that very day and maintained the two markets inactive until January 1976 in Lisbon[107] and January 1981 in Porto.

One of the most important strategic decisions of an Exchange relates to the solutions to be adopted in order to better respond to

---

[105] TARGET = Trans-European Automated Real-time Gross settlement Express Transfer system. At the time of this writing, there are only six Target holidays per year: New Year's Day (January 1), Good Friday, Easter Monday, Labour Day (May 1), Christmas Day (December 25) and Boxing Day (December 26).

[106] WWI began on 28 July 1914 and ended on 11 November 1918.

[107] Lisbon reopened for Bonds in January 1976, but trading on shares were allowed only from the end of February 1977 on.

the particular trading requirements of the different types of issuing companies. Specifically:

- should listing requirements be the same for both large and small firms, and if not, how different?
- how many different trading segments (with different listing and trading rules) should it offer to issuers?
- and, how to differentiate listing and operational requirements for debt instruments from those applicable to equities?

Today most Stock Exchanges are rediscovering the segment of the small and medium enterprise (SME) after a long period in which their attention tended to focus mainly on larger (and multinational) corporations because of their inherent advantages for Exchanges (revenues and economies of scale). But now the world is realising that in all advanced domestic economies the SME segment is equally large when viewed in consolidated terms, and that these firms contribute proportionally more than large ones in terms of innovation, job creation, and flexibility, all important characteristics for investors. Since Exchanges have in place the mechanisms to screen every issue during the phase of admission to their markets as well as the systems (computers and telecommunications) to provide tradability to those issues, different regimes may be offered to different instruments and to different issuers by adopting a multi-tier regime of market segments with distinct rules and levels of visibility and quality, in order to better meet the desires of each particular case.

12. The period without Stock Exchanges in Portugal in the 1970s

The military coup of April 1974 began during the night from the 24th to the 25th and led to the government in power being ousted and immediately replaced by a Salvation Junta (*"Junta de Salvação Nacional"*) in the evening of the 25th. Of course, in the following days there were no conditions for the Exchanges to operate and so the *Junta* issued an informal order to immediately suspend the operations in both centralised markets. The reason was to avoid large price swings triggered by the prevailing uncertainty.[108] That decision was subsequently published in the Official Gazette on 29 April 1974. So the last trading day in both Exchanges was 24 April 1974.

Unfortunately and unexpectedly, soon after that coup the political scene became very confused and increasingly influenced by the communist party and other leftist organisations, all of them advocating a programme of nationalisations in many sectors of the domestic economy — in particular, the whole financial sector. Indeed, in September 1974 the three existing issuing banks — *Banco de Portugal, Banco de Angola*, and *Banco Nacional Ultramarino* — which historically had been private companies with shares listed on the Lisbon Stock Exchange were nationalised, although under more or less market conditions. But in March 1975, a leftist swing in the domestic politics nationalised in turmoil a number of industrial sectors: all banks and insurance companies, all shipping and road transport companies, power utilities, cement industries, and other large corporations, etc.

At the same time, the Portuguese government granted full independence to all its overseas colonial territories during a single year

---

[108] See Chapter 4.10 and 11. On the way to assess volatility see Ross, Westerfield, Jaffe, 2005: 255.

(1975) which had significant impacts in the country, especially in the capital market.

Together, these independencies and those nationalisations implied that:

- all nationalised companies left the Exchanges;
- all listed companies with major activities in the overseas territories were either nationalised by the newly independent governments or went bankrupt;
- to that loss of wealth, investors also saw the market value of the remaining shares[109] tumble heavily in response to the pessimistic mood in the country[110] and also as a consequence of the loss of liquidity brought by the closure of the Exchanges.

The Lisbon Stock Exchange remained closed for share trading for around three years: 25 April 1974 to 28 February 1977[111], but the Porto Exchange remained closed much longer and reopened only on 27 January 1981[112].

---

[109] Actually, the Lisbon Exchange Daily Bulletin for the 25 February 1977 session (Friday) lists the collection of companies whose shares were allowed to resume negotiation from 28 February 1977 on. Probably due to lack of interest from investors, the actual first share trading day occurred on 4 March 1977 and only 2 issues — "*Lisnave*" and "*Fiação e Tecidos Torres Novas*" — witnessed some trading, but with a total of only (respectively) 60 and 50 shares changing hands.

[110] Besides domestic reasons to justify this pessimist mood, the first oil shock coming at the end of 1973 also played a role, as many of Portugal's trading partners entered into recession in 1974 and for some years.

[111] Gossip states that the government that took power after the coup soon realised that the increasing needs to finance accumulating budgetary debts required an organised market to give tradability to the expanding volumes of T-Bonds being placed in the market.

[112] See "*Portaria*" 770/75 dated 18 December 1975 and published in the Official Gazette on 23 December 1975 which determines the first trading day in Lisbon to be 12 January 1976. Mind that only three individual brokers remained on the occasion from those that existed before the suspension in 1974. See also "*Portaria*" 574-A/80, of 4 September 1980 and published in the Official Gazette on 5 September 1980,

However, the legal environment governing these re-installed markets was still that of the simplified Interim Code enacted in the beginning of 1974. For some time, no new laws were issued on Stock markets as, when trading in shares resumed, the number of companies listed was extremely reduced, none were large entities, and investors were very risk averse, due to the traumas brought recently to them by the political and economic events following the revolution. The quotations were below the average, a fact that one would expect after the turmoil associated with the political, social, and economic upheaval.

Meanwhile, a second world oil shock (1979) added to the adjustments brought about by the above events and forced the country to negotiate two standby agreements with the International Monetary Fund (1979 and 1983).

13. Investment Funds

Investment funds were introduced in Portugal just a few years before the 1974 military coup through specific legislation published in 1965 — Decree-Laws nr. 46302 of 27 April 1965 and nr. 46342 of 20 May 1965; subsequently two funds were created by local banks and quickly became very popular: total asset value of € 2.3 million[113].

which determines the first trading day in Porto to be 2 January 1981. Actually it occurred only on 27 January 1981 after three individual brokers were appointed by the Minister of Finance by his Decision of 19 December 1980. Under current Portuguese hierarchy of legislation Decrees are issued by the Council of Ministers, but *"Portaria"* is the legislation signed by a single Minister, normally to detail a general law and allow rapid adjustments to market requirements.

[113] See page 16 of the study *"A Indústria dos Fundos de Investimento em Portugal"*, published in Portuguese by CMVM in September 2002.

- FIA (*"Fundo de Investimentos Atlântico"*) from an initiative of Bank BPA — *Banco Português do Atlântico*;
- FIDES (*"Fundo de Investimentos para o Desenvolvimento Económico e Social"*) due to an initiative of the BT&A — *Banco Totta & Açores*.

Unfortunately, the nationalisation of so many companies that occurred after 1974 meant that these funds lost their *"raison d´être"*, and that forced the government to nationalise both funds in 1976[114] with some compensation being paid to the participants for the value of the units they previously owned. These were open-end funds — *"fundos abertos"* — investing only in securities — *"fundos mobiliários"*.

After the Exchanges resumed their operations and the investor community returned enthusiastically to the share and bond markets, the advantages of diversification and the economies of scale provided by mutual funds again became important to small investors. In 1985 the government introduced new specialised legislation to update the legal framework and also to diversify the types of funds tradable in Portugal to both closed-end versions and funds investing in real estate assets — *"fundos imobiliários"*:

- Decree-Law nr. 134/85 of 2 May 1985: updating the existing legislation concerning open-end funds investing only in securities;
- Decree-Law nr. 246/85 of 12 July 1985: introducing open-end funds for investment in real estate assets or in companies buying selling, renting or exploring such assets.

---

[114] See Decree-Law 539/76 of 9 July 1976.

Later, the experience accumulated and the explosion of this segment of investment led the government to issue a new Decree-Law nr. 229-C/88 of 4 July 1988, introducing closed-end funds — *"fundos fechados"* — reinforcing the disclosure requirements of information to their participants and consolidating into a single diploma the entire Portuguese legislation on investment funds and their managing entities.

For a country with small savers who also have a reduced level of financial literacy, mutual funds offered to small portfolios again the possibility of lowering both the credit and volatility risks along with reduction of transaction costs. Mutual funds also offered the capacity to use hedging techniques that are normally available only to large and professional investors.

Another reason behind the success of these mutual forms of investment stems from the aggressive marketing used by most resident banks toward their depositors via the management institutions they created to explore this segment of the market. Banks benefitted from the different commissions that investors pay to the banks and/or to those affiliated entities.

An important step was taken later with the creation of two types of investment funds aiming at the retirement age of the Portuguese population. Anticipating problems with the two official obligatory pension schemes[115], the government offered considerable tax incentives for the application of individual savings in a special type long--term investment fund — called PPR funds[116] — which should only be wound down by its beneficiary after his/her retirement. Later,

---

[115] One for Civil and Military Servants and a different one for the general employee of private firms. Nunes, 2007.

[116] The PPR acronym stands for *"Planos Poupança Reforma"*. See Decree-Law nr. 205/89 of 27 June 1989.

another fund — PPA[117] — was introduced with this same objective, but in this case with the restriction of investing predominately in shares.

14. Pension Funds

Portugal introduced social security systems in the middle of the twentieth century. The first legislation dedicated to this area is dated from 1935 and the old political regime — *"Estado Novo"* — basically improved the legislation and expanded the system until the revolution in 1974. The new regime accelerated that process much more, but until the 1990s that evolution concentrated mostly on widening the coverage of the system so that any national citizen could receive a minimum support both before and after his/her retirement.

In any case, the Portuguese social security system has always been operated in a regime of *"pay-as-you-go"*, in which the proceeds provided by the current contributors are used immediately to pay the pensions of those already retired, ill, or the widow of a contributor. The system only marginally accumulated some excess contributions as current pensions were (and still are) calculated from a legally defined mathematical formula without an individual account where each beneficiary periodically "deposits" his/her contributions year after year (and accumulates any gained interests), and from which his/her future pensions will be paid out. Only in the 1980s did the government start giving signs that this social security system will inevitably collapse in the future, without capacity to pay pensions and other benefits to future generations.

---

[117] The PPA acronym stands for *"Planos Poupança Acções"*. See Decree-Law nr. 204/95 of 5 August 1995. Markowitz, 1952.

One big change in the Portuguese society behind this future insufficiency is the rapid and significant reduction of the number of children per woman — now slightly above 1 — meaning that increasingly in the future there will be not enough contributors to the system to finance the retirees. Figure 14 illustrates total fertility rate in Portugal in the last five decades.

Another factor is the extension of life expectancy due to the constant improvement in the health system, which forces the system to pay benefits for longer periods of time. Increasing levels of welfare meant increasing life expectancy.

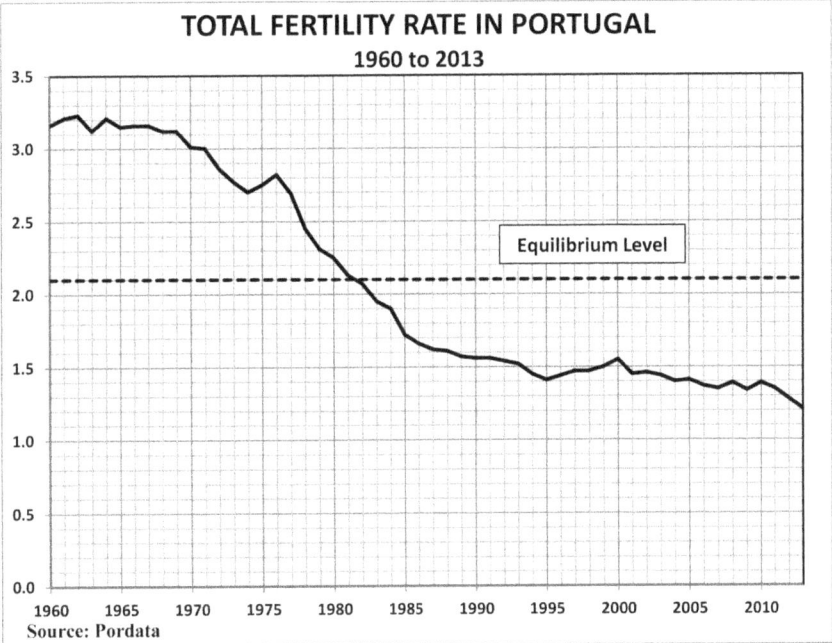

Figure 14 — Total fertility rate in Portugal

Finally, the expansion of the education system forces the young generations to enter the labour market and start paying for the system much later than their parents.

It was in 1985 with the Decree-Law nr. 323 of 6 August 1985 that these pension funds received their official blessing, and the first pension funds were placed in the market only in 1987.

In order to complement the official social security system, the government initiated a campaign to promote pension schemes at the corporate level — so that firms offer some complementary mechanism to the official system — and at the individual level — individuals being able to participate in private pension funds. Both initiatives were awarded some tax incentives[118], at least in the beginning with the purpose of motivating the domestic minds that traditionally were fully dependent on the official scheme for the retiring age, and to cover a potential incapacity to make a living out of working.

Now both segments — companies and individuals — complement the official system via pension funds operated privately by insurance companies and by specialised independent financial management companies[119]. Therefore, the number of alternative funds jumped from zero in 1987 to a maximum of 237 funds in 2010, and the volume of capital mobilised grew from zero to a maximum of €21.9 billion in 2009, representing 12.5% of GDP[120]. The financial crisis triggered in the US by the real estate bubble has affected this segment of the financial market, as Table 5 shows. More important is the low value of capital the Portuguese pension funds still manage in terms of GDP, as this opens an immense market for issuers, intermediaries, and families to explore more intensively this long-term mechanism of saving to hedge the uncertainties of the future.

---

[118] For example, corporations, under determined circumstances, could consider as fiscal cost twice the amount they invested in their pension funds.

[119] Denominated "*Sociedades Gestoras de Fundos de Pensões*" or Pension Funds Management Societies.

[120] Mind that in the UK, Switzerland, and Holland, this percentage hovers above 100% of their respective GDP. Blinder, 2013.

IMPORTANCE OF PENSION FUNDS IN PORTUGAL

	2 006	2 007	2 008	2 009	2 010	2 011	2 012	2 013
Nº of Managing Societies	227	224	230	236	237	229	228	224
Capital under management (000)	€ 21,184,992	€ 22,356,037	€ 20,281,921	€ 21,917,738	€ 19,724,644	€ 13,237,867	€ 14,470,997	€ 15,157,989
Shares	€ 6,307,000	€ 5,669,802	€ 2,587,232	€ 3,335,083	€ 2,793,317	€ 2,039,917	€ 1,233,119	€ 1,525,104
Deposits + Commercial Paper	€ 1,007,000	€ 1,123,410	€ 2,860,649	€ 1,290,783	€ 2,261,887	€ 2,139,548	€ 2,069,519	€ 1,844,751
Real estate	€ 1,655,000	€ 2,696,034	€ 3,020,279	€ 3,112,868	€ 3,124,061	€ 3,262,272	€ 2,787,146	€ 2,696,322
Bonds (T, M, C)	€ 7,273,000	€ 8,159,056	€ 8,647,666	€ 10,594,415	€ 8,365,965	€ 5,914,637	€ 6,020,723	€ 6,072,700
Other funds	€ 4,656,000	€ 4,263,124	€ 3,387,412	€ 3,660,650	€ 3,256,198	€ 2,824,017	€ 2,589,147	€ 2,981,540
Other assets	€ 287,000	€ 444,612	-€ 221,317	-€ 76,061	-€ 76,783	-€ 2,942,524	-€ 228,656	€ 37,571
GDPmp (000)	€ 166,248,715	€ 175,467,717	€ 178,872,582	€ 175,448,190	€ 179,929,812	€ 176,166,578	€ 169,668,162	€ 171,211,072
Capital/GDP	12.7%	12.7%	11.3%	12.5%	11.0%	7.5%	8.5%	8.9%

Sources: BdP and ISP

Table 5 — Importance of listed companies compared to annual GDP

15. The Role of the Exchanges in the Privatisation Programme

As mentioned above, the political regime empowered after the April 1974 military coup decided to nationalise large segments of the domestic economy following a philosophy of state control of many crucial industries, such as finance, utilities, transports, etc.

Later and as a result of our accession to the then European Economic Community, that extended role of the state in the domestic economy had to be reversed under the constraints of the state budget and the pressure of the rule of competitive rules in Europe whereby companies must survive without any support from member states.

Therefore, an ambitious programme was developed to return all nationalised firms to private hands and the first significant step[121] occurred when the commercial bank — *"Banco Totta & Açores S.A."*

---

[121] Although it was in 1987 that the first companies were sold, these were very small firms, and only on 10 July 1989 the government sold 49% of *"Banco Totta & Açores S.A."* in a special trading session of the Lisbon Stock Exchange. Clemente, 2002.

— saw 49% of its share Capital sold to private investors in July 1989.

The relevance of this privatisation programme to the Stock Exchanges stems from:

a) The decision to favour the two Stock Exchanges (Lisbon and Porto) to execute most of the public offers of the different corporations in order to benefit from the transparency and the credibility of organised markets;

b) The sale of each slice of capital — large companies were sold in two or more tranches distributed over several years. This was used to promote this type of investment in the domestic society, which had been so badly affected by the Revolution and its aftermath;

c) The wish to develop and professionalise the human structure of both Exchanges and the banking sector (through which buying orders were collected and the securities sold were deposited in the accounts of the individual investors); also the brokerage community received an impulse to strengthen their capital base and to institutionalise their legal status.

Year	Number of Operations	New Cias Privatised	Total Proceeds (€ 000)
1 987	4	4	4,782
1 988	4	4	9,060
1 989	16	16	393,383
1 990	19	13	845,814
1 991	23	20	875,771
1 992	24	19	1,563,968
1 993	26	24	401,088
1 994	20	17	938,343
1 995	35	28	1,814,239
1 996	14	7	2,415,216
1 997	11	7	4,324,555
1 998	8	3	3,853,222
1 999	8	4	1,607,945
2 000	10	6	3,393,517
2 001	3	0	547,703
2 002	3	3	260,359
2 003	2	0	53,554
2 004	2	0	832,363
2 005	2	1	403,200
2 006	3	0	1,505,409
Total	237	176	26,043,491

Table 6 — Year of the main privatisations

Table 6 summarises privatisation operations, total proceeds, and the number of privatised companies. From 1987 until 2006 a total of 237 operations were executed mobilising more than €26 billion with most of the large companies offered to the public in special trading sessions organised in the two Exchanges.

In total 175 companies returned to the private sector, with the state maintaining small amounts of capital in a few cases to control strategic decisions for some years.

16. The Government's role

Government tends always to play an important role in Capital Markets and in the domestic Exchanges because it performs different functions:

- as an issuer of large amounts of debt instruments that are frequently listed on Exchanges;
- normally it shares some legislative powers with the local parliament, and both define the whole legal framework that regulates these markets and their operations;
- in particular, taxation of the profits from capital market investments and of the commissions collected by the different intermediaries are a prerogative of governments that may profoundly affect the market, as it reduces the net gains individuals extract from financial investments;
- supervision and detailed regulation of these markets often resides in specialised bodies whose management is normally appointed by the government;
- some governments prefer to explore certain important domestic economic activities — often under the excuse of these being natural monopolies — with large state companies whose capital is controlled, at least partially, by the government as any other risky investor in search of annual returns.

This multiple presence has changed over time, and some experimentation has occurred in different places. Initially individuals' associations in Britain and Northern continental Europe freely discovered the best organisational and governance principles by themselves without any state regulation. Political economy textbooks included definitions of Stock Exchanges as centralised markets located in large urban trade centres where businessmen met for negotiations and transactions involving large amounts of capital.[122] And the rules for operations and penalties pertaining to brokers' activity were meticulously described, especially regarding unfair competition (amongst them) and false rumours.[123]

In the second half of the nineteenth century Commercial Codes established in most of the European countries included some chapters regulating Stock Exchange operations, from listing to trading. Penalties were prescribed, and textbooks commented on these various issues, thereby spreading information and financial literacy.[124] Detailed regulations for Stock Exchange and/or brokers' codes sometimes even included the opening hours, duration of the sessions, timing for short-selling, and the schedule for transactions on derivatives.

However, in the late nineteenth century and early 1900s, voices calling for state regulation became loud and quite effective[125]. This meant that governments could no longer be blind toward Stock Exchanges, but should keep them under the scrutiny of the central state. Such a concept is close to regarding Stock Exchange functions as a public good, to be preserved, implemented, and regulated. Today the idea that stock markets contribute to any country's economic and financial health is firmly established, and *"governments wish to prevent major catastrophes from occurring"* and *"regulations are meant to curtail some untoward behaviour"*.[126]

---

[122] Colson, 1903, vol. 2.

[123] Moysen, 1904. Carreras, 1865.

[124] Thaler, 1900.

[125] Nineteenth century bibliography, (Hayaux du Tilly, 1901, for example), argues that while trading in commodities interests only some people, everybody must recognise that financial assets serve everybody. This was not the common opinion in the early days, when self-regulated Exchanges arose following merchants' and traders' initiatives, and these competed for their intermediation role.

[126] Hafer; Hein, 2007: 120.

The recognition of the utility of Stock Exchanges for the economic system comes also from the need to collect small-pocket savings for government loans in public debt because confidence in governments increases bond prices[127], and from the fact that stock markets reflect a nation's vigour and credibility. Additionally, as capital mobility is an important condition for private businesses and public credit in all countries, its efficient provision by Stock Exchanges for public works and collective improvements make governments dependent on them as well, while regulating their activity, simultaneously.[128] *"Governments (...) are even more complex stakeholders than are entrepreneurs or families. They are both the largest issuers and largest institutional investors in most markets, controlling state-owned banks and influencing major financing decisions"*.[129]

Taxes on Stock Exchange operations were (and still are) a difficult matter. On the one hand, it is considered that the access to stock market services should be simple, cheap, and attractive. On the other hand, financial operations provide a means for increasing production, distribution, and selling, and the opportunity for such benefits should be taxed.[130] Which taxes might be adopted (and at what rates), and which effects on financial operations may be acceptable had triggered technical discussion as early as the beginning of the twentieth century.

The entire history of Portugal shows the central role always played by the successive governments in its domestic economy and consequently upon the Stock Exchanges. In the beginning of the twentieth century, according to the 1888 Commercial Code and the 1901 Regulations, the two local Exchanges were a private

---

[127] Ulrich, 1906, p. 55, quoting Piccinelli, 1897.

[128] Ulrich, 1906, 65, quoting Laveleye, 1898.

[129] Morel, et al., 2013: 6.

[130] Weil, 1902.

initiative administered by private Commercial Associations, even if here the government had a controlling mechanism upon them, besides the normal regulatory and supervisory functions. Mind that this interference did not change significantly when the political regime in the country changed from a monarchy to a republic or even when the Estado Novo regime was installed in 1926 with its authoritarian philosophy. Of course the presence of the government increased substantially after nationalisation of the two Exchanges in 1974 under the guidance of the Interim Code issued in January 1974. And, when it was decided to relax the state control in 1991, the Exchanges were transferred to two not-for-profit civil associations, not into fully for-profit companies. Full privatisation of the Portuguese Exchanges occurred only in 2000, following the previous merger between Lisbon and Porto Associations. This was a precondition for a subsequent transfer of ownership to the Euronext Group in February 2002.

17. Supervision of the Markets, Intermediaries, and Investors

In the beginning of the twentieth century, the Portuguese Exchange markets were supervised by the local Commercial Associations and the Government[131]. After nationalization of them in 1974 (before the revolution), only the government remained in supervision via the Ministry of Finance.

---

[131] An important role was played here by a specialised General Inspection established in the Ministry of Finance in 1947 and initially concentrated in the banking sector, but which in 1949 (by Decree-Law 37470) expanded to oversee the entire financial market — banks, insurance companies, and the capital market — under the name of *"Inspecção-Geral de Crédito e Seguros"*. With the 1974 Revolution this inspection was disbanded in 1975 (by Decree-Law 107/75), the Central Bank receiving most of its responsibilities, and leaving the inspection of the insurance sector in the Ministry of Finance. But in all this legislation the capital market seems to be the poor member of this three-tier inspection. Sanchez, 2012.

The first step to introduce a specialised body for this function occurred in 1988 with the Decree-Law that created the so called *"Auditor-Geral do Mercado de Títulos"*. With the first full Securities Code (1991) this body was developed to become a true securities and exchange commission denominated *"CMVM-Comissão do Mercado de Valores Mobiliários"*.

Mind that Portugal opted for the three-segment model of supervision, in which insurance companies have a specialised supervisor — *"Instituto de Seguros de Portugal"* — the banking industry is overseen by the Central Bank, and the capital market by CMVM commission, all three coordinating their operations via the domestic *"Conselho Nacional de Supervisores Financeiros"*[132].

In an effort to simplify the complex evolution of the legal environment that ruled the workings of the organisational infra-structures of this market, one can identify three different periods, as Figure 15 shows.

a) 1st period: from the end of the nineteenth century until the middle of the 1960s

A new (the second) Commercial Code was published in Jun/1888[133] to be implemented from the beginning of 1889. It is nick-named *"Código Veiga Beirão"* after the principal author and Minister of Justice of the government, *Francisco António da Veiga Beirão*. As a broad code — it encompasses four books[134] — it aimed to cover all commercial activities

---

[132] National Council of Financial Supervisors. Câmara, 2011.

[133] Approved by "Carta de Lei" dated from 28 June 1888, which includes the Code and states its implementation from 1 January 1889.

[134] Book 1: covers commerce in general (*"Do Comércio em Geral"*). Book 2: covers special contracts in commerce (*"Dos Contratos Especiais de Comércio"*). Book 3: deals with maritime commerce (*"Do Comércio Marítimo"*). Book 4: deals with bankruptcies (*"Das Falências"*).

in Portugal including the operation of Exchanges and their Brokers.

Exchanges are covered in the following parts:

- Book One ("*Livro Primeiro*")

    ◦ "*Título VII — Dos Corretores*", Articles 64 to 81
    ◦ "*Título VIII — De Lugares Destinados ao Comércio*"
        Chapter I — "*Das Bolsas*", Articles 82 to 92

- Book Two ("*Livro Segundo*")

    ◦ "Título VIII — Das Operações de Bolsa", Articles 351 to 361.

From this overall framework a number of Laws and Regulations were subsequently published pertaining to the operations of the Exchanges and their Brokers:

TIME LINE OF MAJOR LEGAL STEPS

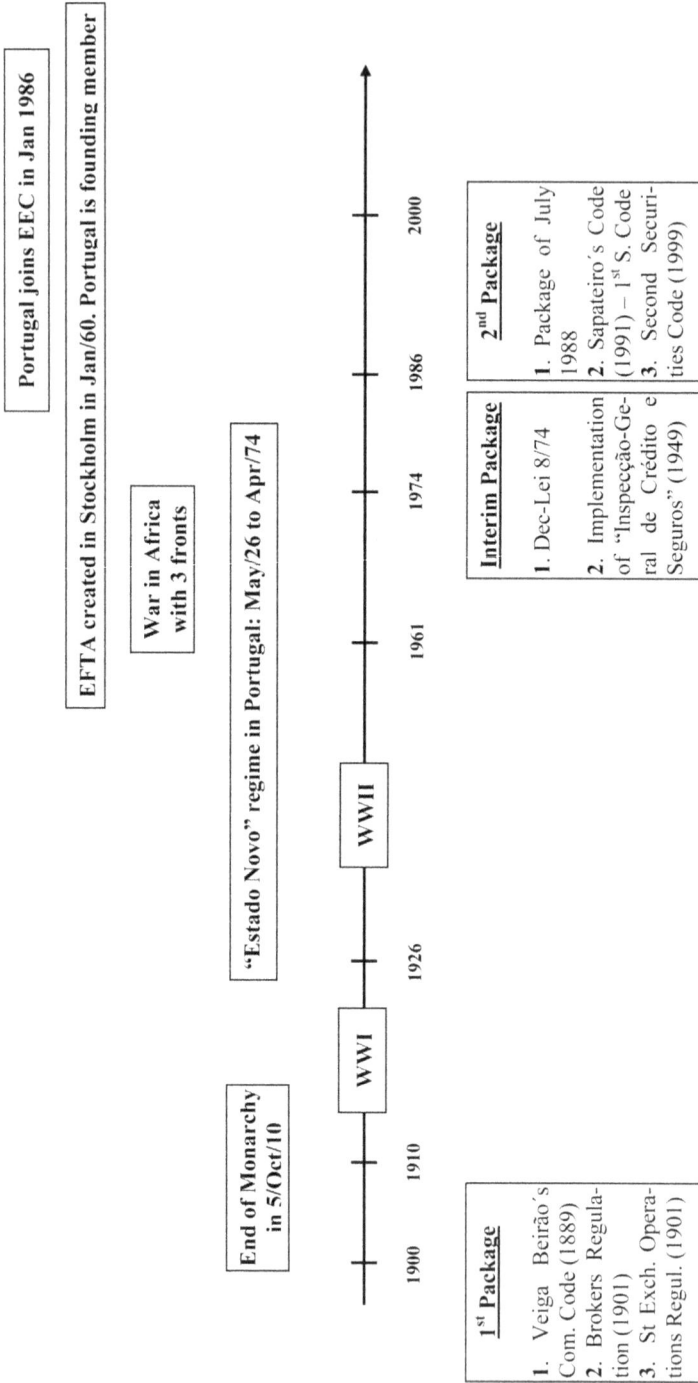

Portugal joins EEC in Jan 1986

EFTA created in Stockholm in Jan/60. Portugal is founding member

War in Africa with 3 fronts

"Estado Novo" regime in Portugal: May/26 to Apr/74

End of Monarchy in 5/Oct/10

WWI

WWII

1900 1910 1926 1961 1974 1986 2000

1ˢᵗ Package
1. Veiga Beirão´s Com. Code (1889)
2. Brokers Regulation (1901)
3. St Exch. Operations Regul. (1901)

Interim Package
1. Dec-Lei 8/74
2. Implementation of "Inspecção-Geral de Crédito e Seguros" (1949)

2ⁿᵈ Package
1. Package of July 1988
2. Sapateiro´s Code (1991) – 1ˢᵗ S. Code
3. Second Securities Code (1999)

Figure 15 — Summary of main legal steps in 1900s

- Regulation of 8 October 1889[135]: regulates in detail article 83 of the Commercial Code regarding the application for opening an Exchange; it also indicates that it is up to the Brokers Chamber to decide about the listing request for any security (except for domestic tradable treasury instruments, which are automatically entitled to be listed);

- Law of 11 April 1901: adds to the three types of commercial firms defined in the Commercial Code (Article 105) a fourth type named *"Sociedades por Quotas"*, a special and simpler legal form of corporation designed to simplify small initiatives in which nominal capital is represented not by equal shares but by individual — potentially dissimilar — parts; in any event, this special legal form of corporation can also issue bonds and have them listed on an Exchange;

- Decree of 10 October 1901 issues two important Regulations:

  - Regulation of the Operation of Stock Exchanges[136]
  - Regulation of the Brokers' activities: brokers are private physical persons appointed by the government who were required to intermediate in any Exchange operations; three types are defined: for trading in securities, for trading in shipping, transports, and insurance, and for trading in commodities;

---

[135] Published in Government Gazette nr. 230, on 11 October 1889. Mind that after the Republican Revolution on 5 October 1910, the Government reset the numbering of this Gazette to 1 from 6 October 1910 on.

[136] It is interesting to note that this Regulation establishes a precise maximum amount of 2,400$000 for the total annual costs for BVL (Article 66) along with an indication (Articles 61 to 65) that Exchange income belongs to the Ministry of Finance from which operational costs were covered; but any surplus would be used by the Government for purposes unrelated to that Exchange market.

○ Decree of 24 December 1901[137] introduces slight modifica-
tions in Articles 13, 41, and 59 of the above Regulation
of Exchanges, and in Articles 42 and 97 of the above
Regulation of Brokers;

○ Decree of 30 October 1903 regulates the supervisory role
of the Commercial Association of Lisbon over the Lisbon
Stock Exchange (BVL) and how it relates with the BVL's
Brokers Chamber.

Three more legal diplomas are worth mentioning, the first to
stress the controlling policy the government maintained over private companies and the Exchanges, the other two showing that
even innovation in financial products needed the agreement from
the government.

○ Decree-Law nr. 37 470 of 6 July 1949: creates the
"Inspecção-Geral de Crédito e Seguros" which merges the
two existing supervisors of the credit institutions and
the insurance companies, but also extends its scope to
include the capital market;

○ Decree-Law nr. 46 342 of 20 May 1965: creates and regulates open-ended investment funds restricted to portfolios
of securities, along with their managing societies.

b) **2ⁿᵈ period**: from the middle of 1960s to 1991

The expansion of the domestic market forces the government
to initiate a complete modification in the overall legal environment for companies and Exchanges, but lack of time permitted only some "improvisations" and the military coup in 1974
imposed a delay of around two decades:

---

[137] Published in the Government Gazette nr. 292 of 26 December 1901.

- Decree-Law nr. 55/72 of 16 February 1972: determines the rules to be fulfilled by commercial societies to issue shares in Portugal;
- *"Portaria"* nr. 103/72 of 21 February 1972: for the first time requires a prospectus to be published before a public placement of shares in Portugal;
- Decree-Law nr. 8/74 of 14 January 1974: interim Securities Code, which nationalises the Lisbon and Porto Exchanges;
- *"Portaria"* nr. 262/74 of 10 April 1974[138]: Internal Regulation of the Lisbon Stock Exchange.

The general practice of investors was to buy to hold. People trusted companies, there were only a few trading operations, settlement occurred in three days. At the end of the 1960s the number of trades increased greatly, and three-day settlements were no longer possible, Exchange operations need to be accelerated with the 1974 ruling:

"When Mr. Cota Dias became minister, he invited me to join his State Secretary for the Treasury (1972-74), and asked me to work on that ruling for the Exchange, as it was a responsibility of that State Secretary according to the law. (Today it is up to the Minister to define such responsibilities).

According to the complaints I was receiving, investors bought shares but received them only six months later, and that could not be allowed to continue because with the scheduled IV Development Plan (*"Plano de Fomento"*) things would become

---

[138] Mind that this regulation was enacted just 15 days ahead of the military coup of 25 April 1974, so without much practical impact upon the market and its agents.

even worse when the Exchange would be unable to cope with its added demands. Therefore, I wrote the Decree-Law in cooperation with the General Inspectorate for Credit and Insurance ("*Inspecção Geral de Crédito e Seguros*"), that is, with Mr. Carlos Rosa, who was the Director at the time."[139]

Due to the acceleration brought about by the accession of Portugal to the European Economic Community on top of the profound revolution underwent by the country following the political events of 1974, it was necessary to complement the interim innovation centred on Decree-Law 8/74 with a package of laws in July 1988 that bridged the existing legal framework to a new one still to be developed. This package comprised eight Decree-Laws — nrs. 229-A/88 to 229-I/88 — plus six "*Portarias*" — nrs. 422-A/88 to 422-D/88 plus 480/88 and 481/88 — whose main topics covered were the following:

- Changes in the 1986 Corporate Code
- Improvements in the Investment Funds regime by introducing real estate funds and closed-end funds
- Dematerialisation of securities to facilitate issuance and trading, and to reduce risks and costs of settlement
- Internalisation of some European rules relative to listing of securities in a Stock Exchange and relative to Take Over Bids and Public Offers to Sell.
- It also forced local brokers to incorporate their activities through one of two types of financial intermediaries that were created — broker houses and dealer houses.

An important initiative taken by the government in the years 1986 to 1988 was an "invitation" for private corporations to open

---

[139] Interview by *Dr. José Luís Sapateiro*.

or increase their capital and list their shares in the Portuguese Exchanges. In fact the government not only published a set of diplomas[140] giving incentives to issuers and investors in shares, but the Minister of Finance himself took the initiative to write a letter to many local firms inviting them to consider the use of the capital market and the listing of their shares.

c) **3rd period**: since 1991

Finally, in 1991, a brand new and comprehensive Securities Code was published with Decree-Law nr.142-A/91 of 10 April 1991. The main ideas behind this code were to:

- update the Portuguese legal framework for the Capital Market, in particular "importing" all European directives applicable to this business
- liberalise the market
- reduce the role of the government in the daily activity of issuers and intermediaries
- semi-privatise the two Exchanges by transferring their ownership and management from the state to two private civil associations
- allow banks to participate on a voluntary basis in the management of Stock Exchanges but without full membership rights
- automate Exchange trading and interconnect the two Stock Exchanges

---

[140] See Decree-Laws nr. 172/86 (30/June/1986), and 130/87 (17/March/1987), along with the Law nr. 2/88 (26/Jan/1988). As an example, the first DL reduces income tax for corporations offering shares to the public, reduces taxation upon dividends paid by listed shares, and introduces a tax deduction of 10% of the amount invested in subscribing and buying listed shares. Also SMEs received tax benefits to increase their share capital.

- launch a domestic Central Securities Depository responsible for the registration of all listed securities and for the settlement mechanisms
- institutionalise a local supervisor and regulator — *"CMVM — Comissão do Mercado de Valores Mobiliários"* to substitute the incipient and tiny *"Auditor-Geral do Mercado de Títulos"*[141].

The practical use of this extensive and all-encompassing Securities Code and the continuous production of new laws at the European level soon suggested the need for a new one that should be much more flexible, less detailed, and incorporate the most recent European legislation. Therefore, in 1999 the Second Securities Code was published via Decree-Law 486/99 (13 November 1999).

It is interesting to mention that when the Portuguese Exchange joined the NYSE Euronext group from 2007 on, no legal changes in the domestic framework were introduced, as the merger agreement between Europe and the US was designed to preserve the isolation between the two jurisdictions.

---

[141] Created by Decree-Law nr. 335/87 (15 October 1987) as a person charged with the responsibility of supervising the capital market in order to *"degovernmentalise"* that activity.

CHAPTER 6
GLOBALISATION AND STOCK EXCHANGES

The early twentieth century was a very special moment for Europe regarding its capacity to lead the world trade, dominate the export capital to all continents, and advance a number of free-standing companies to operate in the global context.[1] British leadership in industrialisation and the catching-up process followed by other nations dominated the international scene and contributed mightily to the expansion of the globalisation process.[2] Railways already crossed all continents, sail and steam shipping connected all main seaports, trade fuelled the world international division of labour, and the adoption of the gold standard provided an accurate system for international payments. Main actors in this scene were private corporations, operating in all sectors, both in Europe and elsewhere.[3] From mining to farming, transportation to commerce, industrial production to the provision of utilities, private corporations raised large amounts of capital from a multitude of small-pocket savers who sought to maximise their rewards in stock markets through investment as shareholders. [4] Local, regional, and national Stock

---

[1] Amatori; Jones, (editors), 2003.

[2] Rodrik, 1999.

[3] Jones, 2005. Alquist, 2010, 2012.

[4] Bauer, Pool, and Dexter, 1972.

Exchanges were part of a world network of financial relationships, in which London and New York were leading the markets.[5]

The sophisticated financial culture of the time resulted from accumulated expertise in domestic production and trade, in international commercial links, insurance contracts, currency transactions, share trading, bond issuance, and derivative contracts.[6] Vast financial elites operated businesses, commanding the urban centres and their role in the large networking system of information, expectations, investment, and transactions.[7] Dealers, accountants, brokers, bankers, and finance experts in general, formed a technical staff that operated according to behavioural rules derived from codes of honour intended to inspire confidence, transparency, and trust, as the Daily Bulletins of stock markets demonstrate.[8]

1. Panorama worldwide. Rationale for the Consolidation of Exchanges

History explains the initial Exchanges as natural responses of local commercial entities to the needs of the markets around them — tradability for the issued securities and information disclosure about the respective issuers. Therefore these centralised markets were initially run by private organisations.

On the other hand, many countries that arrived to the capitalistic world only after the 1960s — the case of eastern countries in Europe after the fall of the Berlin Wall in 1989 and some former African

---

[5] Chandler, 1962/1998. Dalton, 2001.

[6] Courtois, 1902: 80-90.

[7] Cassis, 2006.

[8] In Lisbon as in London. For example, London Stock Exchange Intelligence, *Burdett's Official Intelligence,* several issues. British Library of Political and Economic Science, BLPES, London School of Economics.

colonies — obtained their current national Exchanges through an administrative initiative of their domestic governments (which therefore owns them). Initiative and ownership by a national government accelerates the procedure to implement a Stock Exchange but deprives the organisation of the typical dynamism of private firms, and makes them more vulnerable to the political interests stemming from any government. The theoretical benefit of commercial neutrality usually attached to a government may easily be overcome by the huge levels of debt that many national Treasuries have now issued, along with the fact that governments in most young countries tend to control large numbers and sizable enterprises.

In mature countries, the twentieth century has witnessed a number of experiments in which ownership and legal status of Exchanges were developed as a tentative response to the new requirements brought about by the evolution in size and sophistication of their domestic markets, and also under the influence derived from the internationalisation of many markets.

As usual, there is as yet no best solution to these ownership and organisational problems as all different alternatives have advantages for some stakeholders, but important drawbacks for others.

This explains why some experimentation is still seen here and there around the world — and in different levels — seeking to determine whether Exchanges will better be as for-profit endeavours or, on the opposite, as not-for-profit organisations. Probably the best alternative is to design a model in which all parties with some form of interest have a word within the organisation without anyone having a majority vote, and to organise the operations in such a way that the community can receive most of the positive inputs from every side, but remain largely immune to the negative interests of each one.

The typical model of a historical Exchange can be described as a kind of club created by a certain number of financial intermediaries — commonly known as brokers — to facilitate their business of finding counterparties to execute the buy and sell orders they receive from their clients. Probably the best known example is the foundation, in 1792, of the great-grand-father of the current New York Stock Exchange, when 24 brokers institutionalised that exchange via the famous Buttonwood Accord.

In this initial model the interests of this intermediation community prevail over all the other stakeholders, in particular, the Exchanges are typically closed to banks. That is, banks cannot operate directly in their trading floors, implying an inherent reduced capacity of those centralized markets to reach geographies far away from the physical building where that market operates. Mind that, in opposition to most brokerage houses (because most are tiny firms) banks often offer extensive distribution networks that permit capturing orders to an Exchange from very distant (and therefore large) areas.

In a number of European countries and in the US there are historical registers that indicate that, before the twentieth century, many mid-size towns developed local Exchanges as a natural response of traders and investors to improve liquidity and tradability of securities and, in many cases, also of commodities.

Of course, these local trading centres catered basically to local issuers and to local investors, and their restricted geographical coverage was determined by the physical limitations to collect orders from distant parties and to receive updated information from issuers headquartered far away from them. Switzerland is a good example, as there were seven Exchanges spread over that small country, each one catering essentially to its cantonal market. High mountains did not facilitate communications between even close by towns.

Around WWI but mainly after it, better communications within most countries led some local Exchanges to begin a move aiming at establishing connections with similar ones located in neighbouring towns in order to replace tiny local markets with a larger regional one. There was a strong rationale for these first-level consolidation moves:

a) to avoid the duplication of infrastructures, such as buildings and knowledgeable man-power;
b) stronger competition between the various merged markets to capture additional issuers and more orders from larger constituencies;[9]
c) to improve liquidity due to the concentration of larger and more diversified interested parties (issuers, investors, and intermediaries);
d) therefore, enhancing their capacity to attract large corporate and governmental issuers;
e) to improve the economic representativeness of the quotations discovered in their centralised markets;
f) to gain economic dimension to benefit from the attention of additional broadcasting channels, such as nation-wide newspapers;
g) to offer more visibility to issuers, thereby attracting more stakeholders.

Later, these advantages were "rediscovered" when telecommunications made it possible to go one step further and merge most regional Exchanges in each national country into one single domestic central market — second consolidation move. And the introduction of computers to match buy and sell orders further pressed toward consolidation due to their enormous calculating capabilities, together with the cost savings brought about by common use of a single machine. The UK is a typical example: from 22 regional Exchanges

---

[9] Shy, Tarkka, 2001. Katovich, 2011. Kaheman, 1992.

immediately after 1914 there was a succession of consolidations until only the London and Liverpool Exchanges remained operational in the beginning of the 1970s. But the big-bang introduced in 1986 then ended that process by concentrating in the London Stock Exchange the whole UK market[10].

Of course, some countries with more regionalised economies and political structure tended to resist this concentration move as each region enjoys having its own centralised market. The case of Spain is the perfect example of this as the centralism of Madrid led the four Spanish regions with Stock Exchanges — Madrid, Basque Country, Catalonia, and Valencia — to decide to keep their regional Exchanges as independent juridical entities in spite of sharing one single computer to trade in an integrated manner the entire Spanish market. Another singular case in Europe is Germany, where the history of the country and her particular form of federalism justifies that a number of länder maintain an independent Stock Exchange, not even participating in an interconnected electronic system as in Spain. But this regionalism did not preclude Frankfurt from playing a nation-wide role similar to London's with a kind of monopoly of all big business in Germany.

A similar approach was recently used by Euronext when France, Belgium, and Holland decided to merge their domestic Exchanges in 2000 in order to offer a much larger market to international issuers and investors while avoiding some triplications: each country maintained its national Exchange as a local entity but the three markets are interconnected via a common telecommunication network and a

---

[10] See Huggins, 2014: *"... However, by the 1970s the changing industrial regional order across the UK — leading to the economic divides we see today — deemed a situation where the remaining regional exchanges were absorbed into the international LSE in 1973".*

single trading platform[11]. This was the third level of consolidations, for the first time a cross border type within the European Union.

This initiative fructified even further — fourth level, cross Atlantic — when the American group of Exchanges constructed around the NYSE acquired control of the Euronext Group in 2007. But the local influence of each side was considered so important that this step was designed with the idea of guaranteeing that, in spite of a unified infrastructure that interconnects the different poles of the group, there was an absolute legal separation between the two continents in the sense that the laws applicable to issuers and investors in US did not apply to the European side and vice-versa.

However, this brief experience in a number of countries revealed a number of problems stemming from these overextended organisations, an important one being the reduced attention paid to the smaller parts of the spectrum, meaning the retail investors and the smaller issuers. Also, the differences between distant markets in terms of traditions, laws, and financial systems seem to introduce "noise" into the daily workings of those Exchanges that are integrated into geographically extended groups. This may explain the recent (2014) "divorce" of the former Euronext from the Americans, which basically re-established the European group of Exchanges (except for LIFE) as it was in 2002.

---

[11] The Portuguese Stock Exchange joined the Euronext Group in February 2002 together with the British Derivatives Exchange LIFFE (which, in 2014, left the group, following the split between the European and US groups of Exchanges).

2. The Case of Small and Medium Enterprises. The Case in Portugal

"Central to a market's effectiveness is confidence among investors that it can absorb orders to buy and liquidate shares at prices which reflect the intrinsic values of the underlying claims, and that the availability of the trading mechanism will not be disrupted."[12] In fact, liquidity influences people's participation in securities markets, influencing the deepening of stock markets. That is, liquidity attracts liquidity and that explains part of the greater attention these markets attach to large issues, either of shares — big corporations — or of bonds — T-Bonds and similar public debt.

However, the world is currently re-focusing on Small and Medium Enterprises (SME) for a number of reasons:

    a) SMEs face the very same type of financial needs of large company[13] but they make up the vast majority of the firms incorporated in any domestic economy;

    b) because their size does not allow them to benefit from many different economies of scale, they use a proportionally larger percentage of labour than Large Enterprises (LE), thus creating proportionally more jobs; also they lay off labour less frequently in case of economic crisis; that is,

---

[12] Rousseau, 2008: 15.

[13] In particular:
    1) it is crucial to maintain permanent access to short-term sources of funds to finance the vast majority of their daily activities of buying inputs, paying salaries, granting credit to its clients, paying in due time a number of periodic costs, etc.
    2) although less frequent, now and then, they also need to tap long-term sources of funds to finance their investments in infrastructures — buildings, machinery — and in research and development of new products and services.
    Berger, 2005.

they make a more than proportional contribution to reduce unemployment;

c) their small size makes them more flexible than LEs, that is, they adapt better and more quickly to the market swings occurring frequently in any domestic economy;

d) their survivorship depends very much on an offer (of products or services) that differentiates them from what LEs already are offering to their clientele; precisely because of that, innovation is more often found in such small companies than in larger ones;

e) most LEs began their lives as SMEs since only rarely does a firm initiate activities with a very large scale of operations; SME are the seeds of most LEs;

f) SMEs tend (and have to) to remunerate investors significantly above LEs operating in the same field (or risk) because their investors need to be able to withstand larger swings in both quotations and tradability (liquidity risk).

The current crisis enfolding since the summer of 2007 has had the advantage of emphasising the financial difficulties faced by SMEs in many countries worldwide: not only their lack of stable funds — equity and debt financing — for infrequent long-term purposes, but even their acute shortage of working capital for their permanent short-term operations. In fact, for a significant number of SMEs, the end result of the current credit crunch (implemented by the banking sector in many countries) has been the failure of some of them in spite of being very profitable firms, simply due to credit constraints — quantity and price of the working funds available to them.

Europe is particularly vulnerable to problems developed in its banking system since, opposite to the case of the United States of America, most countries in the European Union base their financing of their corporate fabric on funds provided by the banks. With the exception of the UK and to some extent the Netherlands, capital markets in Europe are significantly smaller in GDP terms than their bank counterparts and much more restrictive for SMEs seeking to raise money.[14] This means that smaller European corporations are much more vulnerable to the periodic (so history indicates) credit crunches that affect the banking systems in different countries. In most of Europe, funding alternatives to firms and especially to SMEs either do not exist or are less effective than in the US.

Reasons that may explain this European preference for the intermediated channel to supply financing to companies come, in part, from "natural" limitations proper to small issuers, but also in another part, from the different subjective *"liabilities"* attached to any direct mobilisation of savings for productive purposes. Examples of the first type are:

a) large issuers have more capacity to directly tap any segment of savers due to their visibility, credibility, and political and commercial connections;

b) large issues benefit from a number of economies of scale both at issuance and during their lives, which tend to negatively affect smaller placements of either debt or equity;

c) admission of any issue to a Stock Exchange is extremely demanding to any issuer in terms of bureaucracy, cash costs, and information disclosure, but that means proportionally much more for a smaller organisation;

d) there are many requirements to be fulfilled on a permanent basis to remain listed on an Exchange: payment of annual fees, periodic disclosure of information, availability of an Investors' Relation Department within the issuer organisation, etc.

---

[14] Costa; Mata, Justino, 2016. Bivens, 2011. Gorton, 2010.

Coupled with the privatisation programme during the 1990s, Portugal executed the miracle of being able to call the attention of some other European Exchanges in less than two decades, a fact that led to the merger of Portugal's two domestic markets into a centralised national market that would go on to join the innovative Euronext Group in February 2002. In fact, institutional convergence assured that in a few years it was possible to overcome most of the fears regarding small size, and establish a "normalised" capital market fully open to foreign investors and mature enough to accommodate the ambitious aims on capital-free circulation in a global perspective. This is a good example that even though legal origins and framework affect finance, politics and globalisation dictate the tools to build markets and advance economically.

3. The Consolidation Movement in Portugal. The Euronext Singular Case

Although the Portuguese legal framework allowed the extension of the services of the two traditional Exchanges — Lisbon and Porto — to other domestic towns via the so called "Regional Trading Centres" delegated from one of them, in fact the country always concentrated transaction on securities in only those two organised markets[15], mainly Lisbon. The explanation may be found in the over-size of the Lisbon conurbation in relation to the whole country and the concentration in Porto of most of the financial activity of the northern region. Also, Portugal never developed regional

---

[15] This does not exclude the fact that, at least in the euphoric periods of the early 1970s and in 1987, spontaneous and illegal markets appeared in some cafés around the Lisbon Exchange in order to bypass some trading costs and to explore some price misalignments between the official market and these "private" initiatives.

towns large enough to accommodate viable local banks and other intermediaries.

The first step to integrate the two domestic Exchanges occurred with the introduction, in 1991, of a common automated system for Trading and Post-trading: a single computer system was selected and installed — TRADIS — connecting the two regional markets and a new company *"Interbolsa"* (physically headquartered in Porto) was formed precisely to be responsible for all of the operative side of those post-trading functions (see p. 226).

Only in the beginning of 2000 did the two Portuguese Exchanges merge into a single legal entity then named BVLP — *Bolsa de Valores de Lisboa e Porto*[16]. It happened that almost at the same time (March 2000), the EURONEXT project was launched in Paris, Brussels, and Amsterdam. The Portuguese single Exchange joined only two years later, on 1 February 2002 after negotiations that led to a memorandum of understanding signed on 13 June 2001 and the agreement on the financial conditions for the subsequent merger. Mind that later on Portugal renamed its Exchange as Euronext Lisbon in a manner similar to the other three partners.

In April 2007 this pure European Euronext Group merged with the NYSE Group — New York Stock Exchange and the Archipelago Group — to form the transatlantic NYSE Euronext Group. At this point it may be worth remarking that Portugal was the last European country to enter this multinational group, a fact that deserves some reflection from all sides[17].

---

[16] The new firm *"BVLP — Sociedade Gestora de Mercados Regulamentados, S. A."* was formed through a public contract signed on 10 February 2000 that transformed the existing *"Associação da Bolsa de Valores de Lisboa"* and *"Associação da Bolsa de Derivados do Porto"* into a private corporation with a capital of €6.0 million (see daily bulletin 17217 dated from 28/Feb/2000). The first day of the new BVLP firm was 1 March 2000.

[17] Note that the Euronext Group also acquired LIFFE — London International Financial Futures and Options Exchange in 2002, but this did not add a fifth Stock Exchange (in UK) but rather expanded the scope of activities of the group into the

4. Increased Integration of Portugal in the World Market

The 1889 Commercial Code — Article 351 — and especially the subsequent 1901 *"Regulation of the operation of Stock Exchanges"* determined that foreign securities — shares and debt instruments — could be listed in Portugal contingent upon government approval[18], which later allowed some Brazilian T-Bonds to be admitted to Lisbon. Besides that, some resident companies that were listed on the Lisbon Exchange until 1974 were also listed on Paris Bourse and (mainly) on Brussels. Finally, London always played an important role in the external economic and financial relations of Portugal with significant flows of funds between the two countries.

However, the succession of political and economic crises in Portugal during the entire nineteenth century implied some spill over of financial problems and impacts to the following century, restricting the external flows to those connected with the commercial trade and with financing of the growing public deficit. The two world wars also contributed to that isolationism of the country, which only began to subside with the Marshall Plan after WWII and mainly from 1960 on, following the participation in EFTA.

But the true opening of the Portuguese financial borders occurred only after 1986 with the accession of the country to the then EEC — European Economic Community. Combining this with the fact that the true modernisation began only with the 1st Securities Code in 1991 (including the important introduction of computers and telecommunications in the Exchanges and banks), can explain

---

derivatives segment which, until then, had only a minor expression in its turnover and was due mainly to the Paris and Amsterdam financial centres. Caves, 2007. Duning and Lunden, 2008.

[18] See Article 24 of the *"Regulamento do Serviço e Operações das Bolsas de Fundos Públicos e Particulares e Outros Papéis de Crédito"*, published with the Decree of 10 October 1901.

that comparisons with external Stock Exchanges tend to begin only after this later date.

We now turn to the main results found by Vilanculos[19], who analysed eight international equity foreign indices in comparison with the Portuguese PSI-20 index throughout the period from 19 April 1993 to 31 March 2009. She used daily closing prices of the main indices from the Stock Exchanges in Madrid (the IBEX-35), Paris (the CAC-40), Brussels (BEL-20), Amsterdam (AEX-25), London (FTSE-100), Frankfurt (DAX-30), Tokyo (NIKKEI-225), and New York (S&P-500).

Correlation of First Differences of the Daily Log values of the Equity Indices
Daily Closing from 19 April 1993 to 31 March 2009

	ΔLOG AEX	ΔLOG BEL	ΔLOG CAC-40	ΔLOG DAX-30	ΔLOG FTSE-100	ΔLOG IBEX-35	ΔLOG NIKKEI-225	ΔLOG PSI-20	ΔLOG S&P-500
ΔLOG AEX	1.000								
ΔLOG BEL-20	0.788	1.000							
ΔLOG CAC-40	0.876	0.742	1.000						
ΔLOG DAX-30	0.813	0.691	0.820	1.000					
ΔLOG FTSE-100	0.842	0.731	0.844	0.754	1.000				
ΔLOG IBEX-35	0.799	0.675	0.829	0.758	0.773	1.000			
ΔLOG NIKKEI-225	0.318	0.329	0.310	0.277	0.31	0.295	1.000		
ΔLOG PSI-20	0.593	0.55	0.605	0.557	0.585	0.624	0.294	1.000	
ΔLOG S&P-500	0.468	0.431	0.471	0.506	0.462	0.429	0.101	0.285	1.000

Table 1 — Linear correlations between eight international equity indices and PSI-20 for the whole period

During that period all nine indices showed a positive trend, with some level of positive linear correlation of their daily log-returns[20]. The Portuguese market was most sensitive to Madrid and much less to Tokyo and New York although this latter finding may derive from the large time differences between the two markets. Paris and Amsterdam follows Madrid in close steps.

---

[19] Vilanculos, 2011.

[20] First differences of the natural logs of daily closing prices.

This degree of internationalisation improves if the period is restricted to a more recent interval: 2 January 2003 to 31 March 2009. Dividing the whole sample at the end of 2002 reflects the participation of the Portuguese Stock Exchange in the Euronext Group of Exchanges from February 2002 on, as that implied sharing a common trading platform and, more importantly, the operation in Lisbon of most of the large members of the other three Exchange partners.

Correlation of First Differences of the Daily Log values of the Equity Indices
Daily Closing from 2 January 2003 to 31 March 2009

	ΔLOG AEX	ΔLOG BEL	ΔLOG CAC-40	ΔLOG DAX-30	ΔLOG FTSE-100	ΔLOG IBEX-35	ΔLOG NIKKEI-225	ΔLOG PSI-20	ΔLOG S&P-500
ΔLOG AEX	1.000								
ΔLOG BEL-20	0.860	1.000							
ΔLOG CAC-40	0.938	0.870	1.000						
ΔLOG DAX-30	0.855	0.780	0.885	1.000					
ΔLOG FTSE-100	0.894	0.841	0.913	0.818	1.000				
ΔLOG IBEX-35	0.863	0.816	0.908	0.823	0.866	1.000			
ΔLOG NIKKEI-225	0.364	0.411	0.391	0.349	0.386	0.384	1.000		
ΔLOG PSI-20	0.658	0.667	0.683	0.590	0.694	0.697	0.408	1.000	
ΔLOG S&P-500	0.517	0.491	0.510	0.565	0.499	0.495	0.111	0.316	1.000

Table 2 — Linear correlations between eight international equity indices and PSI-20 (second interval)

Using a linear regression model to explain the daily log-returns of the Portuguese index by the corresponding returns of the other eight indices throughout the whole sample[21], again Madrid drags most the Portuguese market (1% change in Madrid tends to "force" a 0.24% change of the PSI), followed by Brussels and London in almost equal terms, but much below Madrid. Interestingly, this degree of explanation improves for the more recent time interval — the adjusted R^2 jumps from 0.451 to 0.548 — with Madrid having a slightly larger influence (0.27% instead of 0.24%), but with London (0.26%) almost equalling Madrid.

---

[21] Mind that the adjusted R^2 is 0.451 including in the regression a one-day lagged return of PSI-20 as explanatory variable. Page 18 of Vilanculos' Master Thesis.

"*With the purpose of assessing if stock indexes of the countries in study have similar trends through time, the co-integration test was performed*". The conclusions are that the indices are co-integrated with 95% significance level, and (again) that co-integration becomes stronger in most recent times[22].

---

[22] Vilanculos, 2011: 15 and 16.

CHAPTER 7

THE LISBON EXCHANGE AS AN INTERNATIONAL REFERENCE CASE

Introduction

Of course, organised markets can only work smoothly under a known set of rules defined and imposed by a government or self--imposed by the markets themselves. But the natural development of capital markets led those ruling authorities to write ever expanding and increasingly complex laws and regulations in order to discipline the new financial activities being invented — e.g., new instruments like the multiple derivatives now common — and to clarify special details of market operations.

However, today any such market has to operate under many layers of legislation issued by multiple rule makers:

a) **Governments**: in many countries these markets and their domestic Stock Exchanges are now governed by an overall framework that results from a long process of increasing specialisation that mirrors the many layers of an onion; in the beginning, Portugal only had a Civil Code that included the general principles of contracting between individuals; next, a Commercial Code was found necessary and written to better cover all commercial activities, although keeping the rules governing these markets simple; then, part of this last Code was isolated to form a Commercial Companies Code; and finally, further developments in the financial activities of those societies led to an autonomous Securities Code, which is now the "top" layer of rules governing Capital Markets and Exchanges;

b) **Supervisors**: due to the ever increasing technicalities of financial instruments and their markets, governments seem to prefer to transfer the regulation of its own laws to a specialised and autonomous entity, responsible also for the daily supervision of these financial markets; but in many countries (and Portugal) there is more than one financial Supervisor, forcing all participants in such market to report to more than one regulator;[1]

c) **Exchanges**: practical rules of operation are normally defined by the respective Exchanges; but the rapid pace of their evolution in Portugal added a trace of instability to those domestic rules;

d) **Accounting**: demands of corporate transparency, the newly introduction of an option for marking-to-market both assets and liabilities of firms, and the internationalisation of markets forced a number of recurrent updates in sophisticating accounting rules in many jurisdictions;

e) in Europe markets are also subject to the rules emanating from the European Union legislating bodies — the **Commission** and the **Parliament**; Portugal joined the European integrating process in 1986;

---

[1] The case of the super abundant US market with many supervisors is probably the paradigmatic situation, but even the previous UK model with only the FAS — Financial Services Authority — did not eliminate the frequent multiple scrutiny conducted by this institution upon most financial intermediaries and issuers. Rotheroe, 2005.

f) finally, investors are subject to **taxation** from different governments, adding a crucial (and often unstable) layer of rules that cannot be neglected; and companies that dare to issue across borders have to deal with multiple tax systems and potentially with some double taxation.

Of course this legal panorama further complicates life when an issuer or an investor considers moving beyond the national domestic borders.

Small and Medium Enterprises (SME) and retail investors are particularly vulnerable to these legal and regulatory increasing demands, but any intention to bring them back to these markets cannot be based only on a simple elimination of some of these layers of rules and/or their stabilisation; nor on introducing standardisation across different geographies, accompanied by some simplification of the whole framework via elimination of duplications and simpler rule writing. To create an environment proper to SMEs the solution may likely be found in a better segmentation of both the issuers and the investors in order to apply very simple rules to less risky situations, while restricting the full burden of the heavy legislation to large companies and to professional investors.

1. The Commercial Companies Code (1986)

For most of the twentieth century, the Portuguese Capital Market was regulated by the 1889 Commercial Code with only minor improvements introduced here and there, during more than 80 years, until 1974 (see Chapter 5.17). Finally the explosion of the share market in 1972 and 1973 revealed a number of limitations and constraints of this legal framework and led to the publication of an interim Securities Code in 1974 to quickly bring a minimum updating to the Portuguese legislation covering the issuing of securities by local corporations and their trading.

Unfortunately, this improvement was enacted only about 15 days before the 1974 military coup that led to the "suspension" of the operations in the two Portuguese Exchanges and to the nationalisation of many segments of the local economy.

Even when the domestic politics brought back a minimum set of conditions for reinstating the local capital market (around 1976), the main concern of the government was simply to have the market working again, not to continue the modernisation of the legal framework.

As the 1889 Commercial Code covered a wide range of areas of legislation, inevitably some of them were treated in a rather simplified and generic way, soon requiring further development to update the code's contents and enter into many more details. This was the case of the part dedicated to commercial societies. It was felt that it would be better to develop an autonomous code of Commercial Companies than to update and expand that part of the Commercial Code. As a result in 1986 the government published the so called *"Código das Sociedades Comerciais"* by Decree-Law 262/86, of 2 September 1986.

Another reason for this Code was the decision of Portugal to join the then European Common Market[2]. In 10 June 1985 Portugal signed the accession treaty and became a full member on 1 January 1986. Europe had meanwhile produced a number of Directives covering this corporate sector that were to be included in this Code.

> By regrouping dispersed and ancient legislation, this (corporate) Code aims to provide a global and systematic regulation on

---

[2] Portugal submitted its request to join the European Communities on 28 March 1977. Azevedo et all., 1996.

commercial companies: divided into eight chapters, it contains a set of legal provisions which are applicable to all types of companies (Part I, arts. 1 to 175), a regulation for each one of these different types (Part II to Part V) — with a particular emphasis on stock corporations (Part IV, Arts. 271 to 464) — and a specific regulation concerning affiliate companies (Part VI, Arts. 481 to 508-E). Although adopting a few original solutions from a comparative law perspective, it has been profoundly inspired by some foreign legal orders (mainly, the German and French company laws) and takes into account a good deal of the Community Directives on company law (including some among them which have not been finally approved, as the proposal for a 9th Directive on Groups of Companies)[3].

Although this Code regulates a number of items related to the issuing of securities by corporations and the information that they are required to disclose to the general market, the perspective here is the firm and not the securities market.

2. The 1988 Legal Package

As the local market reacted very positively to all measures and incentives offered by the government since 1977, soon the country returned to the point where it had been when the 1974 revolution closed the two Exchanges and nationalised many listed companies. Therefore, while waiting for a new and comprehensive Securities Code to be studied and produced, the government decided to enact interim pieces of legislation to improve the working conditions of the market and the Exchanges.

---

[3] See Antunes, 2009.

First, the government introduced slight changes in the 1974 Interim Code on 12 December 1975 (Decree-Law 696/75) when it decided to reopen the Lisbon Exchange only for Bond trading. Then the first independent supervisor of the market was created — *"Auditor-Geral do Mercado de Títulos"* — by Decree-Law 335/87 of 15 October 1987. The Decree-Law 210-A of 27 May 1987, later replaced by Decree-Law 59/88 of 27 February 1988, created a compensation system for the operations in requiring the deposit of the involved assets in financial institutions, to treat them as fungible assets.

In July of 1988, the government issued an extended collection of diplomas[4] — eight Decree-Laws plus six *"Portarias"* — of which it is worth mentioning the following four:

- Decree-Law nr. 229-C/88: defines the regime governing all types of Investment Funds — open-end, closed-end, securities, and real estate;
- Decree-Law nr. 229-D/88: creates the dematerialised form of shares.

According to *Manuel Ricciardi*, de-materialisation was a very important practical aspect. He remembered an episode of his professional experience, when a transaction of paper stocks in a large-capital amount required a truck (*"camioneta"*) to move them to their new owners. As he was responsible for this operation, "if the paper stocks would disappear for any reason, I would be in a serious financial situation. I called home to say I would sleep in the office".[5]

---

[4] Decree-Laws of 4 July 1988: nrs. 229-A, 229-B, 229-C, 229-D, 229-E, 229-F, 229-G, 229-I, and *"Portarias"* nrs. 422-A, 422-B, 422-C, 422-D. Plus two additional *"Portarias"* of 22 July 1988: nr. 480 and nr.481,

[5] Interview kindly concedet to us at his son's brokerage office, at Rua do Comércio. We evoke here the memory of his great contributions to the Lisbon Stook Exchange.

- Decree-Law nr. 229-I/88: regulates the constitution and operation of Dealer and Broker societies, forcing former individual brokers to transform their offices into corporations
- *"Portaria"* nr. 422-A/88: regulates public offers of securities — Takeover Bids and Public Offers for Sale.

3. The Revolution brought on by the 1991 "Código Sapateiro" (1st Securities Code)

After so many years of quasi-immobilism, in 1987 the government and the market were in a favourable condition to order a new and comprehensive Securities Code[6] that would, on one hand, expand the 1986 Commercial Companies Code into the markets' operative rules and, on the other hand, segregate another part of the very old Commercial Code into a new autonomous Code. The pressure for this new legislation was also magnified by the 19 October 1987 crash of the Portuguese Exchanges, a crisis that in Portugal had its own roots, especially the new limitations found with the recent explosion of share quotations observed during the months preceding that date.

> "The events between 1974 and 1989 were very serious and when *Dr. Miguel Cadilhe* was Finance Minister he asked me to produce a new securities Code. After the 1986-87 crash he called me and asked to write, in the context of a specific commission, a new law that would refound the Exchange ... . We (myself,

---

[6] With nr. 5 of article 2 of the Decree-Law nr. 335/87 of 15 October 1987, the Finance Minister Miguel Cadilhe determined the constitution of a Specialised Section within the *"Conselho Nacional das Bolsas de Valores"* to submit a project to review the old Decree-Law nr. 8/74 (the Interim Code). That section was headed by *Dr. José Luís Sapateiro*, the main author of the previous Interim Code.

Eduardo Catroga and *Morais Leitão*) were promoted to enlighte-
ned individuals. I thought that it would not make sense to revisit
the 1974 Code. Our Exchanges still operated manually and came
from the nineteenth century and some trades were only settled
after seven months. In the new Code I defined 3-day settlements.
I went home and remained indoors for one year writing the Code.
Each chapter was sent to the commission to get feedback. I sought essentially to close all loopholes that could later be used to
jeopardise the operations of the Exchanges. I got a lot of pleasure
to write the Code. I told *Minister Cadilbe* that I would collaborate
for free and I did not receive a single penny. I received some
help for that part relative to the disclosure of information from
the Exchanges. I was awarded a *"Comenda da Ordem Militar de
Cristo"* by the President of the Republic, *Mário Soares*, on the
recommendation of the Prime Minister *Cavaco Silva"*.[7]

The new philosophy for the capital market permeating this
new Code includes the principle of *"full disclosure consecrated in
the American rule since 1933, (...) autonomy, de-statisation, de-
-governmentalisation, liberalisation (...) professionalisation, de-
-bureaucra-tisation, and dynamisation"*[8].

This law transferred ownership and management of the Lisbon
and Porto Stock Exchanges to two not-for-profit private Civil
Associations[9]. Stock Exchanges returned to their original private
character, but now with the government keeping some say in their

---

[7] Interview kindly concedet to us on 3 November 2009, at Mota Engil, Linda-
a-Velha, Carnaxide.

[8] Preamble of the Decree of April 10, 1991.

[9] Forced to leave the state umbrella and enter the private sector by this 1991
Securities Code, the Lisbon Exchange became a Civil Association by decree of 22
January 1992 and the Porto Exchange by decree of 25 March 1992.

strategic running. Ownership of capital[10] was distributed amongst the brokerage firms that were members of each Exchange, but banks, although not allowed to intermediate any transactions, could also share some minority capital on a voluntary basis. Annual profits could not be distributed to those shareholders but rather should be reinvested in the same business[11] and in case of dissolution any accumulated capital would return to the Treasury[12].

This Code allowed all sorts of methods and systems for trading, from the traditional oral call system to the electronic continuous negotiation regime. More important, it forced a partial interconnection between the two Exchanges by creating a nationwide main market in which a company would be admitted to the two Exchanges. Other segments of the market remained regionalised for some more years until the two Stock Exchanges merged at the end of 1999.

Besides the traditional main market and the segment called of "*without quotations*" to admit companies in difficulties, this Code copied the French model of a Second Market aimed at the small and medium companies with a modest capital distributed in the general public.

De-materialisation of securities was revised, abandoning the formerly adopted Brazilian model to follow the French principles of freedom to preserve the investors' accounting of underwritten securities in any financial intermediation institution.

Issuing of securities by companies became totally free as the previous requirement for administrative authorisation was finally scrapped.

---

[10] Actually, the capital of these civil associations was not represented by common shares, but by ownership titles, each associate having only one such title.

[11] See article 248 of this 1991 Securities Code.

[12] See article 250 of this 1991 Securities Code.

Over-the-counter (OTC) Market and Special Markets were identified as de-regulated possibilities in this Code, and the Minister of Finance is identified as the regulatory entity for the second ones in order to maintain a great flexibility to create and design them and their features (e.g., their specific trading fees)[13].

Financial Futures and Financial Options were regulated and a formal market for Futures was inaugurated in the Porto Stock Exchange on 20 June 1996, while Options began trading a little later on 19 March 1999.

Due to the technical capacities installed, a system for automatic borrowing — *"SEA-Sistema de Empréstimo Automático de Valores Mobiliários"* — was adopted supporting a Repo market from 14 April 1997.[14]

Insider trading and market manipulation were defined along with the respective criminal penalties.

Unfortunately, the purpose of covering and regulating so many matters in a single law led to an extra-long diploma organised in:

- 7 Titles: General Dispositions, Primary Market, Secondary Markets, Public Offers, Financial Intermediaries, Crimes and Sanctions, Final Dispositions
- 16 Chapters
- 686 Articles, many of which with so many indents as from a) to z)
- many cross-references from one article to others in an intricate network of relations that makes it very time consuming reading this law.

---

[13] See Decree-Law 186/94 of 5 July 1994.

[14] After an adjustment to Decree-Law 142-A/91 of 10 April 1991 by Decree-Law 196/95 of 29 July 1995.

One important characteristic of this Code is that it replaces the former supervisor *"Auditor-Geral do Mercado de Títulos"* with a new more structured entity called *"Comissão do Mercado de Valores Mobiliários"*, CMVM for short. It is the true Portuguese Securities and Exchange Commission.

With this Code Lisbon attracted many investors to Portugal's shares, especially the first large scale inflow from non-residents. The Lisbon market then returned to greater number of transactions, but was again negatively influenced by the 1993 crisis.

4. European Directives and the Second Securities Code

The fact that Portugal entered the European Community in 1986 had two important consequences:

- the European legislation — Directives and Regulations — sooner or later had be applicable in the domestic economy;
- the progressive lowering of the legal borders to other member countries and the increasing participation of Europe in the globalisation movement meant that Portugal was increasingly open to the outside world.

The consequence for the Portuguese Exchanges of these developments in Europe was an increasing role of non-resident investors in our Exchange markets, with all indicators expanding significantly and steadily. This market expansion — more issuers, more capital, more instruments — together with the accelerated production of European legislation aimed at this market soon recommended a thorough review of the whole domestic legal framework put in place from the enactment of the 1991 first Securities Code — nicknamed *"Código Sapateiro"*.

In 1999 a second version of the Portuguese Securities Code was thus enacted by Decree-Law nr. 486/99 of 13 November 1999, with five main objectives in mind: codification, simplification, modernisation, internationalisation and increasing the flexibility of its provisions. Additionally, this Code was slimmed down to a little more than half the previous number of articles via a number of measures:

- the parts regulating the *"Conselho Nacional do Mercado de Valores Mobiliários"* (an advisory body of the Minister of Finance for the capital market), the supervisor (CMVM), the entities managing the Exchanges and/or other markets, and the Central Securities Depositories were all treated as separated pieces of legislation;
- *"the drafting technique used: cross-references were minimised to those that were strictly necessary, and the language used is as simple and clear as possible given the complexity of the material; double cross-references were eliminated, as were constant caveats and commentaries that exceed the text's instructive content"*;
- *"the establishment of general principles and rules was prioritised, and frequent use was made of generic concepts and general clauses; insofar as was reasonable, the details of the law were left to regulations of a different kind, in accordance with deregulation criteria that allow ample space for, on the one hand, administrative regulations, particularly those of the CMVM and, on the other hand, a moderate level of self-regulation by other entities that participate in the market"*;
- *"in response to internationalisation and the integration of securities markets, more attention has been devoted to defining the scope of the Code's applicability and deter-mining what laws apply in multi-jurisdictional situations; in parti-cular, "rules were introduced to make possible, and even to*

encourage, the trading of securities regulated under foreign laws in markets located in Portugal";

- *"a distinction is made between institutional investors and non-institutional investors: any other entity that does not benefit from the protections granted to non-institutional investors is considered to be an institutional investor"*;

- *"the structure of the markets is now based on the distinction between regulated markets, which are modelled on stock exchanges, and other organised markets, which can have greatly varying characteristics ... the non-regulated markets are not subject to any authorisation, and their operation is subject only to legal compliance monitoring by the supervisory authorities".*[15]

The Code also transposes the different EEC Directives related to securities matters:

- Directive 79/279/EEC of 5 March, 80/390/CEE of 17 March (1), 82/148/EEC of 3 March, 87/345/EEC of 22 June, 90/211/EEC of 23 April, and 94/18/EC, of 30 March, all of which relate to coordinating the conditions under which securities can be officially listed on a Stock Exchange;

- Directive 82/121/EEC of 15 February, related to information to be published by companies the shares of which have been admitted to official Stock Exchange listing;

- Directive 86/627/EEC of 12 December, related to information that must be published upon the purchase or sale of a significant share in a listed company;

---

[15] All text in italic is copied from the preamble of Decree-Law nr. 486/99 of 13 November available in English in the site of CMVM.

- Directive 89/298/EEC of 17 April, related to the require-ments for the drawing-up, scrutiny and distribution of the prospectus to be published when transferable securities are offered to the public;
- Directive 89/592/EEC of 13 November, related to coordina-ting regulations on insider dealing;
- Directive 93/22/EC, of 10 May, related to investment servi-ces in the securities field, specifically the part that was not transcribed into the General Regime of Credit Institutions and Financial Institutions in Decree-Law nr. 232/96 of 5 December;
- Directive 95/26/EC, of the European Parliament and Council, of 29 June, related to the reinforcement of prudential super-vision, which came to be known as the post-BCCI directive;
- Directive 98/26/EC, of the Parliament and Council, of 19 May, related to the settlement finality in payment and secu-rities settlement systems, transcribing only the portion that applies to securities settlement systems.

This second Securities Code together with Decree-Law nr. 394/99 of 13 October was instrumental to support, the two next steps taken in Portugal in terms of the architecture of the institutions of this market:

- First, and following the same trend seen in recent decades in many European countries where the different regional Exchanges merged into a single nationwide central market, on 20 December 1999 a meeting of the two general assem-blies of the two domestic Exchanges[16] decided to merge

---

[16] The two Portuguese Exchanges were the Lisbon Stock Exchange and the Porto Derivatives Exchange. Indeed, in June 1994 an agreement had been struck

them into a single entity[17] called BVLP — *Bolsa de Valores de Lisboa e Porto*. This was formally constituted by public contract signed on 10 February 2000, transforming the two existing Civil Associations into a single completely private corporation organised as a for-profit entity.

- Second, and responding to the leap forward given in 2000 by Paris, Brussels, and Amsterdam, which put their three Exchanges under a common holding company called Euronext, Portugal entered into this same group in February 2002.

5. Creation of CMVM

Until the 1974 Interim Code the Exchanges with their private character simply provided trading facilities to the market. Supervision was in the hands of the government, which had created in 1949 a specialised department in the Ministry of Finance called *"Inspecção- -Geral de Banca e Seguros"*[18]. During the political regime that lasted from 1926 to 1974, the philosophy was more than supervising as it called for authorising everything, from a securities issue by a corporation to listing on an Exchange.

---

between them to avoid fragmentation of the Portuguese market by the two poles, by concentrating in Lisbon all cash operations in Portugal in return of Porto receiving the responsibility of launching a Derivatives Exchange that would monopolise the centralised derivative market in the country. The last day of cash operations at the Porto Exchange was 22 June 1994.

[17] Evans, 2004: 236. As literature on platform pricing has demonstrated, if various platforms are competing to establish their services in mature markets or product markets that are particularly vulnerable to price competition and commoditisation, services can provide an important source of revenues and profits on subsidising the product, to obtain the desired effect on adoption and customisation in the market. Subsidising is a pricing strategy to be avoided, but as usually buyers paid in advance, the subsidising strategy was very easy. Consumano, 2008.

[18] General Inspector of Credit and Insurance.

That Interim Code gave some supervision duties to the Exchanges as both had been nationalised and were simply a department of the Ministry of Finance.

The first step to give independence to a supervisory body was an initiative of the Minister *Miguel Cadilhe*, who created the *"Auditor--Geral do Mercado de Títulos"* by the Decree-Law nr. 335/87 of 25 October 1987. But this was clearly a transitory step, as the 1991 Securities Code dedicates all of Chapter 3 of Title 1 to the enactment of the brand new *"Comissão do Mercado de Valores Mobiliários"* as a public institute benefitting from administrative and financial autonomy, and charged with powers of supervision and control of the market and its players, and also of producing regulations for that market. It is managed by a Directive Board appointed by the Council of Ministers for 5-year terms.

Mind that the tendency in Portugal is to adapt a model of organisation for the layer of supervision and regulation in which each market segment has its own supervisor: banks are supervised by the Central Bank (*"Banco de Portugal"*), insurance companies by a distinct *"Instituto de Seguros de Portugal"*, and the Capital Market by this CMVM body. The integrated version experienced in the UK some years ago or, on the opposite side, the highly dispersed American model, were not considered appropriate for a market as small as the Portuguese one.

6. Status of the Portuguese Exchanges

During the entire twentieth century Portugal experienced a whole series of statutes attributed to the two Stock Exchanges operating in the country. From the 1888 Commercial Code and the subsequent Regulations, Exchanges in Portugal were a kind of clubs of their individual brokers that were controlled either by the local (same town) Chamber of Commerce, if it existed, or otherwise by the Local Commercial Association. It was up to these entities to appoint the Managing Board to run the Exchange. But the law also mentions the Chamber of Brokers to which a number of duties were assigned, in particular to decide upon the applications received for the listing of any securities.

This private character is however somewhat mitigated by a number of budget constraints detailed in the 1901 *"Regulation of the Operation of Exchanges"*:

- it indicates a maximum value for the annual budget
- it lists the different sources of income of an Exchange, and requires all proceeds to be deposited with the Ministry of Finance
- it indicates that any potential surplus after costs could be used by the Government for purposes not connected to the Exchange.

The first jump into modernisation was the Decree-Law 8/74 which nationalised the two Exchanges with the government appointing the Presidents of the two Directive Boards[19] and making these organisations simple departments of the Ministry of Finance. Even the legacy staff members of the two existing Exchanges were turned into civil servants of that Ministry.

This model remained until 1992 when, according to the very first Securities Code published in 1991, both organisations were semi--privatised through their transformation into two not-for-profit Civil

---

[19] Article 10 indicates the composition of the Directive Commission in which one or two other members were also appointed by the Minister of Finance in order to represent the local credit institutions. The Brokers Chamber also designated its leader as their representative on the Commission and all listed non-financial companies indicated the last member.

Associations[20]. No dividends could be paid to anyone but reinvested in the Exchange. The Members of each Association were the local financial intermediaries.

An interesting characteristic of this model was its two-tier membership: individual brokers (physical persons) and brokerage houses had to be full members of the Exchanges — although each one had to apply for membership to each Exchange (Lisbon and Porto); as for banks they were so-called "*non-members*" as they had no trading rights in the Exchanges, and together could only have minority voting power in the General Assemblies of each Association. As non--members, banks had to convey all orders to the market received from their clients through brokers. This was intended to maintain trading capacity in the hands of the brokers along with a controlling power over Exchanges.

This model of semi-private character of the Associations was challenged almost immediately due to the example coming from the sale, in 1986, of the Stockholm Stock Exchange to a local IT corporation ("*OM Company*"). The concept of Exchanges being run by truly private limited liability corporations began then spreading throughout Europe with the added argument that such a corporation could accept any type of shareholder and therefore could gain the interest of commercial banks in the securities business and so benefit from their inherent widely distributed branch networks. In Portugal this corporate transformation and the consolidation of the two Exchanges were executed simultaneously when the Lisbon and Porto Exchanges were merged into a single and truly private corporation called BVLP - Lisbon and Porto Stock Exchange in the

---

[20] Following authorisation stated in "*Portaria*" nr. 407/91 (12 December 1991), the Association of the Lisbon Stock Exchange was formally constituted on 10 January 1992, but it only started operating the Lisbon Stock Exchange on 26 March 1992 after the "*Portaria*" 81/92 (25 March 1992) transferred the Exchange to its property. Similarly the Association of the Porto Stock Exchange was formalised on 22 January 1992 and started operating the Exchange on the same 26 March 1992.

beginning of 2000. At the same time, the former members (brokers) and non-members (banks) of both Exchanges received a percentage of the share capital of the new firm according to the quotas they owned in the Civil Association they came from[21].

This corporate statute made it much easier to subsequently sell the shares of this new firm to the Euronext Group, in February 2002. It is interesting to note that this European group had begun with three Stock Exchanges in 2000.

7. A new legal approach

Due to steps already executed in the globalisation process and the multi-layer legal framework regulating financial markets, it may pay to consider a completely different legal philosophy to discipline the various players involved:

- instead of designing rules that are suspicious of every and all stakeholders in this market — and which are therefore designed in a very extended fashion in order to anticipate all possible wrongdoings;
- accept that market players always tend to be ahead of the legislators, and so put the emphasis on the sanctioning mechanisms in the hands of the market authorities;
- and allow the supervisors to operate under a discretionary principle where they sanction wrongdoers after an informed judgment instead of following a mechanical application of the written law.

---

[21] Most intermediaries were members or non-members of the two Exchanges at the same time, and therefore received a quota in the total share capital proportional to the sum of their previous individual interests.

Most players follow ethical rules, but for those wrongdoers — there will always exist some of them in any place — any minor fault needs to be so heavily penalised that the resulting losses to the "*sinner*" will far outweigh the potential benefits derived from such attitudes, and the market does not accumulate substantial negative consequences.

Finally, attention should be paid to the stability of all this set of rules including the tax system. All interested parties are more averse to the legal and tax risks stemming from the frequent changes in the laws and regulations than to the contents of a stable law, even if heavily penalising.

8. Trading Systems

Historically, trading in the two Portuguese Exchanges has always been done orally with the physical presence of the member brokers (or their lieutenants[22]) on the respective trading floor. During the established trading hours, any security could be traded at any time that an order was brought to that market — continuous trading. However, trading occurred first on derivatives, and only in a second time slot was trading executed on cash instruments (shares, bonds, etc.).

The explosion of the secondary cash market in 1972 and 1973, revealed a number of problems of this trading system, and in response the Decree-Law 8/74 introduced trading by auction in which each security was called only once per day. During a few minutes all orders targeted to that specific security should be exposed by the brokers in order to search for a single equilibrium price that

---

[22] Called "*proposto*" in the Portuguese legislation.

could match most of the announced buy orders with most of the unveiled sell orders.

This roll-call system remained in use until February 1991 when some equity issues, due to their larger liquidity, were selected to be traded with two calls per day, roughly one in the morning and a second in the afternoon[23]. Bonds and other securities followed the same rule from 1 April 1991 on.[24]

Automation began to be introduced in September 1991 with an electronic platform borrowed from the Rio de Janeiro Stock Exchange (nicknamed in Portugal as *"Tradis"*) with the particularity that it interconnected the Lisbon and the Porto Exchanges (see p. 225). Although a security could be listed in only one of those Exchanges, only one central computer managed all orders introduced by members of each Exchange.

Another characteristic of this computer system was that it included a module responsible for operating a Central Securities Depository (CSD) and its Settlement System. That is, this electronic platform interconnected Markets — that is trading — Custody and Settlement.

However, this Brazilian system diverged significantly from the various standard platforms being developed and implemented at the time in many markets abroad[25], and that singularity introduced a number of difficulties to internationalise the Portuguese domestic

---

[23] See the *"Circular"* nr. 1/91 of the Lisbon Stock Exchange published with the Daily Bulletin nr.14981 of 15 February 1992 which created this second round of trading for shares and established the selection criterion. Also see in the Daily Bulletin of 22 February 1991 the list of the first 20 share issues selected for the second quotation.

[24] See *"Circular"* nr. 3/91 of the Lisbon Stock Exchange published with the Daily Bulletin nr.15007 of 25 March 1992 which extended this second round of trading to bonds and other securities and established the selection criterion. Also see in the Daily Bulletin of 27 March 1991 the list of the first 20 issues of bonds and other securities selected for the second quotation.

[25] One of them (*CATS — Computed Assisted Trading System*) being adopted at the time in many markets around the world had been developed in the middle

market. International players were not accustomed to our computer screens neither to our operating mechanisms, which discouraged them from engaging Portuguese securities and companies.

As a result, in 1996 a new trading platform was purchased from the Paris Stock Exchange — baptised in Portugal as the *List* system — to substitute (only) the trading module of the existing electronic infrastructure. But the Portuguese CSD continued to use that specialised module of the previous *Tradis* which was slightly adapted to be able to connect to the newly purchased trading system (see p. 225 and 297).

The September 1991 automation also allowed reintroducing continuous trading in Portugal (from 16 September on). Beginning with share issues only, bonds were introduced at a later stage. And to smooth that transition only three share issues were involved throughout the first days. The less liquid securities remained in the roll--call system (but now electronic), with one or two auctions executed per day, depending on their liquidity.

When Portugal joined the Euronext Group, the similarity of both trading engines made it very simple to scrap the domestic computer and connect the local terminals to the machine installed in the outskirts of Paris. But again the Portuguese CSD continued using its own electronic platform until today.

Currently the whole list of admitted securities is divided into a number of so-called trading groups, each with a specific trading procedure, either continuous or with one or two calls per day.

of the 1970s (and used from November 1977 on) by the Toronto Stock Exchange. Clever, 2005.

9. Achieving Scale

The economics of multi-sided platform markets (such as Exchanges) brings to light a novel understanding of some stock-market features. The word "platform" became commonly used in management in the late 1980s and applied in the 1990s to product development, and then extended to market equilibrium economics in the first decade of the millennium. [26] *"Platforms are businesses that sell products and need customers of type A to get customers of type B and vice versa. To get both sides on board, businesses operate a 'platform' that connects or coordinates multiple customers".*[27]

The legal framework of the Lisbon Stock Exchange in the historical background of trade opportunities for the financial operations in a global perspective illustrates how the economics of platform competition has implications for antitrust and regulatory policies in multi-sided markets.

Exchanges as platform markets illustrate the high relevance of network effects. A platform's value is an increasing function of the number of users and uses. Network effects imply switching costs, which, compounded by learning costs, imply that users may be subject to lock-in effects once the platform has achieved scale.[28] As long as users anticipate lock-in effects, user investments require the platform to achieve scale.

The interconnection of the four Exchanges that are members of Euronext is an ideal opportunity to check whether the benefits of a common platform are still present in each individual legacy Exchange.

---

[26] Cusumano; Suarez, 2008.

[27] Evans, 2003: 237-238.

[28] Barnett, 2011.

In spite of the crucial importance of having a rational figure for the domestic average Cost of Capital on which to base the estimates of the discount rate to be used in a number of long-term investments, Portugal has not dedicated enough time to produce such a figure, and that is the purpose of this chapter. It is a first approach which still leaves ample space for further improvements and additional estimates. Part of the answer to this reality might be attached to the number of profound impacts that have affected and disturbed its Capital Markets during the twentieth century, especially the break introduced by the Carnation Revolution in 1974.

1. Economic Importance of a Good Estimate for the Cost of Capital

There are several important economic areas today in which a country needs to know its domestic average Cost of Capital, the search for which has triggered a number of other studies in many countries, especially in the UK and the US, due to their cultural environment and their availability of recorded historical data.

Unfortunately, the success of the American economy over the twentieth century in comparison to other national economies may suggest that the American data translate abnormal annual discount rates (too high), which may be misleading other countries if simply extrapolated to them without proper corrections. *"We should be cautious about generalizing from the United States which, over the twentieth century, rapidly emerged as the world's foremost political, military, and economic power. For a more balanced view, we also need to look at investment returns in other countries".*[1]

Therefore, some years ago three professors from the London Business School — Dimson, Marsh, and Staunton (DMS) — published a large study, involving 16 countries (including Spain), that covers the whole twentieth century[2]. This study provided, for the first time, a long-run perspective of the historical Cost of Capital in the world, but it also showed the diverse financial behaviour amongst those sampled countries, as some of them had significantly smaller capital costs in comparison with the historical values for the US or the UK.

Unfortunately, Portugal was not included in that initial study, a limitation that might have led some of our long-term decisions to be taken based on mere extrapolations of the Cost of Capital from countries considered to be similar (e.g., from Spain).

---

[1] Dimson; Marsh; Staunton, 2002: 47. Boldrin, 2009. Costa et al., 2012.

[2] *"The Triumph of the Optimists: 101 Years of Global Investment Returns"*, 2002. This same study became such an important source of information, for both scholars and practitioners, that it has been updated annually ever since — and subsequently expanded to include more countries (now 22) — thanks to a co-operative agreement established between those three authors and initially the Dutch ABN-Amro Bank, but recently altered to Credit Suisse.

The only study that includes Portugal was conducted by Jorion and Goetzmann but it only reports the period from 1931 to 1996, and it suffers from three limitations:

- the authors had to make use of indirect sources of information for Portugal — especially the *"International Financial Statistics"* published by the IMF;
- dividends were not included in the estimates of the equity returns, and this may undervalue that return;
- the risk premium was measured as capital returns in excess of inflation, not above the risk-free rate.

The purpose of the present estimate is precisely to close that gap via an historical analysis identical to the one conducted by DMS. Therefore, this is an investigation into the past of the Portuguese equity market to uncover any potential average return that, if stationary, might be extrapolated into the future. It is not a forecasting exercise such as performed by a number of scholars including, for example, recent works from *Goyal and Welch* (2008) or *Ferreira and Santa-Clara* (2011), in which some past economic/financial variables are used to estimate the near future value of a stock return.

Two reasons dictated our option (non-forecasting). The first is an intention to make simply an historical survey without any special concern for the facts that explain the final numerical result. The second comes from the fact that we are convinced that one of the main characteristics of any efficient market is that any forecasting method accurate enough to deserve the attention of investors is immediately destroyed by the subsequent decisions of those very investors. Therefore, predicting future returns can only produce practical results if non-disclosed. As Ferreira and Santa-Clara wrote *"... to the extent that what we are capturing is excessive predictability rather than risk premiums, the very success of our analysis will eventually destroy its usefulness.*" That is, unless a new and accurate methodology of forecasting is used only by its author — and for a limited period of time — any volatile future is impossible to forecast with certainty. So, only stable values unveiled from the past can be taken into the future but maintaining some risk (a confidence interval).

That is, the fact that this discount rate is not known with certainty in any market does not mean that one cannot make an estimate by observing the history of his own capital markets. With the benefit that, the larger the sample studied, the greater is the probability that it detects something stable in the market.

2. The problem brought about by the Carnation Revolution (1974)

This historical analysis of the Lisbon Stock Exchange covers the very same time window selected by DMS in order to make our results comparable to theirs: our sample starts at the end of 1899 and stretches until the very end of 2013. But this time frame suffers, as in some other countries, from some periods without data simply because the Exchanges were closed for one reason or another.

In the Portuguese case, The Lisbon Stock Exchange maintained its market operating every week, except during two months in 1914, due to the start of WWI in the Summer, and in 1974-1977 due to the Carnation Revolution in April 1974[3].

As a matter of fact, the military coup that ousted the former regime during the night from 24 to 25 April, led the provisional authorities to "*suspend*" the operations in the two domestic Stock Exchanges immediately with the intention of restarting them in a

---

[3] See chapter 3. Costa, Mata, 2009, 2011a.

short while[4]. Unfortunately, that coup soon turned into a leftist revolution, which among other measures, maintained the markets closed for a much longer period. Due to pressures from the Portuguese Treasury, which needed the liquidity brought about by a centralised market to ease the placement of the ever increasing sizes of debt issues, the Lisbon Exchange reopened for Bonds in January 1976, but remained closed for shares and all other types of instruments until 7 March 1977[5].

Therefore, we had to develop a specific methodology to chain the time series extending from 1900 until that revolution, with the new series starting after the market re-opened in 1977[6]. In particular, it was also necessary to include that during that *"suspension period"*, the Exchange market lost value due to the significant number of listed companies that were nationalised plus the fact that all overseas listed firms simply closed their doors.

As for the short period without quotations in 1914, since it is a much shorter period (only two months), there were no companies delisted, and our sampling frequency is only once per week, we simply neglected this interruption. It is as if we had a somewhat longer week than in other normal cases.

---

[4] See chapter 4 Section 10.

[5] Mind that the Porto Stock Exchange was also suspended from April 25, 1974, but remained closed until January 27, 1981.

[6] In fact and due to liquidity constraints of the Portuguese equity market after that restart, the new index series begins only in January 1978. The period without data, therefore goes from April 1974 to December 1977.

3. Literature Review. Historical Risk Premium

Why the CAPM model

There is now a consensus that variability[7] of share returns requires them, on average, to pay somewhat more to an investor than he/she may earn from debt instruments with similar maturity. Such an excess is necessary as a compensation for the uncertainty of the final actual return.

That positive spread above the volatility-free rate depends on the particular issuer under consideration, but for the whole share market of a country there is an average difference that is called the domestic Equity Risk Premium (ERP), or Market Risk Premium (MRP).[8]

There are different models that connect the individual spread of a particular share to:

a) the general mood of the whole market underlying that particular issuer and

b) to other macroeconomic variables of the country, such as the annual GDP growth rate, some factors of the industrial sector involved, etc.

However, any multivariable model requires the computation of a large number of parameters proportional to the number of explanatory variables used by the model. In this respect, the particular case of the Capital Asset Pricing Model (CAPM) is very attractive because it uses only one explanatory variable — the market average

---

[7] Normally termed "*volatility*" in financial literature.

[8] Fernández, 2009, reviews 150 texts on this issue.

return — although this still requires the estimation of the three following parameters:

- the cost of risk-free[9] debt (R_i);
- the particular level of risk of the issuer (β_i)

$$R_i = R_{free} + \beta_i . \left[\overline{R}_{market} - R_{free} \right];$$

- the average risk premium of the surrounding market $\left(\overline{R}_{market} \right)$.

Therefore, the selection of the Capital Asset Pricing Model is a simplification measure justified on the grounds of the level of accuracy that it still permits, and also by the widespread adoption of similar approaches by other scholars.

The Cost of Capital puzzle

All long-term decisions are forward-looking computations that require the use of a discount rate that will be valid for the future, not the Cost of Capital that was in place in the past. However, this single value is not observable in the market and there is as yet no known model that quantifies a guaranteed value for any time-frame ahead. There are many studies that have developed methodologies for predicting the equity premium[10] but their results are not uniform, and even show some considerable inconsistencies.[11]

---

[9] Free of the Volatility Risk of the equity market, but not excluding any potential Credit or Liquidity risks.

[10] Fama and Schwert, 1977, 1981; Rozeff, 1984; Keim and Stambaugh, 1986; Campbell and Schiller, 1988 a, b; Fama and French, 1988, 1989.

[11] Lettau and Ludvigson, 2001, and Schwert, 1998, 2002.

Mehra and Prescott (1985) used an 1889-1978 data base for GDP and Consumption in the US and concluded that Arrow-Debreu asset-pricing models could not explain, at the same time, the high (American) equity risk premium and the small average risk-free return (debt) that was historically observed.

Rietz (1988) respecified that model for a frictionless pure-exchange economy and solved the puzzle in capturing the effects of (potential) market crashes by abandoning the hypothesis that consumption growth rates are symmetric about their mean (and that they fall above their mean as often as they fall below). Reasonable degrees of time-preference and risk aversion were found, provided that plausible severe crashes are not too improbable in the long-term analysis.

Barro and Ursúa (2008) went into full annual data on Consumption for 22 countries (including Portugal) to detect crises, as this is the variable *"that enters into usual asset-price equations"*. To enlarge the sample they also used GDP for 35 countries (maintaining Portugal). For samples that start as early as 1870 (as is the case for Portuguese GDP estimations) a peak-to-trough method was used for each country to isolate economic crises[12]: they identified 87 crises for consumption and 148 for GDP. This led to the conclusion that 3.5 years was the average duration for disasters, having a mean size of the declines of 21% to 22%, under a coincident timing both in Consumption and GDP. The conclusion is that their model accords with *"the observed average equity premium of around 7% levered equity"*, after assuming that 3.5 is the coefficient of relative risk aversion.

---

[12] Defined as cumulative declines in Consumption or GDP by at least 10%. Vecon, 2010.

Historical approach

The frequent use of the past in order to estimate that historical Cost of Capital is based on the idea that the future will not be much different from the observed past[13]. But this raises a number of problems, in particular, nothing guarantees a smooth replication of the past in the long-term future. Additionally, most countries did not accumulate enough information about their past (especially the distant past) to produce reliable estimates of such realised cost.

Ibbotson Associates is probably the best known source of information for the US market, since this country recorded a time series that runs uninterrupted from the beginning of 1926. And for the UK market, Barclays Capital and Credit Suisse First Boston both produced similar historical estimates for the British Cost of Capital from a series that starts in 1919.

The similarity of all three final results led most capital budgeting, fund management practice, and regulators' decisions to be made traditionally from that well known American Equity Return Premium of (around) 8.5% p.a.[14]

However, more recently this single "Anglo-Saxon" value became suspicious after the arguments coming from different grounds. On the one hand, both DMS (2002) and *Goetzmann* (1999) conducted historical estimates for some countries (including the US market) using data covering the entire twentieth century and obtained not a single common historical rate, but a wide range of different domestic average share returns, some of them significantly far from the above US value, even after considering the impact of the various currencies involved. On the other hand, *Schwert* (1998) noted that extending the

---

[13] Campbell and Thompson, 2005, Hillebrand, and Medeiros, 2010.

[14] This is the value indicated in the most recommended book, *"Corporate Finance"* by Richard Brealey and Stuart Myers in its successive editions.

US data base backward to the beginning of the nineteenth century (thus a time series about 200-years long), the American average Cost of Capital becomes much less than the traditional Ibbotson result, a fact that may indicate that the risk premium of a country may be non-stationary, and, if so, the future may be different from the observed past. Finally, an Equity Return Premium of 8.5% is too large to be compatible with both the rate of long-term economic annual growth of any economy (estimated to be around 2%) and the level of risk aversion normally accepted for an average investor (exponent γ between 1 and 2).

In relation to the first criticism, such a time variability of the Cost of Capital within one single country or amongst different countries makes sense, since markets inevitably comprise human beings and it is known that their mood does change in response to the economic and social conditions surrounding that market. That is, human reasons may, now and then, determine an adjustment of the equity spread demanded by investors to take the risk of price volatility in tandem with those environment changes.

But why are the Ibbotson and DMS estimates for the US market (8.5%) so much larger than the *Schwert* estimate (4% p.a.) for the same country? The answer comes from what is now called "*survival bias*".[15] Investors demand an Equity Return Premium not only to cope with the variability of stock returns, but also to compensate them for the potential total loss due to rare but catastrophic crises that are always possible, as recorded in the history of any country. That is, although people require an extra payment to invest in volatile shares precisely because they are volatile, because shares also

---

[15] Brown, Goetzmann, and Ross, 1995.

suffer from a kind of *"credit risk"*, the total premium demanded must be large enough to pay for both sources of risk[16].

Indeed, during the entire twentieth century the US was lucky enough to avoid the great turmoil that affected, for example, Russia — two revolutions — or Germany and Japan collapse of their economies after the loss of world wars and/or invasion by foreign armies. On the contrary, the US economy developed throughout the same years in a rather smooth manner, in spite of some "minor" crises that were observed here and there, such as the Great Depression of 1929 and the two oil shocks of the 1970s and 1980s. In any event, the American financial market never closed for extended periods, there was no major nationalisation affecting large sectors of that economy, and there were no significant social events affecting the nation. On the contrary, in the 1800s there were the 1812-15 War with the British empire and the major Civil War (1861 to 1865), which brought vast devastation to some important regions of the country, and these may explain that, extending the time series backward to include these previous 100 years, the average equity return becomes closer to the observed values in those other more unstable countries.

Under this interpretation, the high Equity Return Premium observed during the twentieth century in the US market would be the result of a pessimistic view of the average American investor during those recent 100 years that required them to demand a compensation to cover the expected volatility of returns plus the risk of a potential total loss. However, in the nineteenth century, the Equity Return Premium realised already incorporates the actual losses of

---

[16] As Jorion & Goetzmann, 2000, stated: *"To the extent that the event causing the break was anticipated, the market seems to have been able to gauge the gravity of the unfolding events. Price declines before breaks is consistent with increasing demand for risk compensation for a catastrophic event"*, page 14. Dejuán, et al., 2011. Frankema, 2010. Hekimian, 2013.

those catastrophic years, and that could explain the much lower premium found ex-post.

As to the criticism about the size of the ERP, there are two economic models that suggest that the 8.5% estimated for the US market must be an excessive figure:

i) Gordon's constant growth model[17] for corporations allows us to estimate the Equity Risk Premium from

$$ERP = g_{real} + \frac{D_1}{P_0} - r_{real}$$

where **g** is the constant growth rate of the company, and **D/P** is the percent return obtained from the amount **D_1** of (next year) dividends received from a share currently priced at **P_0**, and **r** is the cost of debt. For annual dividends on the order of 3% to 4% of **P** and a real return of long-term debt of around 2%, an annual Equity Risk Premium of 8.5% requires a growth rate greater than 6% p.a., which can only exist while a company is still in its infant stages of development[18]. Additionally, that model is over-optimistic since it assumes a constant rate **g** forever. For a more realistic model with growth rates decreasing, as the company matures, from an initial high value, the discount rates of future dividends must be less, meaning a smaller Equity Risk Premium than under the constant **g** model;

ii) Consumption-based asset pricing seeks to estimate the Equity Risk Premium from economic theory, as that premium ought to be the expression of the risk aversion of investors,

---

[17] Gordon, 1959.

[18] Otherwise — if unabated — that company would, sooner or later, become larger than its surrounding economy. Note that the consensus is for a long-term growth rate of any economy of about 2% p.a.

since the securities' extra returns are the price of delaying consumption from today into the future. The appropriate measure of the risk of investing in volatile assets is to assess the impact of that investment on the riskiness of future consumption. This leads us to the recognition that the key to investment risk is the correlation between asset returns and consumption variation: the higher that correlation the more risky are those assets because these investments pay off more to savers precisely when consumption is already high, and vice-versa:

$$\textbf{\textit{Risk Premium for an Asset}} = \gamma.\rho.\sigma_{\Delta C}.\sigma_R$$

where γ is the average investors' risk aversion and ρ is the correlation between the percentage change in consumption ΔC and the asset return $\mathbf{R}$. Once again, for normal values of these four parameters[19], the Equity Risk Premium obtained would be about 100 times lower than the empirical findings. Any accommodation based on accepting values of γ much larger than the classic range[20] is not possible because that would require extremely large real interest rates, which were never found in any market for a prolonged period of time.

It has been suggested that this consumption model might be either too conservative or too rational. As to the conservative side, *Campbell and Cochrane* (1999) proposed a change in the utility functions such that *"as consumption drops toward the accustomed standard of living X, people become more risk averse because they*

---

[19] Normal orders of magnitude: $\gamma = 1$ or 2, $\sigma_{\Delta C}$ is around 1% p.a., σ_R around 20% p.a. and $\rho \leq 20\%$.

[20] Even if we are slightly more generous and accept γ around 10 and ρ around 40%, we find a risk premium of about 0.8% p.a.

are less willing to accept further declines in consumption". That is, γ is not constant and can become much larger than in classic models, especially when consumption falls and approaches that habitual level.

On the psychological front, the development of **Prospect Theory** by *Tversky and Kahneman* (1992) allowed bringing some irrationality to the explanation of market behaviour. This is what *Benartzi and Thaler* (1995) did: investors care more about the *returns* obtained than about the *value* of their portfolios. Since losses are particularly painful, some investors do not evaluate returns every day, but only at large intervals of time, avoiding the useless pains due to temporary losses. Those investors evaluating their portfolios everyday thus require a large risk premium to hold shares instead of bonds, but those leaving large time intervals between evaluations have lower probabilities of losses and require smaller risk premia. Therefore, there are many different risk premia in the market and their values may change over time according to the average time horizon of evaluation of investments.

Because *Tversky and Kahneman* later noted that most people tend to gauge their investment return on an annual frequency, and were also able to quantify the average overvalue π attributed by individuals to the pain received from realised losses — 2.25 times greater than the value felt from alternative gains — Costa (2014)[21] was able to estimate the ERP corresponding to such psychological asymmetry in humans: 6.97% per annum for an average volatility of 20% p.a.

---

[21] See the site of the Portuguese regulator CMVM (www.cmvm.pt) in "*publicações/Cadernos do mercado de valores mobiliários*" April 2014, article 3, or in www.cmvm.pt/CMVM/Publicacoes/Cadernos/Documents/CadernosMVM%2047.pdf

ERP and ERP DENSITY. NON-LINEAR

T = 1 year & r_f = 3% p.a.

π	μ − r_f			(μ − r_f)/σ		
	10%	20%	30%	10%	20%	30%
1.00	0.039%	0.303%	0.986%	0.39%	1.51%	3.29%
1.25	0.945%	2.144%	3.793%	9.45%	10.72%	12.64%
1.50	1.684%	3.646%	6.085%	16.84%	18.23%	20.28%
1.75	2.308%	4.915%	8.021%	23.08%	24.58%	26.74%
2.00	2.847%	6.013%	9.696%	28.47%	30.06%	32.32%
2.25	3.322%	6.979%	11.171%	33.22%	34.89%	37.24%
2.50	3.746%	7.841%	12.488%	37.46%	39.21%	41.63%
2.75	4.129%	8.620%	13.676%	41.29%	43.10%	45.59%
3.00	4.478%	9.330%	14.760%	44.78%	46.65%	49.20%
3.25	4.798%	9.981%	15.754%	47.98%	49.90%	52.51%
3.50	5.094%	10.583%	16.674%	50.94%	52.91%	55.58%
3.75	5.368%	11.142%	17.528%	53.68%	55.71%	58.43%
4.00	5.625%	11.664%	18.325%	56.25%	58.32%	61.08%

ERP and ERP DENSITY. NON-LINEAR

T = 1 year & r_f = 0% p.a.

π	μ − r_f			(μ − r_f)/σ		
	10%	20%	30%	10%	20%	30%
1.00	0.038%	0.295%	0.961%	0.38%	1.47%	3.20%
1.25	0.943%	2.134%	3.764%	9.43%	10.67%	12.55%
1.50	1.682%	3.635%	6.053%	16.82%	18.17%	20.18%
1.75	2.305%	4.903%	7.986%	23.05%	24.51%	26.62%
2.00	2.845%	5.999%	9.659%	28.45%	29.99%	32.20%
2.25	3.319%	6.964%	11.131%	33.19%	34.82%	37.10%
2.50	3.743%	7.826%	12.446%	37.43%	39.13%	41.49%
2.75	4.126%	8.604%	13.633%	41.26%	43.02%	45.44%
3.00	4.474%	9.313%	14.715%	44.74%	46.56%	49.05%
3.25	4.794%	9.963%	15.708%	47.94%	49.82%	52.36%
3.50	5.090%	10.565%	16.626%	50.90%	52.82%	55.42%
3.75	5.365%	11.123%	17.479%	53.65%	55.62%	58.26%
4.00	5.621%	11.645%	18.275%	56.21%	58.22%	60.92%

Table 1 — Theoretical value of the ERP from Behavioural Finance and assuming 20% of annual volatility

Unfortunately, *Tversky and Kahneman* detail only the case of the American investor and also say nothing about the variability of that overvaluation of pain throughout the economic cycle. We are still in the infancy of the new Prospect Theory and it remains to be checked whether it needs some adjustments to these two points.

Summary

Since the known theoretical models are not yet able to supply reliable figures for future values of the ERP, we are left with the classic approach of estimating the future from the recorded past. However, the Ibbotson figure sounds exaggerated, not only for the US market, but also for other countries, suggesting that the best each country can do is to develop its own data base of stock returns and extend it backward as far as possible to improve the quality of the estimate.

However, this avenue raises some problems: is the historical sample large enough to produce estimates falling within narrow confidence intervals? What if the Equity Risk Premium is itself variable?

This question of non-stationarity is crucial for historical estimates, because the simplest analysis has implicit the assumption of stationarity. But there are reasons for suspecting that the true Equity Risk Premium may be changing over time, a fact that is in agreement with some tests that reveal statistically significant changes in market variability. So, unless we have a model of how the Equity Risk Premium varies over time, we may be misled by historical data and/or we obtain extremely large confidence intervals even from century-long time series.

Fortunately, there are also arguments in favour of giving some value to the results linearly extrapolated from those historical series:

a) as mentioned above, one of the most comprehensive analyses was conducted by DMS (2002) for the entire twentieth century and covers 16 countries that represent more than 95% of the free-float market capitalisation of all world equities at the start of 2002; although the historical average of Risk Premium[22] varies amongst those countries, that premium is always positive and covers a range (arithmetic averages) between 3.2% and 10.6% p.a.;

b) this large range of values is compatible with the different histories followed by the various countries in the sample, especially catastrophic events such as revolutions, nationalisations, etc. that have plagued them;

c) the average volatility of returns shown currently by most indices (around 15% p.a.) suggests that 100 years of history is not enough to reduce the uncertainty of the estimated average equity returns; that is, the confidence interval

---

[22] Relative to T-Bills, not to T-Bonds.

anticipated for those averages is still too large[23]; but is also compatible with the above range of values;

d) even if the return demanded from shares does vary over time, it is difficult to accept that it took some fixed value in the past but, from now on, has definitely changed; most likely, it has changed a number of times in the past — following the business cycle — without any up or down trend, and will do the same in the future; therefore, the average past of each country may not be very different from its future, and we can approach that historical average provided our that data base covers a number of different business cycles;

e) although there is a minimum rationality in price formation, recent studies have revealed the degree of irrationality present in this particular area of human behaviour; so, it is possible that the high values of risk premium found in the past series are a simple reflection of some of those irrationalities and, unless we assume that mankind will change in the future and be fully rational from now on, we cannot reject those high ERPs.

All in all, it seems that our low level of knowledge of these matters still recommends the use of the past as the *"least worst"* predictor of the future, and that justifies that, every year, the Ibbotson Group publishes a number of studies updating the statistical information from a number of countries: *Ibbotson Associates - Stocks, Bonds, Bills, and Inflation Yearbook*. Also, since the publication of *"The Triumph of the Optimists"* in 2002, covering "only" 101 years of

---

[23] Cornell, 1999: *"...72 years' worth of data is not enough to measure the risk premium with sufficient precision to satisfy most investors ... even if it is assumed that the future is like the past, the estimates are so imprecise that it is not clear what the risk premium has truly been in the past"*, page 44.

"only" 16 countries, the London Business School has partnered with a bank — initially the Dutch ABN-Amro Bank and more recently the Credit Suisse — to update those historical results every year and to extend that type of analysis to 22 countries. Prof. Damodaran also maintains a page on his website where some statistical data are also accessible, in particular the historical cost of capital.[24]

4. Estimating the Long-term Average Market Equity Return

If we cannot predict with certainty the future premium demanded by investors to withstand the inevitable equity volatility, we better look into the past of that market to collect some evidence of what the Portuguese share market has been. And in order to be comparable to the most universal database being constructed currently — the DMS one — an equal time window starting at the very end of 1899 must be used.

Unfortunately, the known equity indices of the Lisbon Exchange market cover only part of that century long window:

- after the Carnation Revolution and the subsequent "suspension" of the Exchange operations on 25 April 1974, only the BVL-General[25] index is available, but this one starts only on 5 January 1988;

---

[24] http://pages.stern.nyu.edu/~adamodar/

[25] This is the official index developed and published by the Lisbon Exchange from the beginning of the 1990s taking January 5, 1988 as the base date. Later it was renamed PSI-General index, but still expresses the average behaviour of all shares listed in its main market. Initially only the closing quotations were used but recently it is calculated in real time during the trading session.

- before that revolution, the National Statistic Office initiated an index series in 1938[26], but it is not continuous until 1974 and uses a different methodology reducing its comparability to the BVL index;
- and the Portuguese Central Bank index that was computed before 1974 was never resumed after 1974, and in any case begins only in 1928[27], with a monthly frequency (in the beginning with only two points per year).

We therefore decided to calculate a whole new series of a new Equity Index for the Lisbon Stock Exchange market using a methodology as close as possible to that official index but now starting in 1900 (base date on December, 1899).

In reality this computation involved two new series, one for the period 1900 to 1974 and another for those few years from the resumption of operations in Lisbon in 1977 until the end of 1987, so that the time gap without index values would be restricted to a minimum time length ("only" about three years).

Since this extended time series covers 114 years, the use of log--values of the index allows us to express in more detail the time evolution of the market in a single graph.

As explained in Chapter 3 of this book, our approach of line fitting to estimate the annual geometric returns benefits from a more stable succession of results when updating these calculations every additional year by including the most recent data from the last 12 months.

Even if a crisis like the one initiated in the Summer of 2007 hits the market (and similarly for a bull market), the slope of the fitted

---

[26] See *"Taxas de rendimento real, índices de cotações e índices de movimento da Bolsa de Lisboa"*, F. Maia de Loureiro, in *"Estudos n.º 6"* of INE (the Portuguese Statistics Office).

[27] Base date on June 29, 1928 with a base value of 100 points.

line accommodates these new events in the market with only slight change. Therefore, the average growth rate of this index along this 114-year long sample was estimated through the adjustment of a straight line best fitted to the empirical (log) realisation, and from there an average (geometric) return rate was calculated[28]. In reality, three lines were best fitted:

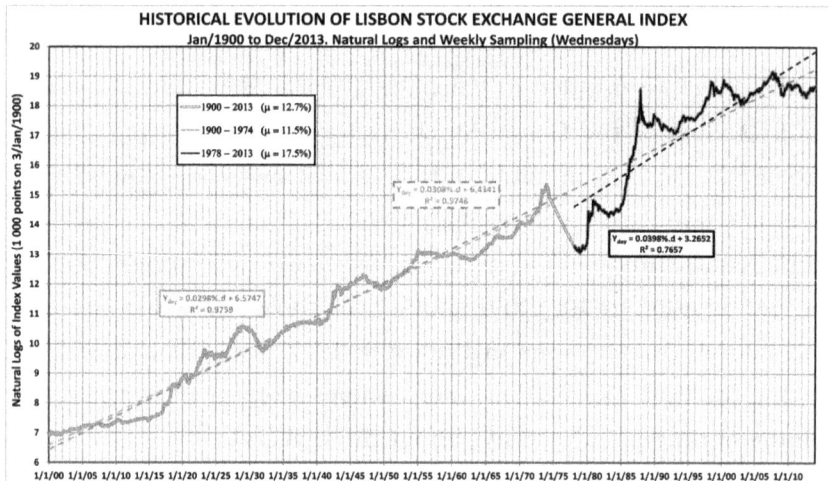

HISTORICAL EVOLUTION OF LISBON STOCK EXCHANGE GENERAL INDEX
Jan/1900 to Dec/2013. Natural Logs and Weekly Sampling (Wednesdays)

- 1900 – 2013 ($\mu = 12.7\%$)
- 1900 – 1974 ($\mu = 11.5\%$)
- 1978 – 2013 ($\mu = 17.5\%$)

$Y_{dec} = 0.0398\%.d + 3.2652$
$R^2 = 0.7657$

$Y_{dec} = 0.0298\%.d + 6.5747$
$R^2 = 0.9759$

Figure 1 – Lisbon Exchange share index from the end of 1899 to the end of 2013

---

[28] Mind that this estimate is the sum of the slope β of the adjusted line with half the annual variance σ^2 according to the Itô's transformation of the accepted model $d[\ln(S)] = (\mu - 0.5\sigma^2).dt + \sigma.dz$. Although, empirical periodic equity returns do not usually follow an exact Gauss distribution, and they tend to show both heteroskedasticity and autocorrelation:
- that non-normality only affects the conversion of the slope of the adjusted line to the estimated annual return: the term $\frac{1}{2}\sigma^2$ is only an approximation, but potential errors from this are usually minimised by the small dimension of the volatility σ.
- autocorrelation and heterokedasticity do not affect the slope β of the adjusted line (but do change the confidence interval of that coefficient), nor the standard deviation σ of the period log-returns.

- for the whole sample, leading to an average (geometric) annual return of 12.7%
- for the window 1900-74, an average (geometric) annual return of 11.5%
- for 1978-2013, an average (geometric) annual return of 17.5%.

This larger return (17.5%) for the period following the resumption of operations is a fact also found in many other countries and is normally interpreted as expressing the need to compensate investors for the recent heavy losses they have suffered, in the Portuguese case, following the Carnation Revolution.

5. The risk-free interest rate in Portugal

In spite of all its deficiencies, the CAPM model is still the most frequently used approach to guide us when estimating a discount rate for valuing volatile shares or other similar assets. Here the Equity Risk Premium (ERP) measures the average market excess return demanded by investors to assume the uncertainty of the subsequent rewards obtained from equities. However, there is no consensus about the maturity of the debt instruments that should be used as the reference basis for comparison: a short-term or a long-term rate.

At first sight, long-term rates would be preferable as they also incorporate a premium for the long maturity of the credit, that is, it compares similar alternatives for funding new projects. However, long T-Bonds also suffer from high volatility of returns due to the variability of the interest rates in the market — which includes the effect of inflation variation — whereas short-lived T-Bills are much less vulnerable to the current price of money, and inflation is rapidly factored in when each new issue is placed in the market.

This justifies the frequent double disclosure of the Equity Return Premium adopted in a number of countries: excess return above T-Bills and above T-Bonds. This is important because in the history of every country there are periods of unanticipated high inflation rates that justify long periods with negative returns from long-term bonds if previously issued with low coupon rates. Those negative returns may mislead us when subtracting the inflated average equity return from such negative debt returns, leading to an excessively large ERP.

It is also not clear which level of credit risk imbedded in that interest rate can be accepted in a real case: the cost of money for operations with a Central Bank (or a National Treasury) or the rates of the Interbank Money Market, which still have some residual credit risk included.

Fortunately, the limitations of the Portuguese money market simplified our decisions in this regard due to lack of alternatives:

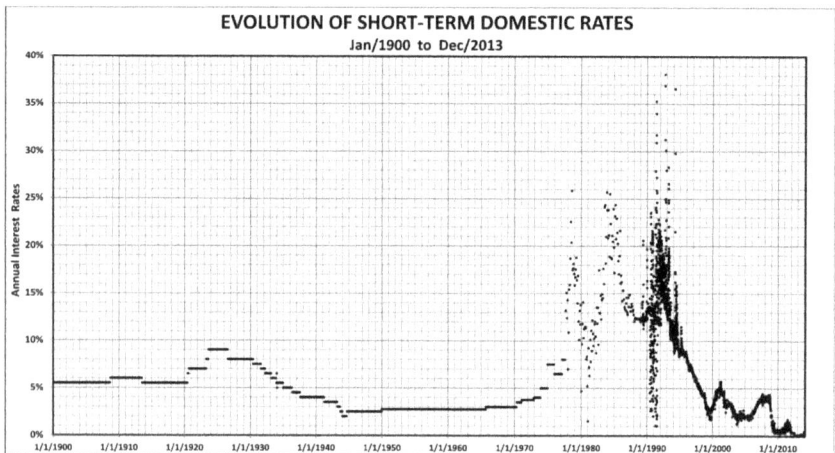

EVOLUTION OF SHORT-TERM DOMESTIC RATES
Jan/1900 to Dec/2013

Figure 2 – Estimates of short-term rates in Portugal during the twentieth century

a) in most countries, the traditional short-term risk-free rate is obtained from the T-Bills market but that instrument in Portugal has a short and troubled history: they existed in the beginning of the twentieth century but were forbidden in 1933 by a government programme introduced to reduce the (almost exclusive) use of short-term funds to finance the state needs; they were reintroduced in 1985, but their issuing was temporarily suspended from 1998 to 2003 due to the launch of the Euro in the euro zone;

b) long-term T-Bonds have a more stable history in Portugal, but an early redemption clause attached to some of the most liquid issues listed in the Lisbon Exchange in the beginning of the century introduces some uncertainty when estimating the actual long-term market rate for these issues; more important was the fact that the Portuguese Government had declared a partial default in 1892, which for many years meant an extra credit risk premium imbedded in the returns demanded from government bonds[29];

c) therefore, we only searched for a proxy series of short-term risk free rates which was constructed using the following different sources:

- from 1/Jan/1900 to 15/Sep/1977: discount rate defined by *Banco de Portugal*, the Portuguese central bank;
- from 15/Sep/1977 to 31/Dec/1988: domestic Interbank Market (IMM) for 24 hours[30] operations (monthly data);
- from 2/Jan/1989 to 31/Dec/2008: domestic Interbank Market for 24 hours operations (daily data);

---

[29] See point 7 of this same chapter.

[30] Although the Portuguese Interbank Market offered operations for maturities ranging from 24 hours to one year, the clear majority of the liquidity was always concentrated in the short-term end of that spectrum.

- from 2/Jan/2009 on: EONIA interest rate defined at the European level; due to the closing of the Portuguese IMM market at the end of 2008, we continued our time series of risk-free rate toward 2009 using the EONIA daily rate as the representative Portuguese short-term interest rate.

The average annual risk-free rate along the whole 114-year sample was calculated for a 365-day year with the following results:

SHORT-TERM DOMESTIC RATES Geometric Average 365-day	
Jan/1900 to Jan/2014	5.90%
Jan/1900 to Apr/1974	4.65%
Jan/1978 to Jan/2014	8.32%

Table 2 – The risk-free rate in Portugal during the twentieth century

6. The Long-term Memory of Defaults

The confidence in Portuguese treasury securities as credit risk--free assets[31] deserves some additional comments. Although it might be thought that Treasuries are risk-free assets because they represent a governmental commitment for the near future, historical events in Portugal during the nineteenth century explain why those treas-

---

[31] Mind that credit risk grows significantly with the time to maturity of the afflicted instrument. So, while T-Bill prices are not strongly impacted by a heightened perceived risk, long-term Bonds, and especially Consols, are profoundly affected by such added uncertainty.

uries cannot be taken as such, at least for much of the 1800s and the initial part of the twentieth century.

In fact, the confidence in our Treasury debt instruments was very low during the second half of the nineteenth century, when the total amount of public debt increased dramatically every year, thanks to a large surplus of public expenditure over the simultaneous tax collection. This negative historical experience ended with the declaration of bankruptcy in 1892 (Decree of 13 June), when government declared that it could not fulfil all the debt contracts signed with its foreign lenders, following the abandonment of the gold-standard just the year before (in July, 1891)[32]. This semi-default meant that:

- all amortisations of Treasuries were suspended (except Consols),
- and the country would pay only 1/3 of all interest due to non-residents under those contracts (except short-term debts).

Of course, even before this partial default the Portuguese credit rating was falling. Specialised newspapers disclosed information on the prices and annual returns of our Bonds and Bills during that pre-bankruptcy period, while the returns demanded from those instruments increased in tandem with the mounting fears on the risk of Portugal. The negotiations with the creditors after June 1892 lasted for ten years, leading to an agreement only when a conversion of the loans was achieved in 1902 (law of 14 May).

The fact that capital markets do have memory means that investors always make their decisions based on a stock of accumulated knowledge, and the reality is that, between 1870 and 1913 the cov-

---

[32] See chapter 2.

erage of all types of news about Portugal in the Times of London reached an annual average of 102 reports. The ratio of bad to good economic news reported was 112%, exceeded only by Russia amongst a sample of the 16 following countries: Argentina, Brazil, Canada, Chile, China, Colombia, Costa Rica, Greece, Egypt, Hungary, Japan, Mexico, Queensland, Sweden, Turkey, and Uruguay.[33]

Such a poor performance closed the doors of all international credit markets to Portugal, and only during the First World War could a loan be obtained from the UK, thanks to the special relationship between the two countries.

So, although returns from domestic Treasuries do not fluctuate as shares — they are volatility risk-free — they still may incorporate some Credit Risk, and the case of Portugal during the first decades of the twentieth century did have some.

7. The Portuguese Historical Equity Risk Premium

The 100-plus years sampled of the history of the Lisbon Stock Exchange provides all the information necessary to estimate, under the adoption of the CAPM model, the average volatility premium for the shares listed in this market.

This study produces three values for that Premium for three different time intervals:

a) for the whole 114-year window (Jan/1900 - Dec/2013): it includes the only two periods without quotations, one lasting about two months in the beginning of WWI, and the second lasting for about 3 years and initiated in April 1974.

---

[33] Magee, Gary, La Trobe University, "*Investors, information and the British world, 1860-1913*", paper presented at the EBHA, Milan, 2009.

b) the initial window from the very beginning until the Carnation Revolution (Jan/1900 - Apr/1974)

c) and the final window after the market resumed operations and to the present days (Jan/1978 - Dec/2013)

Annual Rates	1900-2013	1900-1974	1978-2013
Return$_{365}$ =	12.65%	11.52%	17.49%
R$_{volatilty\ free}$ =	5.90%	4.65%	8.32%
ERP$_{365}$ =	6.75%	6.87%	9.17%

Table 3 – Historical ERP estimated for the three time windows considering 365-day years

Because the sample until 1974 is much longer than the one after 1978, the entire sample produces an average ERP similar to the figure estimated from the 1900-1974 window. The somewhat larger ERP estimated for the period after 1978 may reflect a desire of the market (commonly found) to recover from the heavy losses suffered immediately before. Or, using another perspective, that extra return is the price the companies had to pay to investors to attract them back to volatile securities after the end of a serious crisis. It is like a "credit risk" premium demanded by investors after the extended programme of nationalisations seen in 1974/75.

8. Chaining the two Equity Index Time Series

The fact that the Lisbon Exchange had its operations "suspended" for a few years after the April 1974 coup deprives any time series builder of the necessary market prices of the Portuguese shares. The index time series was thus interrupted on the last trading day — 24 April 1974 — and could be restarted only after shares resumed transactions in March 1977[34]. The question is how to establish a connection between those two time series.

Because markets always consider all the available information for their economic decisions, no investor will ever forget the events of 1974-78, when formulating portfolio strategies. All available historical information matters for these purposes, in particular, the overall Cost of Capital for very long maturities is important, and therefore past evidence does matter. This aim justifies our approach without any ambition of a definitive solution to tackle this lack of data.

Our aproach to connect the two segments of the whole time series was to consider the impact on the wealth of an averge investor who had a position replicating the listed portfolio on 24 April 1974 and measure the loss he/she suffered due to:

- the clear swing to the left in all economic policies of the governments then in power
- in particular, in 1974 and mainly in 1975, a significant part of the domestic economy was nationalised — initially without any compensation whatsoever — involving the financial sector, the utilities, transport companies, among others.[35]
- during 1975 all Portuguese overseas territories gained independence[36] with leftist governments in power in all of

---

[34] Although the government authorisation allowed to resume share trading on the Lisbon Exchange from 28 February 1977, the first trade in shares occurred only on March 7.

[35] Nationalisations of banks and other firms in the main economic sectors (insurance, large industries, and road transports) were carried out in 1975, while land expropriation in the large-property districts of *Alentejo* and *Ribatejo* was also executed.

[36] This determined that half a million Portuguese who were living in the territories, left for Portugal in 1974-75, representing an influx of over 5% to the Portuguese resident population, and requiring the Government to support them in

them, which meant that all local corporations listed on the Lisbon Exchange — the so called Overseas corporations — were either nationalised or closed, implying full losses for their former shareholders.

When the share market resumed operations in March 1977, only a restricted number of the previously listed companies still remained admitted to trading. The comparison[37] between the capitalisation values of the two portfolios is presented in Table 4:

IMPACT OF THE 1974 CARNATION REVOLUTION AND ITS AFTERMATH			
Market Capitalisation in Apr/74	PTE	231 065 277 209$	100.00%
Market Capitalisation in Jan/78	PTE	3 193 835 333$	1.38%

Table 4 – Loss of market capitalisation (shares) after April 1974 and until January 1978

Some years later[38] the Portuguese government decided to compensate the shareholders of the nationalised companies but not of

---

their beginning of new economic activities in the country. On top of that, a severe economic recession in the country brought problems to the balance of payments. Export difficulties led to a currency depreciation in 1977, and an IMF stand-by agreement was required in that year.

[37] Due to the reduced number of trades executed in the first months after reopening and because their prices lacked a minimum economic meaning, we computed the new equity index only from January 1978 on.

[38] The first T-Bonds with a maturity scheduled until 1995 were issued on 15 September 1975 to pay for the nationalisation in 1974 of the three issuing banks. Further nationalisations that occurred in 1975 received compensation only in 1979 and 1980, but because their values were disputed, additional amounts were offered to previous shareholders as late as 1993, although maintaining the initial issuing date of the different T-Bonds offered (some of these later issues were paid out in cash because they had already been amortised).

the overseas firms. For that purpose the Treasury issued a number of T-Bonds[39] that were credited to those affected shareholders but:

- valued those nationalised firms in very low terms;
- the bonds were medium to long-term issues which meant spreading the payment of those compensations over many future years; these long periods were important because of the high inflation rate then prevailing in the country;[40]
- and the coupon rates offered were very low and decreasing for longer maturities.[41]

That is, that compensation was clearly insufficient, meaning that some losses for investors remained even after accounting for those payments.

Fortunately, because these compensating bonds were listed on the Lisbon Stock Exchange it was possible to estimate current market interest rates and use them to discount those bonds back to the beginning of the new index series on 4 January 1978.

---

[39] Compensations awarded were PTE 3,969,269,952 for the nationalisation of the three issuing banks — *Banco de Portugal, Banco de Angola* and *Banco Nacional Ultramarino* — plus PTE 250,585,000,000 for all other nationalisations, and PTE 8,369,412,000 for the existing two mutual funds FIA and FIDES, which lost value due to those nationalisations. The total amount issued had a face value of PTE 262,923,681,952.

[40] The average of the CPI annual inflation rate was 23.6% in 1979 and 16.7% in 1980.

[41] Coupon rates from 2.50% to 17.00% p.a.

IMPACT OF THE 1974 CARNATION REVOLUTION AND ITS AFTERMATH			
Market Capitalisation in Apr/74	PTE	231 065 277 209$	100.00%
Market Capitalisation in Jan/78	PTE	3 193 835 333$	1.38%
Total Compensations (discounted)	PTE	40 848 821 779$	17.68%
Total estimated losses	PTE	187 022 620 097$	**80.94%**

Table 5 – Method used to estimate the average loss due to nationalisations and the delayed indemnities

All in all, the averge portfolio lost almost 99% from 1974 to 1978,
but considering that the government later distributed T-Bonds to
pay for the nationalisations that were valued at about 18% of the
initial portfolio, the average net loss was about 81%. We therefore
chainned the two time series by making the index fall from the level
attained on 24 April 1974 to about 19% of that value on 4 January
1978 (Figure 3).

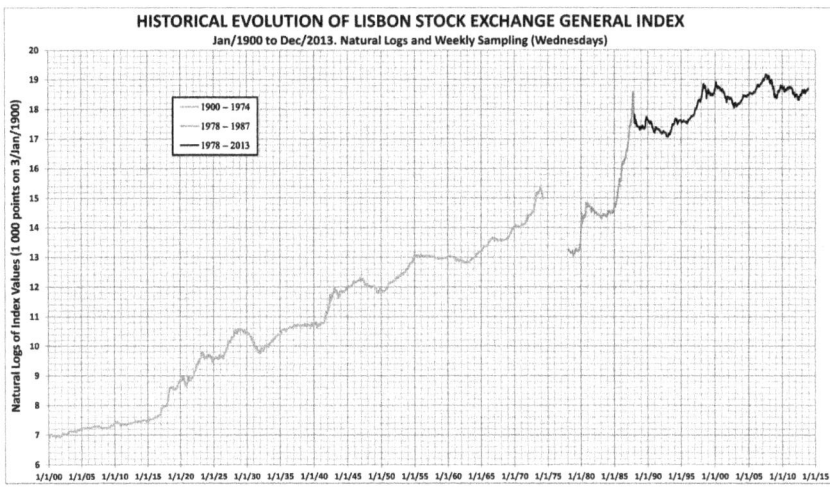

HISTORICAL EVOLUTION OF LISBON STOCK EXCHANGE GENERAL INDEX
Jan/1900 to Dec/2013. Natural Logs and Weekly Sampling (Wednesdays)

Figure 3 – The "jump" between 1974 and 1978 in the whole index
curve translates the average loss due to expropriations, nationalisations, and the effects of the decolonisation.

Table 5 summarises the basic result of all these facts: an average loss suffered by the average investor due to the 1974/78 events of around 81% of his/her initial wealth[42].

The connection between the two ends of the two time series was calculated in order to guarantee the above indicated loss between the index value on 24 April 1974 and its "resuming" value on 4 January 1978.

9. The Equity Risk Premium for Overseas Companies. Liquidity Premium

The large size of the Portuguese empire allowed/required the existence of a few large companies operating essentially in those overseas territories. Most of those companies operated in Angola, Mozambique, and the tiny archipelago of S. Tomé, where some of them had shares (and/or corporate bonds) listed on the Lisbon Stock Exchange. Only one listed company operated in Guiné-Bissau.

---

[42] Mind that the bond issues were intended to compensate not only for the listed companies that were nationalised, but also for many other firms out of the Exchange. The fact that the largest nationalised firms were listed and only small ones were taken by the government, it is estimated that the clear majority of the total bond issues were meant to compensate the listed corporations.

OVERSEAS FIRMS LISTED IN LISBON IN APRIL 1974	Total Overseas Firms Listed	Firms in the Overseas Index
Guiné-Bissau	1	
Fernando Poó Island	1	
S. Tomé e Príncipe	9	
Angola	12	5
Moçambique	11	4
Angola and Moçambique	3	2
Total	**37**	**11**

Table 6 – Number of overseas firms listed in Lisbon with their main operating territories[43]

Those businesses conducted in distant territories added some extra sources of risk to their investors due to:

- transport uncertainties,
- new technologies demanded,
- necessary use of expatriates (recruited in Portugal and in other countries), and their subsequent control from distant headquarters,
- tropical diseases, etc.

One would therefore anticipate that investment in those companies should demand a higher premium to pay for the extra credit risk and for the additional volatility of quotations from those businesses.

Also political risks adversely affecting investors' confidence in the capital market could not be disregarded for activities in, both, the overseas territories and the motherland, as events proved in the 1960s and 1970s. Wars in some territories began in 1961, damaging

---

[43] See also point 13 and Annex of chapter 3.

exports from the disturbed zones due to transport difficulties and the added risks of harvesting (for example, collecting coffee beans in the northern provinces of Angola). The war efforts also led to a different allocation of resources, uncertainty, and even dire perspectives on the future for those firms. In the end, the 1974 Carnation Revolution brought in a new political model based on socialism that was consecrated in the text of the 1976 constitution.

Based on these overseas companies listed in Lisbon it was possible to calculate a brand new equity index — called the "Overseas Index" — intended precisely to gauge the average behaviour of these shares during the 75 years that the Exchange had a minimum of overseas companies listed to be possible producing such an index.

Figure 4 compares the time evolution of this index with the General Index of the Lisbon Exchange during those first three quarters of the century using the same base value (1000 points) for the same base date in 1900.

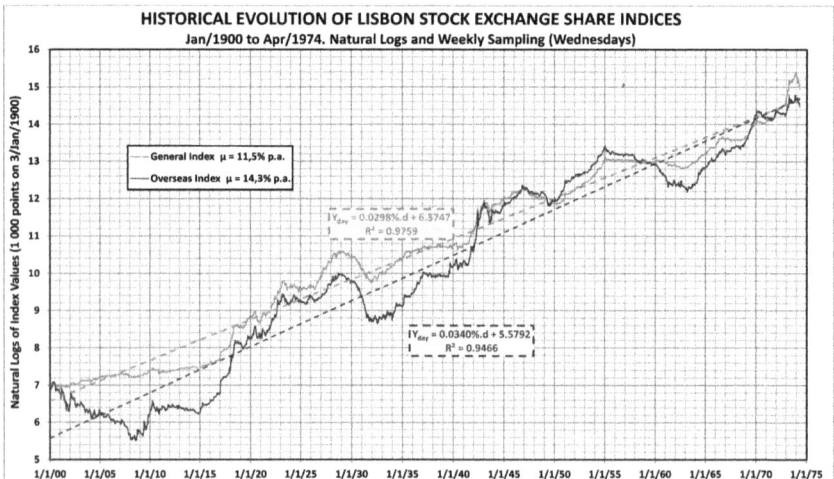

Figure 4 – Comparison between the average behaviour of the overseas firms and the whole Exchange market

Clearly the overseas index was more volatile (2.80% per week) than the general index (1.57% per week) but it also showed a somewhat larger average positive annual return to compensate for that extra uncertainty. The question is whether that extra return paid enough to cover the extra risks due to volatility and credit uncertainties.

Annual Rates	1900-1974		
	General	Overseas	Extra
$Return_{365}$ =	11.52%	14.31%	2.79%
$R_{volatilty\ free}$ =	4.65%	5.65%	1.0%
ERP_{365} =	6.87%	8.66%	1.79%
σ =	1.57%	2.80%	
ρ =	0.611		0.59%
Liquidity premium			1.2%

Table 7 – Decomposition of the extra premium demanded by the average overseas equity

Based on the correlation between these two indices and also considering an estimated extra credit premium of 1%, Table 7 summarises the main findings from this 75-year sampling:

- the sum of the volatility, credit, and liquidity premia amounts to 2.79% p.a.
- additionally, 1% is estimated for credit risk
- since there is some correlation (0.611) between the two indices, 0.59% p.a. is explained by this correlation
- the remaining premium of 1.2% p.a. may be attributed to the reduced liquidity of those shares issued by the overseas companies.

10. Cost of Capital, ERP, and Economic Growth

A bankrupted country in 1892 that was expelled from the international capital markets was able to achieve in the twentieth century the status of a developed country, in spite of its tiny continental dimension and population (between 5 and 10 million inhabitants during the twentieth century). The century brought the diffusion of new technologies and mass-consumption opportunities to the Portuguese people throughout four political regimes: the monarchy, the first Republic, the Estado Novo, and the current democracy. Electricity for all, telephones for all, modern housing for all, the automobile revolution for all, air travel for all, roads and highways for all, and collective social equipment such as hospitals and schools for all, were hallmarks of the Portuguese high standards of living in the twentieth century. From the 1900s until now, the Lisbon Stock Exchange has been a crucial mechanism to facilitate funding and to allocate capital to the best projects within the country (and in the overseas territories until de decolonisation in 1975). In establishing efficient connections between savers and capital users (entrepreneurs and investors in general), information and transaction costs in the capital markets were substantially decreased. The Stock Exchange provided liquidity to the Portuguese economy, meeting the needs of capital for economic activities and new technologies in all sectors. It had a very important energizing role to support the long-run adoption of new technologies in chartered corporations that were associated with the Portuguese economic growth. *"Liquid secondary markets are an important ingredient for economic growth because they induce savers, who are uncertain about their future cash needs, to purchase long-term securities offered in primary markets"*.[44]

---

[44] Ferderer, 2009, p. 2. Madureira, 2007.

The low long-term average ERP and average cost of capital were a stimulant factor for the Portuguese twentieth-century modernisation in promoting limited-liability entrepreneurial initiatives and efforts. *"By and large, where finance leads, enterprise follows"*.[45] Low long-term cost of capital has made it possible that many corporate projects could be implemented, which would not have been promoted without those financial opportunities.

The core miracle was to move from great street dissatisfaction manifestations (from murdering the king in 1908 to organising frequent political revolutions) and from bloody fighting in WWI, to industrialising, adopting new technologies, education, and increasing labour productivity to reap development benefits. Such a miracle was arose from a rural agricultural society of illiterate people, thanks to a capital-deepening process. Economic historians are today more aware of the role of the Portuguese twentieth--century financial system for economic growth, thanks to banking and insurance history contributions.[46] Banking and insurance development also multiplied the securities market of bank shares, which were offered to everybody. The possibility of liquidating an increasing number of security issues at low costs meant greater asset liquidity for investors. The markets of Lisbon and Porto were important sources of energy for propelling industrialisation, transportation modernisation linking the motherland to overseas territories, foreign trade, and massive urbanisation. Stock markets of Lisbon and Porto also were important for fuelling public goods consumption, because public debt and government bondholders supported Portuguese governments throughout the four different

[45] Rousseau, Peter; Sylla, R., 2005: 3.

[46] Laíns, 2011. Faria, 2013. Valério, Nuno et al., 2011.

political regimes of the century to make unbelievable collective facilities available.

Of course there were some stock market bursts and crises associated with the two world wars, the business cycles (such as the Great Depression), domestic politics, and geopolitics. Because of global shocks and shock contagion effects, there is a long-run trend toward synchronization. The business-cycle downturns tend to occur more and more simultaneously, as a high correlation between countries has been discovered, which does not leave space to exceptional regional behaviour. This means that a good definition for synchronisation considers output volatility or output-consumption co-movements, as time-series *"turning points in the corresponding reference cycles occur roughly at the same points in time"*.[47] The negative episodes and losses may generate panic. However, the long-run steady growth of the securities market in Portugal reflects the centennial growth of the Portuguese financial sector, its efficient ability to allocate capital, and growth of the Portuguese corporate economy. In the entire twentieth century the most severe blow to the Portuguese financial system was the 25 April revolutionary period, but even so, recovery from nationalisations occurred after the reset of stock market operations.

The stock market in particular may be pointed out as an example of the efficient organisational adjustments to internationalisation that led Portugal to the EURONEXT. Capital market globalisation illustrates the stock markets' advantage of opening broader opportunities for capital mobility in intermediating international flows of FDI[48].

---

[47] Bordo; Helbeling, 2011: 215.
[48] FDI: Foreign Direct Investment

From an emergent rural economy, it was possible to move to internationalisation in joining supra-national organisations. The Stock Exchange has been and will continue to be a decisive actor in the Portuguese corporate economy and its driving role has not been stressed enough in the Portuguese historiography. Finance is the match for modern economic growth.

ANNEX
STATISTICAL DISTRIBUTION OF 114-YEAR AVERAGE ANNUAL RETURNS

1. Computation methods

The annual return expressed by an Equity Index can be measured by comparing the end value with the corresponding value one year earlier. And because of the log values computed to best fit a straight line, we calculated these annual returns in two different ways:

$$\text{Linear return} = \frac{S_{final}}{S_{initial}} - 1 \qquad \text{Log return} = Ln\left(S_{final}\right) - Ln\left(S_{initial}\right)$$

2. Two Indices (1900 to 1974)

03/Jan/1900 24/Apr/1974	Linear		Log	
	General	Overseas	General	Overseas
-120%	0	0	1	0
-100%	0	0	0	0
-80%	0	0	0	0
-60%	1	0	0	2
-40%	0	2	0	1
-20%	2	6	2	6
0%	18	23	18	22
20%	30	18	33	19
40%	14	12	14	16
60%	5	6	5	4
80%	3	3	2	4
100%	1	3	0	0
120%	1	1	0	0
140%	0	0	0	1
160%	0	0	0	0
180%	0	0	0	0
200%	0	0	0	0
220%	0	0	0	0
240%	0	1	0	0
	75	75	75	75

Table 8 – Comparison between the statistical distributions of the 75 annual returns for the two share indices measured by two similar methodologies (linear and log returns)

3. The General Index (1900 to 2013)

The 114-year window sampled includes the (approximate) three years when the Exchanges had their operations suspended (precluding the publication of any share quotations during those months).

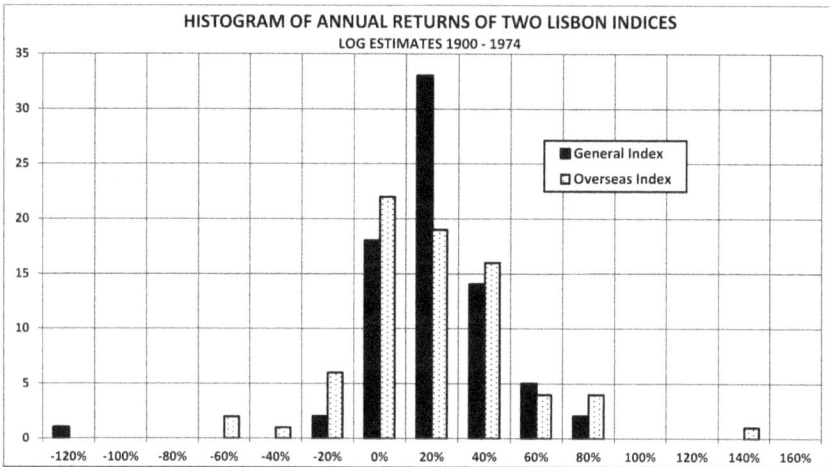

Figure 5 – Histogram of the 75 annual log-returns of the two share indices

We estimated an accumulated loss of around 80% in that period and Table 9 and Figure 6 include the entire years of 1974 to 1977 with that loss evenly distributed in those four years (around 40% loss under linear measurement and around 51% loss under log alternative).

1900-2013	Linear	Log
-120%	0	0
-100%	0	0
-80%	0	0
-60%	0	1
-40%	5	5
-20%	6	7
0%	27	25
20%	39	42
40%	20	20
60%	6	7
80%	4	3
100%	2	3
120%	1	1
140%	0	0
160%	1	0
180%	2	0
200%	1	0
220%	0	0
240%	0	0
	114	114

Table 9 – Comparison between the statistical distributions of the 114 annual returns for the General Share Index measured by two similar methodologies

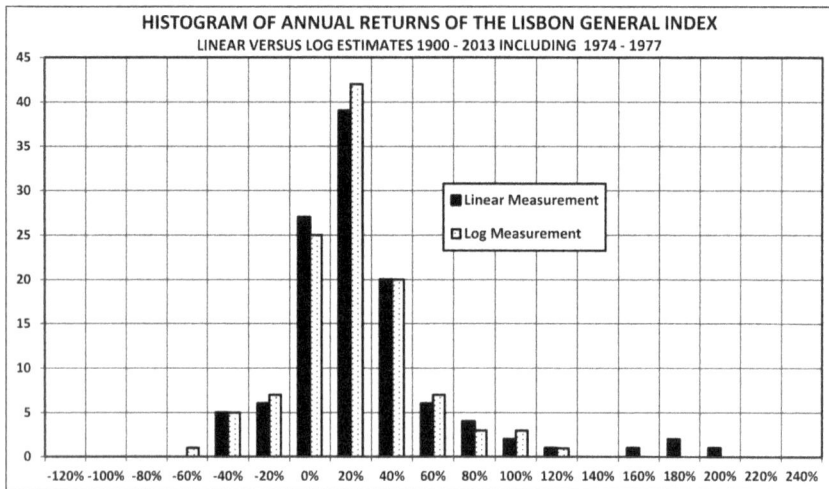

Figure 6 – Histogram of the annual 114 returns of the General Share Index during the twentieth century

346

REFERENCES

Aldcroft, Derek H., *"From Versailles to Wall Street 1919-1929"*, Penguin Books, Middlesex, 1987.

Alexandre, Valentim, *"Origens do colonialismo português moderno: 1822-1891"*, Lisboa, Sá da Costa Editora,1979.

Almodôvar, António; Cardoso, J. L., *"A History of Portuguese Economic Thought"*, London, Routledge, 1998.

Alquist, Ron; Benjamim Chabot, *"Did adhering to the gold-standard reduce the cost of capital?"* Federal Reserve Bank of Chicago, Working Paper 2010-13, 2010.

Alquist, Ron; Benjamim Chabot, *"Institutions, the Cost of Capital, and Long-Run Economic Growth: Evidence from the 19th Century Capital Market"*, Federal Reserve Bank of Chicago, WP17, 2012.

Amaral, Luciano, *"How a Country Catches Up: Explaining Economic Growth in Portugal in the Post-War World (1950s to 1973)"*, Doctoral Dissertation, Florence, European University Institute, 2003.

Amatori, F.; Jones, Geoffrey (editors), *"Business history around the world"*, Cambridge University Press, 2003.

Amatori, Franco, *"Big Business and European Unification: is the Chandlerian Mo--del Still Sustainable?"*, European Business History Association Newsletter 25, 2007.

Amatori, Franco, *"Reflections on Global business and Modern Italian Enterprise by a Stubborn 'Chandlerian'"*, Business History Review, vol. 71, nr. 2, 1997.

Amatori, Franco; Jones, Geoffrey (editors), *"Business history around the world"*, Cambridge, Cambridge University Press, 2003.

Amihud, Y; Mendelson, H., *"Asset pricing and the bid-ask spread"*, Journal of Financial Economics, 17, 1986: 223-249.

Amzalak, Moses Bensabat, *"O tratado de seguros de Pedro de Santarém Lisboa"*, 1958.

Andresen-Leitão, Nicolau, *"The Unexpected Guest: Portugal and European Integration (1956-63)"*, Doctoral dissertation, Florence, 2003.

Antunes, José Engrácia *An Economic Analysis of Portuguese Corporation Law — System and Current Developments*, Coimbra, Coimbra Editora, 2009.

Antwerp, W. C. Van, *"The Stock Exchange from within"*. New York, Doubleday, Page & Cº, 1913.

Appelbaum, E. & R. Batt, *"Private Equity at Work: When Wall Street manages Main Street"*, Russell Sage Foundation, 2014.

Arkes, Hadley, *"Bureaucracy, the Marshall Plan, and the National Interest"* , Prin--ceton: Princeton University Press, 1972.

Asiedu, Elisabeth, *"On the determinants of foreign direct investment to developing countries: Is Africa different?"*, World Development, *30 (1), 2002, pp. 107-19.*

Associação Industrial Portuguesa, Revista da Associação Industrial Portuguesa, 3.º ano, n.º 33, Nov. 1930.

Azevedo, Maria Luísa; Maria do Rosário Azevedo; Luís Bandeira; Miguel Cunha, *"Código do Mercado de Valores Mobiliários e legislação complementar: anotado e comentado"*, Porto, Instituto do Mercado de Capitais, Bolsa de Valores do Porto, 1996.

Bachelier, Louis, *"The Theory of Speculation"*, Paris 1900.

Baptista, Dina; Carlos Martins; Maximiano Pinheiro; Jaime Reis, *"New Estimates for Portugal's GDP 1910-1958"*, Lisboa, Banco de Portugal, 1997.

Barbosa, J. de Vilhena, *"Estudos Históricos e Archeologicos"*, tomo I, Lisboa, Typographia Castro & Irmão, 1874.

Barclays Capital, *"Equity-Gilt Study"*, London, Barclays Capital 1999.

Barnett, Jonathan M., "The Host's Dilemma: Strategic Forfeiture in Platform Markets for Informational Goods", Harvard Law Review, 124, 3, 2011:1863-1937.

Barro, Robert; José F. Ursua, *"Macroeconomic crises since 1870"*, NBER Working Paper nr. 13940, April (2008) available at http://www.nber.org/papers/w13940

Bastien, Carlos, *"A divisão da história do pensamento económico português em períodos"*, in Revista de História Económica e Social, nr. 1, 2nd series, 2001).

Bauer, R. I. Pool; L. Dexter, *"American Business and Public Policy"*, Chicago, Aldine Atherton, 1972.

Baumol, William J.; Robert E. Litan; Carl J. Schramm, *"Good Capitalism, Bad Capitalism and the Economics of Growth and Prosperity"*, Yale, Yale Press University, 2006.

Bedarride, J., *"Des bourses de commerce, agents de change et courtiers"*, Paris, Arthur Rousseau, 1901.

Benartzi, Shlomo; Richard H. Thaler, *"Myopic Loss Aversion and the Equity Premium Puzzle"*, The Quarterly Journal of Economics, MIT Press, vol. 110(1) (1995): 73--92, February.

Berge, Travis J.; Jordá, Òscar, *"A chronology of turning-points in economic activity: Spain 1850-2011"*, The Federal Reserve Bank of Kansas City Economic Research Department, Research Working Paper 11-14, 2011.

Berger A. N.; Gregory F. Udell, *"A More Complete Conceptual Framework for Financing of Small and Medium Enterprises"*, World Bank, Working Paper 3795, Dec 2005.

Berger, Helge; Albrecht Ritschl, *"Germany and the Political Economy of the Marshall Plan, 1947-1952: A Re-Revisionist View"*, in Europe's Postwar Recovery, edited by Barry Eichengreen, 199-245. Cambridge: Cambridge University Press, 1995.

Bergier, Jean-François, *"Histoire Economique de la Suisse"*, Zurich, Cologne, Benziger Verlag, 1983.

Berkowitz, R.; T. N. Toay (Eds), *"The Intellectual Origins of the Global Financial Crisis"*, Fordham University Press, 2012.

Besomi, D. (Ed.), *"Crises and Cycles in Economic Dictionaries and Encyclopaedia"*, Routledge, 2012.

Bethencourt, Francisco; Diogo Ramada Curto (eds.), *"Portuguese Oceanic Expansion 1400-1800"*, Cambridge: Cambridge University Press, 2007.

Billio M.; L. Pelizzon; D. Sartori, *"The European Single Currency and the Volatility of the European stock markets"*, Greta Working Paper 01-02, March 2001.

Birmingham, David, *"The Coffee Barons of Cazengo"*, The Journal of African History, Vol 19, Issue 4/Oct/1978, pp 523 538, DOI: 10.1017/S0021853700016467.

Bivens, J.; *"Failure by Design: The Story behind America's Broken Economy"*, EPI/ Cornell, 2011.

Blakey, George, *"History of the London Stock Market 1945-2009"*, Hampshire: Harriman House Ltd., 2010.

Blinder A.; Andrew W. Lo; R. M. Solow (eds), *"Rethinking the Financial Crisis"*, Russell Sage Foundation, 2013.

Bodenhorn, Howard, *"Large block shareholders institutional investors, boards of directors and bank value in the nineteenth century"*, Working Paper 16955, 2013. http://www.nber.org/papers/w18955

Boldrin, Michelle; Adrian Peralta-Alva, *"What happened to the US stock market? Accounting for the last 50 years"*, Federal Bank Reserve of St Louis Research Division Working-Paper Series, nr. 42-A, 2009.

http://research.stlouisfed.org/wp/2009/2009-042.pdf

Borchardt, Knut; Christoph Buchheim, *"The Marshall Plan and Key Economic Sectors: A Microeconomic Perspective"*, in The Marshall Plan and Germany, edited by Charles S. Maier and Gunter Bischof, 410-451. Oxford: Berg, 1991.

Bordo, M. D.; J. Williamson (eds.), *"Globalization in Historical Perspective"*, Chicago, University of Chicago Press, 2003.

Bordo, Michael; Thomas Helbeling, *"International business-cycle synchronization in historical perspective"*, The Manchester School, vol. 79(2), March 2011: 208--238.

Borges, José Ferreira, *Diccionario juridico-commercial*, 2nd ed. - Porto: Typ. de Sebastião José Pereira, 1856 (1st edition 1833). http://purl.pt/298/3/sc-1369-v_PDF/sc-1369-v_PDF_24-C-R0075/sc-1369-v_0000_capa-426_t24-C-R0075.pdf

Boudon, Georges, *"La Bourse Anglaise"*, Paris, Pedone, 1898.

Boudon, Georges, *"La Bourse et ses Hôtes"*, Paris, Felixm Ciret et Pedone, 1896.

Boxer, C. R., *"The Portuguese seaborne empire 1415-1825"*, New York, A.A. Knopf, 1969. Translated into Portuguse, *"O império colonial português"*, Lisboa, Edições 70, 1977.

Bozerian, Jeannotte, *"La Bourse, ses Opérateurs et ses Opérations"*, vol. I, Paris, E. Dentu and A. Marescq, 1959.

Braudel, Fernand, *"Civilisation matérielle, économie et Capitalisme, XVe- XVIIIe siècles"*, Paris, Armand Colin, 1979.

Brealey, Richard and Stuart Myers, *"Principles of Corporate Finance"*, Lisbon, McGraw-Hill, 2009.

Brito, José Maria Brandão de, *"Estado Novo: Discursos e Estratégias de uma Industrialização Tardia"*, in Manuel Heitor, José Maria Brandão de Brito, Maria Fernanda Rollo (eds.). *Momentos de Inovação e Engenharia em Portugal no Século XX*, Lisboa, Dom Quixote, 2004.

Brown Jr., William; Richard Burdekin, *"German Debt traded in London during the Second World War: A British perspective on Hitler"*, Economica, 69, 2002: 655-669.

Brown, Stephen J.; William N. Goetzmann; Stephen Ross, *"Survival Bias and the Equity Premium Puzzle"*, The Journal of Finance 50(3), 1995: 853-873.

Burhop, Carsten; Sergey Gelman, *"Transaction costs, liquidity and expected returns at the Berlin Stock Exchange, 1892-1913"*, Preprints of the Max Planck Institute for Research on Collective Goods, Bonn 2010/20, May 2010.

Buriat, *"Le Comissionaire contre-partiste en Bourse et spécialement en marchandises"*, Paris, Henri Janne, 1903.

Caetano, António A., *"A Formação de Quadros Empresariais pelo ISCEF depois de 1949"* [The executive education by the Lisbon Institute of Economics and Finance after 1949] (unpublished paper, CD-rom, XXIII Annual Meeting of the Portuguese Economic and Social History Association, 2003).

Cagigal, Juan Carlos Rojo, *"Las origenes de los Mercados Bursátiles en España, 1800-1939"*, Bolsa, 4° trimestre de 2009: 40-46.

Câmara, Paulo, *"Manual de Direito de Valores Mobiliários"*, Lisboa, Sociedade Sérvulo Correia & Associados, 2011, 2nd ed.

Campbell, Gareth; Christopher Coyle, and John Turner *"This Time is Different: Causes and Consequences of British Banking Instability over the Long Run"*, Journal of Financial Hability, vol. 27, Dec 2016: 1-278.

Campbell, John Y.; Robert J. Schiller; Luis M.Viceira, *"Understanding inflation-indexed bond markets"*, Cowles Foundation Working Paper n.º 1696, 2009.

Campbell, John Y.; Samuel B. Thompson, *"Predicting the Equity Premium Out of Sample: Can Anything Beat the Historical Average?"*, NBER Working Paper No. 11468, July 2005.

Campbell, John Y.; John H. Cochrane *"By Force of Habit: A Consumption-Based Explanation of Aggregate Stock Market Behavior"*, The Journal Economy, vol. 107(2), 1999: 205-251.

Campbell, John Y.; Schiller, Robert J., 1988a, *"The dividend-price ratio and expectations of future dividends and discount factors"*, Review of Financial Studies, 1: 195-228.

Campbell, John Y.; Robert J. Schiller, *"Stock Prices, Earnings, and Expected Dividends"*, Journal of Finance, 43, 661-676, 1988b.

Cardoso, José L., , *"Ecos da Grande Depressão em Portugal, Relatos, Diagnósticos e Soluções"*, Análise Social, 203, XVII, 2012: 370-400.

Cardoso, José L., *"Confusion de Confusiones: ethics and options on seventeenth--century stock Exchange markets"*, Financial History Review, vol 9 (2), 2002: 109-123.

Carreras y Gonzalez, Mariano, *"Tratado Didactico de Economia Politica, Filosofía del Interés Personal"*, Madrid, Guijarro, 1865.

Carreras, Albert; Xavier Tafuneli, *"La Gran Empresa en Espana 1917-1974: Una Primera Aproximacion"*, Revista de Historia Industrial 1993, nr. 3: 127-75.

Cassis, Youssef, *"Capitals of Capital: A History of International Financial Centres, 1780-2005"*, Cambridge, Cambridge University Press, 2006.

Cassis, Youssef, *"Big Business: The European Experience in the Twentieth Century"*, Oxford, Oxford University Press, 1997.

Castaño, David, *"Paternalismo e cumplicidade: As relações Luso-Britânicas de 1943 a 1949"*, Lisboa, Associação dos Amigos do Arquivo Histórico e Diplomático, 2006.

Caves, Richard, *"Multinational enterprise and economic analysis"*, Cambridge, Cambridge University Press, 2007.

Chandler Jr., Alfred, *"The Visible Hand: The Managerial Revolution in American Business"*, Cambridge, Belknap Press, 1977.

Chandler, A.; P. Hagdtröm; Örjan Sölvel, *"The Dynamic Firm"*, Oxford, Oxford University Press, 1999.

Chandler, Alfred, *"Strategy and structure, Chapters in the History of the American Industrial Enterprise"*, Cambridge, MA, MIT Press 1962/1998.

Chandler, Alfred, *"Strategy and Structure"*, in Nicolai J. Foss (ed.) Resources, firms and strategies: A reader in the Resource-Based Perspective, Oxford, Oxford University Press, 1997, 40-51.

Chandler, Alfred, *"Scale and Scope. The Dynamics of Industrial Capitalism"*, Cambridge MA, Harvard University Press, 1990.

Chateaudun, Henri Lefevre de, *"Traité des valeurs mobilières et des Opérations de Bourse: Placement et Speculation"*, Paris, Lachaud, 1870.

Chevilliard, G., *"Le Stock-Exchange"*, Paris, Boyveau et Chevilet, 1904.

Clemente, Eloy Fernández, *"El Caso Champalimaud: Análisis de un Contencioso Luso-Hispano"*, in II Encontro International Relações Portugal — Espanha. Uma História Paralela, Um Destino Comum?, Oporto, CEPESE, 8, 2002: 9-27. pdf in castillan - www.cepese.pt/pdf/8actas.pdf.

Clever, Paul; Mario Muth, *"Trends and challenges of electronic trading: from the open outcry to self-execution"*, in Lori Nicholson, The Euromoney, Global Exchanges & Trading Handbook, Deutsche Bank, 2005.

Colson, C., *"Cours d'Economie Politique Professé à l'Ecole des Ponts et Chaussées"*, Paris, Gauthier-Villars et Guillaumin, 1903.

Confraria, João, *"Condicionamento industrial: Uma Análise Económica"*, Lisboa, Direcção-Geral da Indústria, 1992.

Consumano, Michael; Fernando Suarez, *"The role of services in platform markets"*, MIT Digital Centre, Paper 244, Nov 2008.

Cornell, Bradford, *"The Equity Risk Premium"*, New York, John Wiley & Sons, 1999.

Cosack, C., *"Traité de Droit Commercial"*, vol. II, Translated from German by Léon Mis, Paris, Giard et Brière, 1905.

Costa, José Rodrigues da; Maria Eugénia Mata; David Justino, "Serving SMEs via the Stock Exchange: Historical Lessons from the Lisbon Exchange," *Journal of Economic Issues,* September 2016 (Volume 50, Number 3): 851-871.

Costa, José Rodrigues da; Maria Eugénia Mata; David Justino, *"Portugal"*, in Elroy Dimson, Paul Marsh, Mike Staunton (editors), Credit Suisse Global Investment Returns Yearbbook, Zurich, Crédit Suisse Research Institute Publisher, 2014: 35. https://publications.credit-suisse.com/tasks/render/file/?fileID=0E0A3525-EA60--2750-71CE20B5D14A7818

Costa, José Rodrigues da; Maria Eugénia Mata; David Justino, *"Estimating the Portuguese Average Cost of Capital"* Historische Sozialforschung, Historical Social Research. An International Journal for the Application of Formal Methods to History" (Section 'Cliometrics'), n° 140, Vol. 37, 2, 2012: 326-361.

Costa, José Rodrigues da; Maria Eugénia Mata, *"Portugal's 1974 Carnation Revolution and nationalizations: the effects on the Lisbon Stock-Exchange"*, Zeits-chrift für Unternehmensgeschichte (Journal of Business History), vol. 56/1, 2011:29-47.

Costa, José Rodrigues da; Maria Eugénia Mata, *"Stock Exchanges. How to meet the needs of our customers"*, Banks and Bank Systems: Vol. 6, Issue 3, 2011a: 106--120 http://businessperspectives.org/journals_free/bbs/2011/BBS_en_2011_three_Mata.pdf

Costa, José Rodrigues; Maria Eugénia Mata; David Justino (2009), *"Portuguese Average Cost of Capital"* , FEUNL Working Paper 0543, Jul 2009.

Courtois, Alphonse, *"Traité d'Opérations de Bourse et de Change"*, *12ème edition par Emmanuel Vidal,* Paris, Garnier Frères, 1902.

Credit Suisse First Boston, *"The CSFB Equity-Gilt Study"*, London 1999, CSFB.

Crédit Suisse, *"Portugal"*, Source book, Zurich, Crédit Suisse Research Institute Publisher, 2014: 147-152.

Cunha, Alice Monteiro, *"À Descoberta da Europa"*, Lisboa, Instituto Diplomático, MNE, 2007.

Cunha, Rita Campos, *"Mudanças nas empresas privadas: A cultura empresarial"*, in Privatizações e Regulação: A experiência Portuguesa, Lisboa, Ministério das Finanças, 1999: 175-190.

Dahlquist, Magnus; José Vicente Martinez; Paul Söderlind, *"Individual Investor Activity and Performance"*, CEPR Discussion Papers 8744, 2012.

Dalton, John, *"Stock Market Works"*, New York, New York Institute of Finance, 2001.

Damodaran's page in his website — http://pages.stern.nyu.edu/~adamodar

De Long, J. Bradford; Barry Eichengreen, *"The Marshall Plan: History's Most Successful Structural Adjustment Program"*, in Postwar Economic Reconstruction and Lessons for the East Today, edited by Rudiger Dornbusch et al, 189-230, Cambridge, MIT Press, 1993.

Decree from 23 August 1888, with the second *"Código Comercial Português"* also known as *"Código Veiga Beirão"*.

Decree Law 142-A/91 of 10 April 1991, with the First Securities Code.

Decree Law 486/99 of 1 November 1999, with the Second Securities Code.

Decree Law 8/74 of 14 January 1974, with an Interim Securities Code.

Decree Law 57-A/2007 of 1 October 2007, updating the Second Securities Code.

Dejuán, O.; Eladio Febrero; Maria C. Marcuzzo (Eds), *"The First Great Recession of the 21st Century. Competing Explanations"*, Edward Elgar, 2011.

Desai, R., *"Geopolitical Economy: After US Hegemony, Globalization and Empire"*, Pluto Press, 2013.

Dimson, Elroy; Paul Marsh; Mike Staunton, *"The Triumph of the Optimists, 101 Years of Global Investment Returns"*, Princeton, New Jersey, Oxford: Princeton University Press, 2002.

Direcção Geral de Estudos e Previsão, *"Privatizações e Regulação: A experiência Portuguesa"*, Lisboa, Ministério das Finanças, 1999.

Djelic, M. L., *"Exporting the American Model: The Post-war Transformation of European Business"*, Oxford, Oxford University Press, 1998.

Donaldson, Lex, *"For positivist organization theory"*, London, Sage, 1996.

Duarte, Inocêncio de Sousa, *"Dicionário de direito comercial, Comércio Terrestre; Comércio Marítimo"; 2 tomes, Lisboa, 1881.

Duarte, José Matusse, *"A Companhia de Moçambique"*, Masters Thesis, FCSH-UNL, Lisboa, 2000.

Duarte, Rui Pinto, *"Escritos Sobre Direito das Sociedades"*, Coimbra, Coimbra Editora, 2008.

Duffie, Darrel; Nicholae Gârleanu; Lasse Heje Pedersen, *"Securities lending, shorting, and Pricing"*, Journal of Financial Economics, 66 (2002): 307-339.

Duguid, Charles, *"The story of the Stock Exchange, its History and position"*, London, G. Richards, 1901. Available at http://books.google.com/books?id=X-8JAAAAIA AJ&printsec=frontcover&hl=pt-PT#v=onepage&q&f=false

Dunning, John; Sarianna Lunden, *"Multinational enterprises and the global economy"*, Cheltenham, Edward Elgar Publishing, 2008.

ECA, *"Reports to the Technical Commission of the European Commission Administration ECA on the use of the direct help"*, Historical Archive of the Bank of Portugal AHBP, boxes 61-67.

Edersheim, Elizabeth Haas, *"McKinsey's Marvin Bower Vision, Leadership, and the Creation of Management Consulting"*, New Jersey, John Wiley & Sons, 2004.

Eichengreen, Barry; Marc Uzan (1992), *"The Marshall Plan: Economic Effects and Implications for Eastern Europe and the USSR"*, Economic Policy 14 (1992): 14--75.

Eichengreen, Barry ed. *"The reconstruction of the international economy, 1945--1960"*, Brookfield, Elgar Reference Collection, 1996b.

Eichengreen, Barry, *"Institutions and Economic Growth: Europe after World War II"*, in Economic Growth in Europe since 1945, edited by Nicholas Crafts and Gianni Toniolo, 38-70, Cambridge, Cambridge University Press, 1996a.

Eichengreen, Barry, *"Reconstructing Europe's Trade and Payments: The European Payments System"*, Manchester, Manchester University Press, 1993.

Ellis, Howard, *"The Economics of Freedom: The Progress and Future of Aid to Europe"*, New York, Harper & Row, 1950.

European Commission Administration, Reports from the Technical Commission of the ECA, European Commission Administration on the Applications for release of counterpart funds including the Portuguese applications to the Counterpart Fund — Historical Archive of the Bank of Portugal [AHBP] box number 65.

European Commission site on Innovation and SMEs at

http://ec.europa.eu/research/sme/leaflets/en/intro02.html

Evans, David S., *"The antitrust economics of multi-sided platform markets"*, Yale Journal of Regulation, 20, (2), Summer 2003.

Fama, Eugene; Kenneth R. French, *"Business Conditions and Expected Returns on Stock Bonds"*, Journal of Financial Economics, 25, 1989, 23-49.

Fama, Eugene; Kenneth R. French *"Dividend Yields and Expected Stock Returns"*, Journal of Financial Economics, 1988, 22: 3-25.

Fama, Eugene; G. Schwert *"Stock Returns, Real Activity, Inflation and Money"*, American Economic Review, 71, 1981: 545-565.

Fama, Eugene and G. Schwert *"Assets returns and Inflation"*, Journal of Financial Economics, 5, 1977: 115-146.

Faria, Miguel Figueira de; José Amado Mendes (ed.), *"Dicionário de História Empresarial"*, Lisboa, Imprensa Nacional-Casa da Moeda, vol I, 2013.

Ferderer, J. Peter, *"The Emergence of the Modern Over-the-Counter Market for Government Bonds, 1861-1928"*, Macalester College Working Paper, 2009.

Fernández, Pablo, *"The Equity Premium in 150 Textbooks"*, IESE Business School, 2009. *Journal of Financial Transformation*, vol. 27, 2009: 14-18.

Ferraris, Cario F., *"Principii di scienza bancaria"*, Milano, Ulrico Hoepli, 1892.

Ferreira, Miguel A.; Pedro Santa-Clara, *"Forecasting Stock Markets Returns: the Sum of the Parts is More than the Whole"*, Journal of Financial Economics, 100, 2011: 514-537.

Flandreau, Marc, *"Collective Action Clauses before they had Airplanes: Bondholder Committees and the London Stock Exchange in the 19th Century (1827-1868)"*, Graduate Institute of International and Development Studies Working Paper, nr. 01/2013.

Fontaine, Henri, *"La Bourse et ses Operations Légales"*, Paris, Pedone, 1905.

Foreman-Peck, J.; Leslie Hannah, *"Extreme Divorce: the Managerial Revolution in UK Companies before 1914"*, Cardiff Economics, Working Papers, E2011/21, 2011.

Foreman-Peck, J., *"A history of the world economy: international economic relations since 1850"*, Brigton, Wheatsheaf Books; New York, London, Sidney, Tokyo, Singapore: Harvester Wheatsheaf, 1995, 2001 (I, II, V, VI).

Foreman-Peck, J., ed. , *"Historical foundations of globalization"*, Northampton, Elgar, 2001a.

Foreman-Peck, J. (1995, 1999), O'Rourke, Kevin and Jeffrey Williamson, *"Globalization and History, The Evolution of a Nineteenth-Century Atlantic Economy"*, Cambridge MA., The MIT Press, 1999.

Franchi, Luigi, *"Manuale del diritto commerciale italiano"*, Vol. I, Torino, Unione typografica editrice, 1890.

Frankema, Ewout, *"Raising Revenue in the British Empire, 1870-1940: How 'Extractive' Were Colonial Taxes?"*, Journal of Global History 5(3) 2010: 447-477.

Freire, Pascoal José de Melo, *"Institutiones iuris civilis lusitani"*, Coimbra, 1789 (translated by Miguel Pinto de Menezes [revised by A. M. Hespanha], in Boletim do Ministério da Justiça, 161 [1966], 94. Available at http://www.fd.unl.pt/docentes_docs/ma/amh_MA_3849.pdf

Frey, Bruno S.; Marcel Kucher, *"History as Reflected in Capital Markets: The Case of World War II"*, The Journal of Economic History, Vol. 60, No. 2 (Jun., 2000), pp. 468-496.

GAFEEP, Gabinete para a Análise do Financiamento do Estado e das Empresas Públicas, *"Privatizações em Portugal Uma reforma estrutural"*, Ministério das Finanças, Lisboa, 1995.

Galvarriato, Juan Antonio, *"La Bolsa de Madrid. Fundación por la Ley de 10 de Septiembre de 1831. Desenvolvimiento histórico de la Ley y de la Bolsa a través de la primera centuria"*, Madrid, Bolsa de Madrid, 1935.

Garrett, T. A. Almeida, *"Um governo em África, Inhambane, 1905-06"*, Lisboa, Empreza da História de Portugal, 1907.

Gederblom, Oscar; Abe Jong; Just Jonker, *"The formative years of the Modern Corporation: The Dutch East India Company VOC, 1602-23"*, The Journal of Economic History, vol. 73(4), Dec 2013: 1050-1076.

Ghemawat, P.; Tarun Khanna, "The Nature of Diversified Business Groups: A Research Design and Two Case Studies", *Journal of Industrial Economics* 46, 1 March 1998: 35-61.

Giannetti, Renato; Michelangelo Vasta, *"Evolution of Italian Enterprises in the 20th century"*, Heidelberg, New York, Physica-Verlag, 2006.

Giesecke, Kay; Francis A. Longstaff; Stephen Schaefer; Ilya Strebulaev, *"Corporate bond default risk: a 150–year perspective"*, Journal of Financial Economics, 102, 2011: 233-250.

Gimbel, John, *"The Origins of the Marshall Plan"*, Stanford, Stanford University Press, 1976.

Godinho, Vitorino Magalhães, *"Estrutura da Antiga Sociedade Portuguesa"*, Lisboa, Arcádia, 1980.

Godinho, Vitorino Magalhães, *"Finanças Públicas e Estrutura do Estado"* in Dicionário de História de Portugal, vol. II, Lisboa, Iniciativas Editoriais, 1971: 244-264.

Goetzmann, William N.; Philippe Jorion, *"A Century of Global stock Markets"*, Working Paper 5901, NBER, 2000.

Goetzmann, William N.; S. J. Brown; R.G. Ibbotson, "*Offshore Hedge Funds: Survival and Performance*", Journal of Business, Vol. 72, No. 1, 1999: 91-117.

Gordon, Myron J., (1959), "*Dividends, Earnings and Stock Prices*", Review of Economics and Statistics 41: 99-105.

Gorham, Michael; Nidhi Singh, "*Electronic Exchanges, The Global Transformation from Pits to Bits*", Elsevier, 2009

Gorton, Gary, "*Questions and Answers about the Financial Crisis*", Prepared for the U.S. Financial Crisis Inquiry Commission, Yale and NBER, 2010.

Goyal, Amit; Ivo Welch 2008, "*A comprehensive look at the empirical performance of equity risk premium prediction*", Review of Financial Studies 21: 1455-1508.

Griffiss, Bartow, "*The New York Call Money Market*", New York, The Ronald Press C°, 1925.

Griffiths, Richard T., ed. "*Explorations in OEEC History*", Paris 1997.

Grossman, Richard S., "Bloody Foreigners! Overseas Equity on the London Stock Exchange, 1869-1928", *Economic History Review*, May 2015, 68(2): 471-521.

Grossman, R.S., "*Unsettled Account: The Evolution of Banking in the Industrialised World Since 1800*", Princeton, Princeton University Press, 2010.

Gründt, "*I contratti di Borsa apud Manuale di diritto commerciale, marítimo, cambiário, redatto del Dott. Guglielmo Endeman*", vol III, Part I, traduzione dell' Avv. Carlo Betocchi, Napoli, Nicola Jovene & Cª, 1899.

Guillard, Edmond, "*Les Opérations de Bourse*", Paris, n. p. 1877.

Guilmard, Émile, "*De la vente directe des valeurs de bourse sans intermédiaire*", Paris, Guillaumin et Cie, 1904.

Hafer, Rick W.; Scott E Hein, "*The Stock Market*", London, Greenwood Pres, 2007.

Hannah, Leslie, "London as the Global Market for Corporate Securities before 1914", *in Financial Centres and International Capital Flows in the Nineteenth and Twentieth Centuries*, Oxford University Press, 2011.

Hardach, Gerd, "The First World War 1914-1918", Penguin Books, Middlesex, 1987.

Haugen, R., "*The New Finance: The Case against Efficient Markets*", (second edition), Upper Saddle River, NJ: Prentice-Hall, 1999.

Hautcoeur, Pierre-Cyrille; Amir Rezaee; Ângelo Riva, "*How to regulate a financial market? The impact of the 1893-1898 regulatory reforms on the Paris Bourse*" Ecole Normale Supérieure PSE Working Papers number 2010-01.

Hautcoeur, Pierre-Cyrille; Amir Rezaee; Ângelo Riva, "*Stock exchange industry regulation, The Paris Bourse, 1893 — 1898*", 2010. Available at

http://eh.net/eha/wp-content/uploads/2013/11/Hautcoeurb.pdf

Hayaux du Tilly, Jean, "*Du marché financier et de sa réglementation*", Paris, L. Larose, 1901.

Hekimian, Raphael, "*A study of contagion between French and American stock markets. The inter war example*", University Paris West, WP, 2013.

Hertner, Peter; Geoffrey Jones eds., "*Multinationals: Theory and History*", Aldershot, Gower, 1986.

Hillebrand, Eric; Marcelo C. Medeiros (2009), *"The Benefits of Bagging for Forecast Models of Realized Volatility"* Econometric Reviews, 29(5), 2010: 571-593.

Hilt, Eric, *"When did ownership separate from control? Corporate Governance in the Early Nineteenth Century"*, Journal of Economic History, 68- 3 (2008): 645--685.

Hirschman, Albert O., *"Fifty years after the Marshall Plan: Two posthumous memoirs and some personal recollections"* in Albert Hirschman "Crossing Boundaries", selected writings, New York, Zone Books, 1998: 33-43.

Hogan, Michael J., *"The Marshall Plan: America, Britain and the reconstruction of Western Europe, 1947-52"*, Cambridge, Cambridge University Press, 1987.

Horta, Paulo; Carlos Mendes; Isabel Vieira, *"Contagion effects of the subprime crisis in the European NYSE Euronext markets"*, Portuguese Economic Journal (2010) 9: 115-140. DOI 10.1007/s10258-010-0056-6.

Houpt, Stephan; Juan Rojo Cagigal, *"The origins of the Bilbao Stock Exchange 1891--1936"*, Universidad Carlos III, Madrid, Working Papers 10-5, Apr. 2010.

http://mpra.ub.uni-muenchen.de/11864/

Huggins, Robert, *"Regional Stock Exchanges in the UK: adressing the Mirage of Global Markets, Mondovision Worldwide Exchange Intelligence"*, 7/06/2014.

Ibbotson Associates, *"Stocks, Bonds, Bills, and Inflation Yearbook"*, several years.

Imprensa Nacional, *Diário do Governo*, several issues. http://www.dre.pt

Instituto Nacional de Estatística, *"Estatísticas das Sociedades"*, Lisboa, INE, several years.

Instituto Nacional de Estatística, *"Principais Sociedades"*, Lisboa, INE, 1972.

Instituto Nacional de Estatística, *"Estatísticas Monetárias e Financeiras"*, Lisboa, INE, several years.

Jones, Geoffrey, *"Multinationals and global capitalism from the nineteenth to the twenty-first century"*, Oxford, Oxford Univ. Press, 2005.

Jones, Geoffrey; Harm Schröter eds., *"The Rise of Multinationals in Continental Europe"*, Aldershot, Edward Elgar, 1993.

Jones, Geoffrey, *"Merchants to Multinationals"*, Oxford, Oxford University Press, 2000.

Jordà, Ò., Schularick, M. and Taylor, A. M. "Financial Crises, Credit Booms, and External Imbalances: 140 Years of Lessons". *IMF Economic Review* 59 (2) pp. 340--378.

Jorion, Philippe and William Goetzmann, *"Global Stock Markets in the Twentieth Century"*, The Journal of Finance, vol. LIV, 3, 1999: 953-980.

Judt, Tony, *"Postwar: A History of Europe Since 1945"*, New York, Penguin Books, 2005.

Justino, David, *"História da Bolsa de Lisboa"*, Lisboa, Inapa - Bolsa de Valores de Lisboa, 1994.

Kaheman, Daniel; Amos Tversky, (1992) *"Prospect Theory: An Analysis of Decision under Risk"*, Journal of Consumer Research 19 (June 1992): 14-25.

Katovich, J., "*Alternative capital financing for the 99% (of business)*", FOCUS, nº 226, December 2011, World Federation of Exchanges.

Keim, Donald B.; Robert F. Stambaugh (1986), "*Predicting Returns in the Stock and Bond Markets*", Journal of Financial Economics, 17: 357-390.

Keynes, John Maynard, "*The economic consequences of the peace*", MacMillan, London 1924.

Kindleberger, Charles P. "*Marshall Plan Days*", London, Allen & Unwin Cº, 1987.

Kindleberger, Charles P., "*The World in Depression 1929-1939*", Penguin Books, London, 1987.

Knobl, Peter, "*Securities Trading and recent developments in the exchanges marketplace*", in Lori Nicholson, The Euromoney, Global Exchanges & Trading Handbook, Deutsche Bank, 2005: 27-31.

Krugman, Paul, "*The Return of Depression Economics, and the Crisis of 2008*", N. York, WW Norton & Cº, 1999, 2009.

La Porta, R.; F. Lopez-de-Silanes; A. Shleifer; R.W. Vishny, "*The Quality of Government*", Journal of Law, Economics and Organisation 15, 1 (1999), 222-279.

La Porta, Rafael; Florencio Lopez-de-Silanes; Andrei Schleifer; Robert Vishny, "*Law and Finance*", Journal of Political Economy, 1113, 1998.

La Porta, R.; F. Lopez-de-Silanes; A. Shleifer; R.W. Vishny, R.W, "*Legal Determinants of External Finance*", 52 Journal of Finance 3 (1997), 1131-1150.

Lafargue, M. Paul, "*La fonction économique de la Bourse*", extrait di *Devenir Social*, April 1897.

Laíns, Pedro, "*Structural change and economic growth in Portugal, 1950-1990*", in Sakari Heikkinen and Jan Luiten van Zanden (Eds.), Explorations in Economic Growth, Amsterdam, Aksant, 2004, pp. 321-340.

Laíns, Pedro, "*An account of the Portuguese African empire, 1885-1975*", *Revista de Historia Económica*, (Madrid), vol. 16, 1998: 235-63.

Laíns, Pedro, *História da Caixa Geral de Depósitos 1974-2000*, Lisboa, Imprensa de Ciências Sociais, 2011.

Lambert, Eliezer, "*Dictionnaire de legislation et de jurisprudence sur les opérations de bourse*", Paris, 1902, Giard et Brière.

Laveleye, Emile, "*Éléments d'Économie Politique*", Paris, Hachette, 1898.

Le Bris, David, "*What is a Stock Market Crash? 20 French Crashes since 1854*".

https://www.eurofidai.org/Le_Bris_2010.pdf retrieved on June, 30, 2014.

Le Bris, David; Hautecoeur, Pierre-Cyrille, "*A challenge to triumphant optimists? A new index for the Paris stock exchange (1854-2007)*", LEA-INRA Working paper nr. 21, 2008.

Lenine, Vladimir I., "*Imperialism, the Highest Stage of Capitalism*", London, Routledge, 1993, 1917.

Lettau, Martin; Sydney Ludvigson, 2001, "*Consumption, Aggregate Wealth, and Expected Stock Returns*", Journal of Finance, 56, 815-849.

Lisbon Stock Exchange, *Boletins de Cotações*, Lisboa, several issues.

London Stock Exchange Intelligence, *Burdett's Official Intelligence,* several issues. British Library of Political and Economic Science, BLPES, London School of Economics.

Loureiro, F. da Maia, *"Taxas de Rendimento Real, Índices de Cotação e Índices de Movimento da Bolsa de Lisboa"*, Estudos do INE, 6, 1943.

Machuqueiro, Pedro Urbano, *"Nos Bastidores da Corte, o Rei e a Casa Real na crise da Monarquia 1889-1908"*, PhD dissertation presented at FCSH, UNL, 2014.

MacPherson, Myra, *"The Bewitching Brothers Victoria Woodhull, Tennessee Claflin, and Women's rights on Wall Street"*, Financial History, Museum of American Finance, Winter 2014a: 12-15.

MacPherson, Myra, *"The Scarlet Sisters: Sex, Suffrage, and Scandal in the Gilded Age"*, New York, 2014.

Maddison, Angus, *"The World Economy. A Millennial Perspective"*, Paris, OECD, 2001.

Madureira, Nuno L., *"Enterprises, Incentives and Networks: The Formative Years of the Electrical Network in Portugal, 1920-47"*, Business History, Oct 2007, 49, 5: 595-615.

Magee, Gary, *"Investors, information and the British World 1860-1913"*, EBHA, Milan, 2009.

March, Michael, *"The future of clearing: improving the market infrastructure"* in Lori Nicholson, The Euromoney, Global Exchanges & Trading Handbook, Deutsche Bank, 2005: 11-14.

Markowitz, Harry, *"Portfolio Selection"*, Journal of Finance, Vol. 7, nr. 1. Mar., 1952: 77-91.

Marques, A. H. de Oliveira, *"Portugal na Crise dos Séculos XIV e XV"*, Vol. 4 of Nova História de Portugal, Lisboa, Presença, 1st edition, 1987.

Martín-Aceña, Pablo; Ángeles Pons; Concepción Betrán, *"Financial crises and financial reforms in Spain: what have we learned?"*, Working Papers in Economic History, Universidad Carlos III de Madrid, Departamento de Historia Económica e Instituciones, WP 10-01 January 2010.

Martins, Maria Belmira, *"Sociedades e Grupos em Portugal"*. Lisboa, Estampa, 2nd edition, 1975.

Mata, Maria Eugénia; José Rodrigues da Costa, *"From finance to management: Rui Ennes Ulrich, a Portuguese scholar of the early twentieth century"*, Busines History, DOI: 10.1080/00076791.2013.809525; 2013.

Mata, Maria Eugénia, José Rodrigues da Costa, David Justino, "Justificação da Nova Edição da Obra", *"Prefácio"*, *in Da Bolsa e Suas Operações*, Ruy Ennes Ulrich, Coimbra, Imprensa da Universidade de Coimbra, 2nd edition, reviewed and augmented, 2011 (1st edition 1906): 7-14; 15-28, ISBN: 978-989-26-0131-1.

Mata, Maria Eugénia, *"As small events may have large long-run effects on business perspectives (Portugal, 1940s)"*, Problems & Perspectives in Management, Vol 8, Issue 3, 2010: 17-31.

Mata, Maria Eugénia, *"Portuguese Public Debt and Financial Business Before WWI"*, Business and Economic Horizons, 3, 2010a: 10-27 http://ideas.repec.org/a/pdc/jrnbeh/v3y2010i3p10-27.html

Mata, Maria Eugénia, "*A forgotten country in Globalisation? The role of foreign capital in nineteenth-century Portugal*", Margrit Müller; Timo Myllyntaus (eds.), Small European countries responding to Globalisation and De-globalisation, Bern, Berlin, Bruxelles, Frankfurt am Main, New York, Oxford, Vienna, 2008: 177-209.

Mata, Maria Eugénia "*Large Portuguese firms from the Marshall Plan to EFTA: Early stirrings of Managerial Capitalism?*", Imprese e Storia, 2009, 38: 121-153.

Mata, Maria Eugénia "*Foreign joint-stock companies operating in Portuguese colonies on the eve of the First World War*", South African Journal of Economic History, 2007, Vol 22, nr. 1 and 2, Sep.: 74-107.

Mata, Maria Eugénia; Nuno Valério, "*História económica de Portugal — uma Perspectiva Global*", Lisboa, Presença, 2003.

Mata, Maria Eugénia, "*As finanças públicas portuguesas da Regeneração à Primeira Guerra Mundial*", Banco de Portugal, Economic History Series, nr. 4, Lisboa, 1993.

Mata, Maria Eugénia, "*Actividade revolucionária no Portugal contemporâneo - uma perspectiva de longa duração*", Análise Social, nr. 112-113, vol XXVI, 1991: 755--769.

Mata, Maria Eugénia, "*Câmbios e política cambial na economia portuguesa 1891--1931*", Cadernos da Revista de História Económica e Social nr. 8, Livraria Sá da Costa Editora, Lisboa, 1987.

Matthews, John O., "*Struggle and Survival on Wall Street*", Oxford, Oxford University Press, 1994.

Mehra, Rajnish; Edward C. Prescott (1985), "*The Equity Premium: A Puzzle*", Journal of Monetary Economics: 15, 145-161.

Michie, Ranald C., "*The London and New York Stock Exchanges*", New York, Routledge, 1987, 2011.

Michie, Ranald C., "*Stock Exchanges since 1960*", Focus, March 2010:11-14.

Milward, Alan S., "*War, Economy and Society 1939-1945*", Penguin Books, Middlesex, 1987.

Milward, Alan S., "*The Reconstruction of Western Europe, 1945-1951*", London, Methuen, 1984. E.040-309/A

Ministério do Comércio, Indústria e Agricultura, "*Bolsa de Mercadorias de Lisboa: organização e regulamentação*", Lisboa: Ministério do Comércio, Indústria e Agricultura, 1933.

Morel, Philippe; Nick Gardiner; Robert Grübner; Gwenhaël Le Boulay; James Malick; Sukand Ramachandran; Shubh Saumya; Eriola Shehu, "*Global Capital Markets 2013: Survival of the Fittest*", The Boston Consulting Group BCG Perspectives, April, 2013.

Morris, Gregory, "Heard on the Street, and around the world, The Wall Street Journal turns 125 years old", *Financial History,* Museum of American Finance, 109, Winter 2014: 20-22.

Moysen, André, "*Le coulissier contrepartiste en bourse devant la loi pénale*", Paris, E. Cassegrain, 1904.

Neal, Larry, "*The Rise of Financial Capitalism: International Capital Markets in the Age of Reason*", Cambridge, Cambridge University Press, 1990.

Neves, João César das, "*The Portuguese Economy. A Picture in Figures. XIX and XX centuries*", Lisboa, Universidade Católica Editora 1994.

New York Stock Exchange Committee on Public Relations, New York stock Exchange, New York, New York Stock Exchange, 1936.

Nunes, A; C. Bastien; N. Valério; R. Sousa; S. Costa, "*Banking in the Portuguese Colonial Empire*", Économies et Sociétés, AF n.º 44, 9, 2011: 1483-1554.

Nunes, Anabela; Carlos Bastien; Nuno Valério, "*Privatization, and Transnationalization in Portugal (1980-2005)*", W.P. 26, GHES, 2006.

Nunes, José Pavão, "*Pension Funds in Portugal*", World Forum OECD, 2007.

http://www.oecd.org/site/worldforum06/38787240.pdf

O'Brien, P; Escosura, Leandro Prados de la, "*Balance Sheets for the Acquisition, Retention and Loss of European Empires Overseas*", Itinerario, Vol 23, 3-4, 1999: 25-52.

O'Rourke, Kevin H.; Jeffrey G. Williamson, "*Globalization and history: the evolution of a nineteenth-century Atlantic economy*", Cambridge, MA: MIT Press, 1999.

OEEC, "*Dix ans de Coopération: Réalizations et Perspectives*", Paris, 1958.

Office for National Statistics of UK:

http://www.smallbusiness.co.uk/channels/technology-in-business/news/110threethreethree2/smes-drive-innovation.thtml

Oliveira, Eduardo Freire de, "*Elementos para a História do Município de Lisboa*", Lisbon, Typographia Universal, 1891.

Osório, António; Vitor Santos "*A eficiência económica nas empresas públi-cas e privadas*" in Privatizações e Regulação: A experiência Portuguesa: (1999) 191--215.

Passos, John R. dos, "*A treatise on the law of stock-brokers and stock-exchanges*", Vol. 1, New-York, The banks law publishing Cº, 1905.

Pedreira, Jorge, "*O Sistema das Trocas*", in Francisco Bethencourt and Kirti Chauduri, eds., História da Expansão Portuguesa, vol. IV, Do Brasil para África (1808-1930), Lisboa, Círculo de Leitores, 1998, pp.213-301.

Perkins, Edwin J., "*Wall Street to Main Street: Charles Merrill and middle-class investors*", Cambridge, Cambridge University Press, 1999. FEUNL, N21-001.

Peroni, Chiara, 2009, "A Non-Parametric Investigation of Risk Premia", *Studies in Nonlinear Dynamics & Econometrics*, Vol. 13, nr. 4, Article 2.

http://www.bepress.com/snde/vol13/iss4/art2

Phillips, Peter C. B.; Shu-Ping Shi; Jun Yu, "*Testing for Multiple Bubbles 1: Historical Episodes of Exuberance and Collapse in the S&P 500*", Singapore Management University, research collection School of Economics, Working Paper 8, July 2013. http://ink.library.smu.edu.sg/cgi/viewcontent.cgi?article=2509&context=soe_research

Piccinelli, Ferdinando, *"Apprezammento dei valori publici e delle operazioni di borsa"*, Milano, Ulrico Hoepli, 1897.

Pinheiro, Maximiano (ed), *"Séries Longas Para a Economia Portuguesa"*, Lisboa, Banco de Portugal, 1997.

Poitras, Geoffrey, *"Security Analysis and Investment Strategy"*, Oxford Blackwell Publishing, 2005.

Preda, Alex, *"Informative Prices, Rational Investors: The Emergence of the Random Walk Hypothesis and the Nineteenth Century Science of Financial Investments"*, History of Political Economy, 36 (2), Summer 2004: 351-86.

Proudhon, P. J., *"Manuel du spéculateur à la Bourse"*, Garnier Frère. Paris, 1857.

Raffalovich, Arthur, *"Bourse"*, in Leon Say and Josef Chailley, eds., Nouveau Dictionnaire d'économie politique, vol. I. Paris, Guillauman, 1900.

Rambaud, Prosper, *"Du placement des capitaux en valeurs de bourse"*, Paris, Ernest Thorin, 1884.

Rathinam, Francis Xavier; A. V.Raja, *"Stock Market and Shareholder Protection: Are They Important for Economic Growth?"*, The Law and Development Review Volume 3, Number 2, 2010: 304-325.

Reddy, Michael T., *"Securities Operations. A Guide to Operations and Information Systems in the Securities Industry"*, New Jersey, Prentice Hall, 1995.

Regnault, Jules, *"Calcul des chances et philosophie de la Bourse"*, Paris, 1863.

Reinhart, C.; K. Rogoff (2009), *"This Time is Different. Eight centuries of Financial Folly"*, Princeton University Press, Princeton, NJ, US.

Reis, Jaime, *"The historical roots of the modern Portuguese economy — the first century of growth 1850s-1950s"*, in Richard Herr, The new Portugal, Democracy and Europe, Berkeley, 1993.

Rietz, Thomas A. , *"The Equity Premium: A solution"*, Journal of Monetary Economics, 22, (1988): 117-131.

Ritschl, Albrecht, *"The Marshall Plan 1948-1951"*, EH.Net Encyclopaedia, edited by Robert Whaples, 2004. http//eh.net/encyclopedia/article/ Ritschl Marshall.Plan

Ritschl, Albrecht; Samad Sarferaz, *"Crisis? What Crisis?"* Currency vs. Banking in the Financial Crisis of 1931", SFB Discussion Paper 2010-014 n° 649, 2009.

Roberts, Richard, *"Saving the City: The Great Financial Crisis of 1914"*, OUP Oxford, 2013.

Rodrik, Dani (1999), *"The New Global Economy and Developing Countries: Making Openness Work"*, Overseas Development Council, Washington, DC.

Roe, Mark J., *"Legal Origins and Modern Stock Markets"*, Harvard Law Review, 120 (2006): 460-527.

Rojo, José Angel, *"José Bonaparte (1808-1811) y la legislacion mercantil e industrial española"*, Revista de derecho mercantil, 1977, nr. 143-144: 121-184.

Rollo, Maria Fernanda, *"Portugal e o Plano Marshall"*, Lisboa, Estampa, 1994.

Rosenberg, Jerry M., *"Inside the Wall Street Journal, The history and the power of Dow Jones & Company and America's most influential newspaper"*, London, MacMillan, 1982.

Ross, Stephen; Randolph Westerfield; Jeffrey Jaffe, *"Corporate Finance"* McGraw Hill, Boston, 7th edition, 2005.

Rotheroe, Charles, *"Change actually: the restructuring of European financial markets — what does it mean?"* in Lori Nicholson, The Euromoney, Global Exchanges & Trading Handbook, Deutsche Bank, 2005: 15-18

Rousseau, Peter L., *"Share liquidity, participation, and growth of the Boston market for industrial equities, 1854—1897"*, Explorations in Economic History, XXX, 2008.

Rousseau, Peter L.; Richard Sylla, *"Emerging Financial Markets and early US growth"*, Explorations in Economic History, 2005, vol 42: 1-26

Rousseau Peter L.; Richard Sylla, *"Financial Systems, Economic Growth, and Glo--balization"*, in Globalization in Historical Perspective, M. Bordo, A. Taylor, and J. Williamson (editors), Chicago, Chicago university Press, 2003.

Royal Commonwealth Society, *"Anglo-Portuguese relations in south-central Africa 1890-1900"*, London, 1962.

Rozeff, Michael S., *"Dividend Yields Are Equity Risk Premiums"*, Journal of Portfolio Management, 11, 1984: 68-75.

Saldanha, Eduardo de Almeida, *"Estudos sobre o direito comercial português"*, Coimbra, Imprensa da Universidade, 1896.

Sánchez A.; Arantxa Álvarez, *"Los Cambios Regulatórios Inundan los Mercados Financeros"*, BOLSA, Revista de Bolsa y Mercados Españoles, nr. 191, 1st qtr 2012.

Santarém, Pedro de, *"Tractatus de Assecurationibus et Sponsionibus....* 1552 [Tratado muito útil e quotidiano dos seguros e promessas dos mercadores publicado pelo jurisconsulto português, Doutor Pedro de Santarém], Lisboa: Edição Grémio dos Seguradores, 1961.

Santos, Ana Filipa Cruz Seabra dos, *"Historical Equity Risk Premium in Portuguese Market"*, Master Degree thesis approved in June 2008 at The School of Economics, New University of Lisbon

Say, Horace, *"Agents de change"*, apud Dictionnaire d'économie politique publié sous la direction de Ch. Coquelin et Guillaumin — T. I, Paris,— Guillaumin et Cie, L. Hachette et Cie, 1854.

Sayous, André, *"Les bourses Allémandes de valeurs et de commerce et les lois impériales des 22 Juin et 5 Julliet 1896"*, Paris, 1898, Arthur Rousseau, 1898.

Scherer, Charles, *"La bourse de Paris"*, Paris, Librairie Nouvelle,1886.

Schularick, M. and Taylor, A. M. (2012) "Credit Booms Gone Bust: Monetary Policy, Leverage Cycles, and Financial Crises, 1870-2008". *American Economic Review*, 102(2): 1029-61.

Schwert, William (1998), *"Stock Market Volatility: Ten Years After the Crash,"* NBER Working Papers 6381, National Bureau of Economic Research, Inc. Brookings Wharton Papers on Financial Services, I (1998): 65-114.

Schwert, William, *"Anomalies and Market Efficiency"*, in Handbook of the Economics of Finance, edited by M. Harris and R. Stulz, North Holland, Amsterdam (2002), 2012.

Shy, Oz; Juha Tarkka, "*Stock exchange alliances, access fees and competition*", Working paper nr. 22, Bank of Finland, Helsinky 2001.

Smith, Gervase Clarence (1985), "*The third Portuguese Empire 1825-1975: A study in Economic Imperialism*", Manchester: Manchester University Press.

Smith, Gervase Clarence, (1979), "*Slaves, peasants and capitalists in southern Angola 1840-1920*", Cambridge, CUP.

Sousa, Carlos Hermenegildo de, "*O Plano Marshall: A Reconstrução Económica da Europa Ocidental; A Posição Económica de Portugal*", Brotéria, vol. XLVI, 2, 3, Feb, March 1948: 4-37.

Spierdijk, Laura; Jacob Bikker; Pieter van den Hoek, "*Mean Reversion in Interna-tional Stock Markets:An Empirical Analysis of the 20th Century*", De Nederlandsche Bank NV, Working Paper nr. 247/2010, April 2010.

Stringham, Edward Peter (2002), "*The Emergence of the London Stock Exchange as a Self-Policing Club*", Journal of Private Enterprise 17(2) Spring: 1-19.

Stringham, Edward Peter (2003), "*The extralegal development of securities trading in seventeenth-century Amsterdam*", Quarterly Review of Economics and Finance, Volume 43, Issue 2, Summer 2003: 321-344.

Supino, Camilo, "*La borsa e il capitale improdutivo*", Milano, Hoepli,1898.

Supino, David, "*Le operazioni di borsa seconda la pratica, la legge e l'economia politica*", Torino, Fratelli Bocca, 1875.

Sylla, Richard, "*Early U.S. Struggles with Fiscal Federalism: Lessons for Europe?*", Comparative Economic Studies, 01/2014, 56(2): 1-19.   DOI: 10.1057/ces.2014.10.

Sylla, Richard, "*Financial Foundations: Public Credit, the National Bank, and Securities Markets*", in Douglas Irwin and Richard Sylla, (editors), Founding Choices: American Economic Policy in the 1790s, Chicago, Chicago university Press, 2010: 59-88.

Sylla, Richard, "*Comparing UK and US financial systems 1790-1830*", in Neal, L. (ed.), The Origins and development of Financial Systems and Institutions, Cambridge, Cambridge University Press, 2009: 209-240.

Sylla, Richard; Jack Wilson; Robert Wright, "*Integration of Trans-Atlantic Capital Markets 1790-1845*", Review of Finance, 2006 (10): 613-644.

Sylla, Richard, "*U.S. Securities market and the Banking System 1790-1840*", Review, Federal Reserve Bank of St. Louis, May/June 1998: 83-98.

Sylla, Richard; Wilson, Jack; Wright, Robert, "*America's first Securities Markets, 1790-1830: Emergence, Development, and Integration*", Cliometrics Conference, Toronto, Ontario, 1997.

Tedeschi (Avv. Prof. Felice), "*Dei contrati di borsa detti diferenziali in Italia ed all' Estero*", Torino, Frateli Bocca, 1897.

Teixeira, Pedro, "*The value of political connections in the closing years of authoritarian Portugal*", Master Dissertation presented at Faculdade de Economia da Universidade Nova de Lisboa, 2011 (Supervisor: José Tavares).

Temin, Peter (1997), "*The golden age of European growth: A review essay*", European review of Economic History, I:127-149.

Thaler, E., *"Traité Élémentaire de Droit Commercial"*, Paris: Arthur Rousseau, 1900.

The Salazar Archive, Arquivo Nacional da Torre do Tombo, ANTT, Lisboa; Arquivo Histórico-Diplomático, AH-D, MNE, Lisboa; British National Archives, Foreign Office.

Tversky, Amos and Daniel Kahneman, *"Advances in Prospect Theory: Cumulative Representation Uncertainty"*, Journal of Risk and Uncertainty, vol. 5(4), 1992: 297-323.

Ulrich, Ruy Ennes, *"Da Bolsa e Suas Operações"*, Coimbra, Imprensa da Universidade, 1906. **Ulrich**, Ruy Ennes, *"Da Bolsa e suas Operações"*, Coimbra, Imprensa da Universidade de Coimbra, 1906. Maria Eugénia Mata; David Justino; José Rodrigues da Costa, *"Da Bolsa e suas Operações"*, Coimbra, Imprensa da Universidade de Coimbra, 2nd edition, 2011.

Valério, N; A. Nunes; C. Bastien; R. Sousa; S. Costa (2011), *"O Sistema Bancário Português"*, Lisboa, Banco de Portugal.

Valério, Nuno (2004), *"Nationalizations and Privatizations in Portugal During the Last Quarter of the 20th Century: Were They Profitable to the State?"*, Revista de História Económica e Social, 2ª série, nr. 7, 2004: 129-143.

Valério, Nuno, P. Tjipilica, *"Economic activity in the Portuguese Colonial Empire: a factor analysis approach"*, Économies et Sociétés, Série Histoire économique quantitative, AF, nr. 39, 9, 2008: 1765-1808.

van der Wee, Herman, *"Prosperity and Upheaval: The World Economy, 1945-1980"*, Berkeley: University of California Press, 1986.

Vecon, *"A new stock market crash, a pattern?"*, Tijdschrift voor economisch onderwijs [magazine for economics education], a monthly publication of the VECON, February 2010, the Netherlands.

Vidal E., *"Agents de change"* — apud — Dictionnaire du commerce, de l'industrie et de la banque, publié sous la direction de Yves Guyot et A. Raffalovich, T. I, Paris, 1901 — Guillaumin et C.ie

Vidal, Emmanuel, *"Bourse des valeurs mobilières"* in Yves Guyot and Arthur Raffalovich eds., Dictionnaire du Commerce, de l'industrie et de la banque, Paris, Guillauman & Cª, 1896.

Vilanculos, Chiluva, *"Globalization and the Convergence of Stock Markets"*, Master Dissertation presented at Faculdade de Economia da UNL, 2011. (Supervisor Maria Eugénia Mata).

Vilar, Emílio Rui; et alii (Grupo de Trabalho Interministerial para Análise e Avaliação da Situação e das Perspectivas de Evolução do Sector Empresarial do Estado) [Interministerial Working Party for Analysing and Assessing the Current Situation and the Prospects for the Evolution of the State Enterprise Sector] (1998). Livro Branco do Sector Empresarial do Estado [White Paper on the State enterprise sector]. Lisbon: Ministério das Finanças [Ministry of Finance].

Waldenström, Daniel; Bruno Frey, *"How Government Bond Prices Reflect Wartime Events. The Case of the Stockholm Market"*, SSE/EFI Working Paper Series in Economics and Finance nr. 489, 2002.

Weil, Edmond, *"L'impôt sur les Opérations de Bourse"*, Paris, Rousseau, 1902.

Werner, Walter; Steven T. Smith, "*Wall Street*", New York, Columbia University Press, 1915, 1991.

Wexler, Immanuel (1983), "*The Marshall Plan revisited: The European recovery program in economic perspective*", Westport, Conn.: Greenwood Press.

Wheeler, Douglas L.; René Pélissier, "*Angola*", London, 1971.

Wilkins, Mira; Harm Schröter eds., "*The free-standing company in the world economy, 1830-1996*", Oxford, Oxford Univ. Press, 1998.

Wolfson, Martin; Gerald A. Epstein (eds), "*The Handbook of Political Economy of Financial Crises*", Oxford, 2013.

Zahra, Shaker A.; R. D. Ireland; M. A. Hitt, "*International expansion by the new venture firms: International diversity, mode of market entry, technological learning and performance*", Academy of Management Journal, 43 (5), 2000.